Self-Organizing Complexity in
Psychological Systems

Psychological Issues

Series Editor: Morris N. Eagle

Psychological Issues is a monograph series that was begun by G. S. Klein in the 1950s. The first manuscript was published in 1959. The editors since Klein's death have been Herbert Schlesinger, Stuart Hauser, and currently, Morris Eagle.

The mission of Psychological Issues is to publish intellectually challenging and significant manuscripts that are of interest to the psychoanalytic community as well as psychologists, psychiatrists, social workers, students, and interested lay people. Since its inception, a large number of distinguished authors have published their work under the imprimatur of Psychological Issues. These authors include, among many others, Erik Erikson, Merton Gill, Robert Holt, Phillip Holzman, David Rapaport, and Benjamin Rubinstein. Psychological Issues is fortunate in having an equally distinguished Editorial Board consisting of leaders in their field.

Other Books in the Series

Erik Erikson and the American Psyche: Ego, Ethics, and Evolution
    Daniel Burston
Help Him Make You Smile: The Development of Intersubjectivity in the Atypical Child
    Rita S. Eagle
The Embodied Subject: Minding the Body in Psychoanalysis
    edited by John P. Muller and Jane G. Tillman

Self-Organizing Complexity in Psychological Systems

Edited by Craig Piers,
John P. Muller, and Joseph Brent

JASON ARONSON
Lanham • Boulder • New York • Toronto • Plymouth, UK

Published in the United States of America
by Jason Aronson
An imprint of Rowman & Littlefield Publishers, Inc.

A wholly owned subsidiary of
The Rowman & Littlefield Publishing Group, Inc.
4501 Forbes Boulevard, Suite 200, Lanham, Maryland 20706
www.rowmanlittlefield.com

Estover Road
Plymouth PL6 7PY
United Kingdom

British Library Cataloguing in Publication Information Available

Library of Congress Cataloging-in-Publication Data

Self-organizing complexity in psychological systems / edited by Craig Piers, John P.
   Muller, and Joseph Brent.
    p. cm. — (Psychological issues)
   ISBN-13: 978-0-7657-0525-9 (cloth : alk. paper)
   ISBN-10: 0-7657-0525-7 (cloth : alk. paper)
   ISBN-13: 978-0-7657-0526-6 (pbk. : alk. paper)
   ISBN-10: 0-7657-0526-5 (pbk. : alk. paper)
   1. Psychology—Philosophy. 2. Complexity (Philosophy) I. Piers, Craig, 1964–
II. Muller, John P., 1940– III. Brent, Joseph.
   BF38.S45 2007
   150.1—dc22   2006102101

Printed in the United States of America

∞™ The paper used in this publication meets the minimum requirements of
American National Standard for Information Sciences—Permanence of Paper
for Printed Library Materials, ANSI/NISO Z39.48-1992.

~

Contents

Introduction   vii
John P. Muller

Chapter 1   Complexity Theory as the Parent Science of
            Psychoanalysis   1
            Stanley R. Palombo

Chapter 2   A Biological Theory of Brain Function and Its
            Relevance to Psychoanalysis   15
            Walter J. Freeman

Chapter 3   Neurodynamics, State, Agency, and Psychological
            Functioning   37
            Jim Grigsby and Elizabeth Osuch

Chapter 4   Emergence: When a Difference in Degree
            Becomes a Difference in Kind   83
            Craig Piers

Chapter 5   Emergence and Psychological Morphogenesis   111
            Jeffrey Goldstein

Chapter 6   The Dynamics of Development   135
            E. Virginia Demos

The Language of Complexity Theory 165
Craig Piers

Author Index 173

Subject Index 179

Contributors 183

Introduction

John P. Muller, Ph.D.

Some of us represented in this monograph met in seminars on complexity theory organized by the Forum on Psychiatry and the Humanities at the Washington School of Psychiatry. The forum provided an opportunity to examine a wide range of developments in a new paradigm of inquiry: chaos and catastrophe theory, self-organizing complexity, closure, and emergence—all examples of the broad discipline dealing with nonlinear dynamic systems. This emerging discipline shows many points of convergence with psychological theory and practice, emphasizing that history is irreversible and discontinuous, that small early interventions can have large and unexpected later effects, that each life trajectory is unique yet patterned, that measurement error is not random and cannot be justifiably distributed equally across experimental conditions, and that change is more likely to emerge under conditions of optimal turbulence. For these and other reasons, this volume will, we hope, be of interest to those looking for a contemporary perspective on the mind and the making of meaning.

Making meaningful links in experience is crucial to the development of "closure," that process whereby a living organism as a center of movement achieves self-maintenance through recursive self-referential acts. Closure does not mean closing a system, but rather establishing a reliably variable internal context from which one's environment can be interpreted. Such interpretive activity is based on the development of "syntactic autonomy," the ability to sustain "an internal vehicle for classification" of environmental conditions grounded in feedback from actions based on the classification

(Rocha 2000, 210). In this way, a distinction between "within" and "without" and a boundary between "self" and "other" can be maintained.

In his overview of pertinent studies, Guastello (2001) provides a useful survey of how nonlinear dynamical systems theory has impacted psychology in three broad areas: cognitive science, social organization, and clinical studies. He calls attention to the work of Hardy (1998) on semantic networks as promising, for their continual elaboration may be the most pervasive dimension of self-organizing complexity. I find the work of Charles Sanders Peirce (1992) especially relevant here. By proposing a triadic model for the generation of signs and meaning, Peirce establishes a cogent foundation for the spontaneous, unpredictable, and self-organizing aspects of interpretive action. Signs not only stand for their objects in some respect, but they also generate their meanings, which Peirce called their "interpretants." Such interpretants are the effects produced by the sign on the receiver's feelings, actions, and ideas. These effects, largely unconscious, become new signs, in turn producing their effects on both oneself and others. In this way, Peirce provides a useful and perhaps even testable model for the unconscious clustering of associations as well as for the emergent properties of therapeutic speech.

At the end of this monograph, readers will find a useful glossary of terms that bridges distinctions drawn by this evolving perspective and joins them to some terms we now take for granted as part of an evolutionary framework. This framework properly emphasizes that nothing evolves in isolation but rather in coevolution with the complexifying entities and their energy fields that constitute the nested systems of the universe. In this coevolutionary landscape, we can say, joining Julian Huxley, that in us "evolution was at last becoming conscious of itself" (1959, 20). This mutation is primarily an effect of language, for language has altered the development of the human brain (Deacon, 1997) and thereby the landscape of the Earth itself. Language has become the dominant systematizing force on our planet, and perhaps eventually in our solar system, and maybe beyond. The web of human culture not only differentiates and consolidates us but it also extends our sphere of influence. The Internet, exemplifying a self-organizing, complexifying system, signals the emergence of what Teilhard de Chardin (1955) called the "noosphere," with its worldwide webbing and "hyperpersonal" organization. This is to say that many of the ideas favored by nonlinear dynamical systems theorists have their own history of emergence. For example, Julian Huxley writes of Teilhard de Chardin's work as follows:

> He speaks of complexification as an all-pervading tendency, involving the universe in all its parts in an *enroulement organique sur soi-même*, or by an alternative

metaphor, as a *reploiement sur soi- même*. He thus envisages the world-stuff as being "rolled up" or "folded in" upon itself, both locally and in its entirety, and adds that the process is accompanied by an increase of energetic "tension" in the resultant "corpuscular" organizations, or individualized constructions of increased organizational complexity. For want of a better English phrase, I shall use *convergent integration* to define the operation of this process of self-complexification. (1959, 15)

Complexity as a process "rolling itself up" or "folding in on itself" converges on what we now call fractal dimensionality, reentrant mapping, self-similarity, and so forth. For Teilhard de Chardin, as for Charles Sanders Peirce, consciousness evolves in conjunction with the complexification of physicochemical and biological systems whose "within" or closure includes traces of a type of consciousness already present in the most primitive, least organized systems (hence Peirce refers to matter as "effete mind"). Self-organized complexity theory disputes this claim by asserting that there is no preemergent trace of what emerges as novelty, there is no inscribed plan or aim being achieved, and novelty emerges spontaneously and unpredictably from the operation of very rudimentary computational laws. Of course, whether such "laws" are themselves pregiven or perhaps also evolve in some spontaneous manner is debatable, but not in this monograph. This book aims to provide a partisan overview to a rapidly changing and emerging field that will likely be with us for some time.

References

Deacon, T. 1997. *The Symbolic Species: The Co-Evolution of Language and the Brain.* New York: W. W. Norton and Company.

Guastello, S. 2001. "Nonlinear Dynamics in Psychology." *Discrete Dynamics in Nature and Society* 6: 11–29.

Hardy, C. 1998. *Networks of Meaning.* Westport, CT: Praeger.

Huxley, J. 1959. "Introduction." In *The Phenomenon of Man,* P. Teilhard de Chardin, 11–28. New York: Harper Torchbooks, 1961.

Peirce, C. S. 1992. *The Essential Peirce: Selected Philosophical Writings.* Vol. 1, 1867–1893. Ed. N. Houser and C. Kloesel. Bloomington: Indiana University Press.

Rocha, L. M. 2000. "Syntactic Autonomy: Why There Is No Autonomy without Symbols and How Self-Organizing Systems Might Evolve Them." In *Closure: Emergent Organizations and their Dynamics.* Vol. 901, 207–23. New York: New York Academy of Sciences.

Teilhard De Chardin, P. 1955. *The Phenomenon of Man.* Trans. B. Wall. New York: Harper Torchbooks, 1961.

~

CHAPTER ONE

Complexity Theory as the Parent Science of Psychoanalysis

Stanley R. Palombo, M.D.

This chapter is based on material from my book, *The Emergent Ego: Complexity and Coevolution in the Psychoanalytic Process*. My objective in writing *The Emergent Ego* was to construct a more detailed and coherent theory than we have had before about the psychoanalytic process and how it works, using some important new advances in scientific thought. The sciences of complexity have given us a new perspective on the nature of the evolutionary process. Seen from the vantage point of complexity theory, a living system evolves through an integrating series of reorganizations that raise it to new levels of structure and function. In what follows, we will be looking at the progression of a psychoanalytic treatment as an evolutionary process.

The patient and the analyst are components of a therapeutic ecosystem. Complexity theory explains how the interaction of the components of such a system can give rise to new properties in the system as a whole. The system as a whole, in turn, is an environment that selects from among the properties of its components those that are fittest for maintaining the larger system. These new properties of the components lead to another round of interactions that may produce a higher level of organization in the larger ecosystem. The process is continuous. Over time, the component systems become better adapted to one another, and the ecosystem becomes more stable and efficient.

Complexity is intrinsic to all systems that occur in nature. Nearly all objects and structures in the universe have affinities for other objects and structures at the same level of organization. The rule applies at all levels of structure, from particles and atoms to ideas and people. While there are affinities between objects at every level of organization, the nature of the affinity at each level is specific to that level. Because of these natural affinities, aggregates of objects and structures tend to be self-organizing.

The psychoanalytic process promotes the self-organizing properties of the ideas and feelings that make up the contents of the patient's mind. This happens in a series of phase transitions. At first, only smaller disordered aggregates become organized. Then aggregates of these new organizations are themselves organized into larger units, and so on, for many generations. All of this happens in many separate and asynchronous trajectories that give rise to nonlinear change overall. In this way, the analytic process moves through a series of self-organizing events, each one based on the outcomes of many previous events at lower levels.

The application of complexity theory to the psychoanalytic process will extend the power of psychoanalytic theory to account for the full range of phenomena, large and small, that characterize the therapeutic relationship. My goal in *The Emergent Ego* was to explain more clearly than has been possible before how the patient can benefit from taking part in this prolonged and intimate therapeutic interaction.

The new stage in the development of scientific self-consciousness marked by complexity theory should be a cause for excitement among psychoanalysts. Science today is moving away from the reductionism that blunted its usefulness to psychoanalytic theory in the past. Biology is going beyond the molecular level to a new understanding of the whole organism and its detailed development through self-organizing events.

Science is now in a much better position to learn from psychoanalysis than it has been in the past. The wealth of data generated by the analyst's interaction with the patient can be organized and examined in new ways. These data illuminate the patient's most urgent and most personal concerns. The stakes are high in analysis. At risk is the ultimate success and quality of the patient's emotional life. Analysis requires a mutual commitment to the completion of the process, a deep commitment often matched in human life only in the most intimate of family relationships. These are matters of the greatest scientific interest.

The conditions of an analysis are well controlled for the observation of an interaction of such intensity and longevity. With the development of complexity theory, the data of psychoanalysis can be used to study interactions between people at very high levels of seriousness and subtlety. The data generated by the psychoanalytic process is the ideal material for these new theoretical tools to work on. Psychoanalysis is a natural laboratory of complex interactions.

Complexity theory has created a common ground for theories of organic evolution and evolution in other spheres. The psychoanalytic process is one of these other spheres. The psychoanalytic partners form a loosely coupled self-organizing ecosystem. The components of the ecosystem, in turn, are two tightly coupled self-organizing systems. Patient and analyst are each coevolving within the analytic ecosystem.

For science to give anything like a complete account of the world, it has to apply the same vision to the most complex systems as to the simplest units of matter and energy. Human minds and brains are the most complex systems we know of. Murray Gell-Mann, the discoverer of the quark, is a Nobel laureate in physics (1969) and cofounder of the Santa Fe Institute. As he says in *The Quark and the Jaguar* (1994):

> The point is that human psychology, while no doubt derivable in principle from neurophysiology, the endocrinology of neurotransmitters, and so forth— is also worth studying at its own level. Many people believe, as I do, that when staircases are constructed between psychology and biology, the best strategy is to work from the top down and from the bottom up. (117)

The evolution of complex systems began at the moment of the Big Bang, when the universe started expanding from a point of infinite temperature and density. The universe has been cooling ever since. As it cooled, ever more highly organized structures have emerged from the original homogeneous concentration of radiation. At some point in the expansion, matter emerged in the form of quarks and gluons (or their even simpler precursors). The early stages of this evolution are easy to identify—quarks and gluons joined to make protons and neutrons, which combined in turn to make atomic nuclei, which joined with electrons to make atoms. Atoms formed molecules, and then biological macromolecules, simple organisms, the one-celled protista, the nucleated eukaryotes, and finally the efflorescence of multicellular life. It is a story of successive escalations in complexity that created larger, more intricate, and more diversified interactive systems.

Self-Organization

The properties of complex systems can be observed in our own everyday world even in a pile of sand. Bak, Tang, and Wiesenfeld (1988) studied the behavior of sandpiles. They modeled the fall of individual sand grains on a flat surface from a fixed point above the surface. As a sandpile grows beneath the fixed point, its sides become steeper and steeper, until a critical state is reached. When the sides of the pile can no longer support the addition of one more grain, the next one dropped on the pile causes an avalanche. They found that the extent of the avalanche was quite variable. A single grain might just slide to the bottom of the pile. An avalanche might consist of a few grains, many grains, or even a considerable fraction of the pile.

The piles reached what Bak and colleagues called a state of self-organizing criticality. As each grain fell, it came to rest at some convenient place on the pile, where it might be called on to support the next falling grain. Eventually, the pile as a whole reached the critical state in which it supported the maximum number of grains for its area on the surface. The sandpile had self-organized to an unstable critical state. When another grain was added and the critical threshold surpassed, the organization of the pile broke down.

Self-organized criticality in a sandpile is just at the threshold of complexity in the natural world. Yet it already shows the pattern of punctuated equilibrium we see in biological evolution. The inverse relation between the sizes of biological extinction events and their frequencies is very close to the pattern of sizes and frequencies of the avalanches in a sandpile (Kauffman 1993; Raup 1992). It is also similar to the pattern we see in the progressive reorganization of the patient's mental contents in psychoanalytic treatment.

Cellular Automata

The complex systems found in nature and studied by Bak do not adapt to the world around them, but their complexity is inherited by all complex adaptive systems. Other approaches to the study of complex systems are illuminating. Langton's work on cellular automata has been very influential. A cellular automaton is a lattice of parallel computing elements that can take one of a finite set of values. Each value puts the element in a particular state. States succeed each other as the simulation proceeds. The value of the state of each element is computed from the values of its next door neighbors (including its own value) in the previous state of the system.

Conway's celebrated Game of Life is the most famous and familiar example of a cellular automaton. The Game of Life takes place on a two-dimensional grid of cells, represented as a matrix on the computer screen, but in principle infinite in extent. The transition rules of the game are extremely simple. Each cell has two states, on and off. If a cell is on, and either two or three of its eight nearest neighbors are also on, then the cell stays on after the next computation. If the cell is off and three of its neighbors in its three-by-three element neighborhood are on, then it turns on in the next generation. In all other cases, the cell is off in the next round.

When the game is initiated by a random selection of on and off cells, disconnected groups of connected on cells remain after the first generation. Some of these groups produce gliders—clusters of five cells that move diagonally across the grid to infinity if not obstructed by other patterns. "Glider guns" that produce a steady stream of gliders can be arranged to form a digital computer on the grid (Berlecamp, Conway, and Guy 1982).

The Game of Life computer is a Turing machine. It can compute anything computable by the most powerful supercomputer, given enough time and a large enough grid. Remarkably, such a complex mechanism can be constructed from the three simple transition rules that define the Game of Life. No better demonstration is needed of the organizational power of complex interactions in large arrays of simple parts.

Complex Adaptive Systems

The class of complex adaptive systems (CASs) includes all living things, all organizations of living things, and a growing number of computer programs. CASs are self-organized, like the sandpile and the Game of Life. In addition, their structures can change in response to environmental pressures. The patient and the analyst are each CASs. They share with other such systems a set of properties that determine the most basic aspects of their behavior. Each of them has many component parts, each part with a degree of independence from the larger system it belongs to. The parts interact within each system in a dynamic, nonlinear way. The patterns they form cannot be predicted by the usual methods of mathematical analysis.

CASs are open to the world around them. To maintain or improve their internal structures, they extract energy and information from the outside world. They work constantly, in fact, to maintain a state of disequilibrium with their entropy-drenched surroundings.

The organization of a CAS, its pattern of interaction, is dynamic. It responds to changes both external to the system (in biology, climate changes or the threat of new predators) and internal to it (for example, mutation and recombination). These changes reorganize the components of the system so that it is better able to maintain itself under the new conditions.

An adaptive system responds in a way that improves its fitness for maintaining itself in its environment. The environment confronts it with a set of physical and organizational constraints and, in the biological world, with a population of other systems with conflicting interests. Adaptation is possible only when the pattern of connections within a system can change. Bak

(1994) says, "Fitness is a synonym for self-consistent integration into a highly integrated complex or critical state by any part of the system" (493).

CASs have become well known for their emergent properties and behavior. Emergent properties appear at all levels in the organization of matter, whenever a set of components organizes to become a system. For example, the properties of molecules are emergent with respect to the properties of the atoms they are composed of. In complex adaptive systems, this effect is magnified many times over.

It is still difficult for many people to think of the making of a new object without a conscious human (or superhuman) agent working at it from the top level down. The idea of new properties emerging without the act of a conscious agent has an uncanny feel to it. Complexity theory shows us that in the world of nature, new objects are made through the nonlinear interactions of objects that already exist.

For the broad class of complex adaptive systems, emergent properties and behaviors result from the reorganization of their parts into new kinds of structures with novel functions. Crutchfield (1994) says, "A process undergoes emergence if at some time the architecture of information processing has changed in such a way that a distinct and more powerful level of intrinsic computation has appeared that was not present in earlier conditions" (9). Crutchfield is pointing out that the emergence of a new organization is a computation over the unorganized components. Thus, a computer simulation mimics the intrinsic computation of self-organizing matter.

A patient in analysis gets better when new ways of gathering information emerge from a more effectively connected mental organization. The reorganization of his mental contents makes previously unconscious information available for processing in a new context.

Underlying the psychological changes, the organization of brain activity evolves from a vastly complex interaction among systems themselves containing many interacting parts. The search for computer models of brain activity began with Hebb's (1949) idea for a simulated neural network that laid the foundations for our current understanding of neural network simulations.

Mathematically, neural networks are specialized cellular automata. They are complex adaptive systems similar in many ways to the systems that regulate gene expression. Learning in neural networks has much in common with evolutionary change in organisms, although the time scales are enormously different. The complexity of neural networks in the living brain is also vastly greater than the complexity of those simulated in the computer. What is of great interest is that many functions and properties of the living brain are mimicked on the smaller scale.

Although complexity is characteristic of all living things, higher levels of complexity emerge as evolution moves on. Metazoa and their various organs are complex systems with many cellular components. Yet in simple animals like sponges, interactions between component cells are preprogrammed and limited in their range. A neural network ring opens and closes the mouth of a sea anemone, using a primitive form of experiential knowledge with its genetic programming.

As cognitive capacity increased during the evolution of the vertebrates, new levels of organization beyond that of the single neural network emerged. Many of these are embodied in the evolving anatomy of the vertebrate brain. We can see the development of specialized structures culminating in the differentiated expanse of the human cortex and its vast array of connections.

The brain is superbly equipped to facilitate, optimize, and exploit the opportunities for adaptation created by the complex world in which the organism lives. Freud was correct when he suggested that psychoanalysis works by freeing this rich potentiality from neurotic inhibition. However, the therapeutic process that frees the patient to respond optimally to the world is itself highly complex. In intricate and often very delicate ways, it enters into the self-organizing process already taking place within the patient.

A relatively small change in input from the environment, for example an interpretation, can sometimes lead to a major reorganization of the patient's mental structure at a level of increased complexity. This is typical of complex systems generally.

Without continual reorganization, every analysis would be like the fictional autobiography of Tristram Shandy in Lawrence Sterns's novel of that name. Shandy set out to write his history from birth to the time when he was writing. He spent three days describing the events of his birth. He concluded that his efforts were futile. If he kept up the same pace, he would just fall further and further behind.

The Edge of Chaos

Reorganization is the bootstrapping procedure that makes evolution possible and makes it progressive. A nonlethal mutation that fails to give an organism (or a species) a better ability to reorganize is biologically irrelevant. In the same way, a psychoanalytic intervention that does not contribute to the potential of the patient's mental contents for reorganization is not therapeutic. Sudden and surprising changes in a patient during analysis are evidence of phase changes in the structure of his mental contents. Phase changes occur in complex systems in a configuration often called the "edge of chaos."

One function of the psychoanalytic setting and the therapeutic relationship is to lead the patient's mental activity as close as possible to the edge of chaos, where there is an optimal balance between structure and mobility.

Organized systems of components can be found in either frozen or fluid states. Frozen states are uniform in structure, rigid, crystalline, brittle, and predictable. Local deformations do not propagate through a frozen system, unless they are strong enough to destroy it. Fluid states, by contrast, are chaotic. Lacking internal structure, they are in continual flux. Local perturbations may spread over an entire system in the fluid state within a very short time. Since neither frozen nor chaotic states are differentiated, they cannot be configured to represent or carry information.

Differentiation within systems appears only at the phase transition between frozen crystalline and chaotic fluid states. An example from geology is the coastline of a polar ice cap. Where the uniformly rigid ice cap meets the uniformly chaotic ocean, uniformity disappears. The coastline is a uniquely configured series of promontories, inlets, islands, and icebergs, each with its own finely detailed fractal shape.

So it is with the activities of complex systems overall. Individual forms with stable identities exist only when the system is poised near the edge of chaos, at the phase transition between frozen and fluid states. If a system remains near the edge of chaos, its potential for differentiation and new information content are virtually unlimited.

Successful organisms and CASs in general appear to be driven toward the edge of chaos. When change is advantageous, as it is when the ecosystem changes significantly, organisms tend to evolve in the direction that promotes adaptation.

Clinical Application

The psychoanalytic patient undertakes analysis because he wants to change. Psychoanalysis itself evolved from other methods that failed to provide lasting change in people suffering from psychopathology. Change in psychoanalysis results from an increase in the connectedness and complexity of the patient's mental contents. (This is in contrast with pharmacotherapy, which aims for a tonic and temporary change in the patient's overall state of mind.)

The edge of chaos in the clinical situation is the familiar but hardly ubiquitous state in which the analyst intervenes to open new pathways to the disconnected aspects of the patient's mental content. We see it when a patient produces associations that bring in new material (previously disconnected from the analytic discourse) that creates a new context (through new con-nections) for old material whose meaning had been obscure.

Patients in psychoanalysis, especially in the early stages, may not appreci-ate the adaptive value of working toward the edge of chaos. They may find the hazards of life near the edge of chaos frightening, and may actively seek to avoid them. In that case, trains of associations tend to be short and dis-connected. When this form of resistance is overcome, trains of associations become longer and better connected. Finer and finer distinctions appear be-tween emotionally similar events. The therapeutic ecosystem becomes stabi-lized nearer the edge of chaos.

Near the edge of chaos, associations oscillate between the present and past. These oscillations are not smoothly periodic, of course. An avalanche of associations may come tumbling out of the patient without warning. Their sequence is usually not linear, either logically or chronologically. As in the case of a sandpile, an avalanche of associations is not predictable from what immediately preceded it. However, the new associations always appear in ret-rospect to be ordered, as they clarify the meaning of earlier productions of the patient. An avalanche of associations is a clear-cut sign that the analytic process is moving forward.

Far from the edge of chaos, in the realm of frozen order, the patient's pro-ductions are deterministic and predictable. They are deterministic because we can understand in retrospect where they came from. They are predictable because the number and range of the patient's responses to events are stereo-typed and limited. In the chaotic realm, the patient's productions are neither deterministic nor predictable. No pattern is discernible in them, even in ret-rospect.

Near the edge of chaos, what the patient says is deterministic but not pre-dictable. One can easily understand in retrospect how one statement led to another. Still, at the time the patient speaks, neither patient nor analyst can know where what he says at the moment will eventually lead. New associa-tions enter the analytic discourse, fully determined by the sequence of previ-ous statements but never before encountered in the analysis. A deterministic trajectory of associations leads into the unconscious regions of the patient's mental contents.

The analyst's initial instruction to the patient to say everything that comes to mind without editing or withholding is often called the fundamental rule of psychoanalysis (Kris 1982). Most of the time, the fundamental rule is very difficult for the patient to follow literally. It functions primarily as a baseline from which to measure the obstacles that hinder the patient's spontaneity. However, near the edge of chaos, free association may finally be attainable.

The patient has for the moment lost his need to control what he tells the analyst. His associative process determines what he says, rather than his fears and fantasies about the analyst's response to him.

Because the patient's associations near the edge of chaos are less restricted, trains of associations can be longer, even lasting through an entire hour. A train of associations is an intelligible sequence, in which one association leads to another by a deterministic (though not predictable) route. A train of associations is to be distinguished from an endless series of meaningless details about a single event or interaction, which is characteristic of the chaotic realm.

Away from the edge of chaos, trains of associations are short, ending with one kind of interruption or another. Knowing when an interruption to a train of associations is a break in the flow and not simply the appearance of a new association may be difficult for the analyst. This ambiguity is a major source of uncertainty during the analytic process. Interruptions disguised as associations prolong the periods of quiescence that delay reorganization of the patient's mental contents.

As with other systems undergoing evolution, the periods when the analysis is near the edge of chaos may be brief. The patient may retreat in the direction of frozen order. When he does so, he may claim at such times that he has nothing left to say, or nothing new to say, or that the analyst is not interested in what he says. He finds it difficult to "think of anything." Whatever the analyst has to say seems critical or punitive to him. When the patient's productions become repetitive and predictable in this mode, the analytic situation has moved away from the edge of chaos.

When the productions are unpredictable but no longer cumulative, the situation has moved into the chaotic realm. The patient takes off on a topic that seems unrelated to the issues under discussion. He ignores or evades the analyst's interventions. The analyst may wait for a connection to an earlier topic to appear, but finds himself losing the thread of the associative sequence. He may feel that the patient is putting him down, flooding him with unworkable material, caricaturing the instruction to say everything that comes to his mind.

A shift away from the edge of chaos is usually more subtle than this, however. It may come to the analyst's notice as a modulation of his interest in what the patient is saying. When analysis is working optimally, near the edge of chaos, the analyst is entirely engaged in what the patient is telling him. He experiences the session as flowing in a natural way from topic to topic, each topic illuminating the previous one. New material appears in a meaningful context within the continuous discourse of the analysis. Pauses are brief and lead to new branchings in the patient's associative pathways. In descriptions of the "good analytic hour," such as those of Kris (1951) and Khan (1976), the analytic process is near the edge of chaos.

For the patient, the edge of chaos also has a characteristic feeling. He finds himself discussing thoughts and feelings normally difficult to talk about. Inner resistance is being overcome, with feelings of animation and excitement being generated. His thinking converges with that of the analyst.

When the analyst speaks, the patient may feel he was just about to say the same thing. The analyst seems to be taking the words right out of his mouth. He may wonder why he had not thought of them himself sooner. In the same way, the analyst's planned intervention may be forestalled by the patient's arrival at the same point, just as the analyst was about to speak.

Near the edge of chaos, analyst and patient are in tune. Their contributions, usually complementary, now overlap and reinforce each other. The mother–infant relationship is often evoked to illustrate the attunement of the psychoanalytic process near the edge of chaos. This analogy is misleading, however. It attributes an unrealistic asymmetry to the analytic pair. More apt would be the image of a vocalist and her coach working together at the piano. The analyst's ongoing simulation of the patient's inner life functions as an accompaniment to the patient's vocalizations.

Because the patient near the edge of chaos remembers events of his early life with revived and often vivid feeling, it is often said that the patient is reliving these early experiences in the analysis. Ernst Kris called this reliving of early experience "regression in the service of the ego," a term that makes a useful distinction in psychoanalytic thinking. The idea of the edge of chaos helps us sharpen the distinction even further.

Regression is usually the reenacting of childhood strategies for dealing with anxiety in order to avoid dealing with conflicts in the present. A patient in regression is not experiencing the childhood events that led him to adopt the maladaptive strategy, however, nor is he experiencing the accompanying affects. Regression in the analytic hour is a movement away from the edge of chaos.

The patient who appears to be regressing in the service of the ego, however, is reliving the traumatic events of childhood with a revival of his original feelings. Either he is moving toward the edge of chaos or he is already close to it. This may seem to be a regression in chronological terms, but it is clearly a progression in the coevolutionary development of the analysis.

The analyst learns to distinguish the reliving of traumatic childhood events with their original affects from histrionic reenactment with false but exaggerated feeling. A hysterical reenactment is another move away from the edge of chaos. With the hysterical patient, the events being reenacted are stereotyped traumatic events that have lost their connection with actual experience. They lack plausible detail and they are unrealistically distorted by grandiose fantasies that defend against real trauma.

Unlike memories genuinely relived during an analysis, these hysterical pseudo memories do not open the patient's associations to new material. They only lead back to themselves, and to endless repetition. The false memories of childhood seduction recently in the news lead the patient away from the therapeutic edge of chaos.

Conclusion

Of course, I have barely scratched the surface of complexity theory and its application to psychoanalysis in this chapter. Complexity theory provides a coherent framework for understanding the psychoanalytic process both as a whole and in fine detail. This is because the hierarchy of organizational structures in the mind of the patient is self-similar. The same principles of organization apply at all levels, from the smallest insight to the complex state of mind achieved by the termination of a successful analysis. In conclusion, I propose for your further investigation that complexity theory can provide a new scientific foundation for our hard-won experience with the therapeutic process of psychoanalysis.

References

Bak, P. 1994. "Self-Organized Criticality: A Holistic View of Nature." In *Complexity: Metaphors, Models, and Reality*, ed. G. A. Cowan, D. Pines, and D. Meltzer. Redwood City, CA: Addison Wesley.

Bak, P., Tang, C., and Wiesenfeld, K. 1988. "Self-Organized Criticality." *Physical Review* A 38: 364.

Berlecamp, E., Conway, J., and Guy, R. 1982. *Winning Ways*, vol. 2. New York: Academic Press.

Crutchfield, J. 1994. "Is Anything Ever New? Considering Emergence." In *Complexity: Metaphors, Models, and Reality*, ed. G. A. Cowan, D. Pines, and D. Meltzer, 515–38. Redwood City, CA: Addison Wesley.

Gell-Mann, M. 1994. *The Quark and the Jaguar*. New York: W. H. Freeman.

Hebb, D. 1949. *The Organization of Behavior*. New York: Wiley.

Kauffman, S. 1993. *The Origins of Order: Self-Organization and Selection in Evolution*. Oxford: Oxford University Press.

Khan, M. 1976. "The Changing Use of Dreams in Psychoanalytic Practice." *International Journal of Psychoanalysis* 57: 325–30.

Kris, A. 1982. *Free Association: Method and Process.* New Haven, CT: Yale University Press.

Kris, E. 1951. "Ego Psychology and Interpretation in Psychoanalytic Therapy." *Psychoanalytic Quarterly* 20: 15–30.

McClelland, J. L., and Rumelhart, D. E. 1986. "A Distributed Model of Human Learning and Memory." In *Parallel Distributed Processing,* vol. 2, ed. J. L. McClelland and D. E. Rumelhart, 170–215. Cambridge, MA: MIT Press.

Palombo, S. 1999. *The Emergent Ego: Complexity and Coevolution in the Psychoanalytic Process.* Madison, CT: International Universities Press.

Raup, D. 1992. *Extinction: Bad Genes or Bad Luck?* New York: Norton.

CHAPTER TWO

~

A Biological Theory of Brain Function and Its Relevance to Psychoanalysis

Walter J. Freeman, M.D.

A Brief Review of the Historical Emergence of Brain Theory

Psychiatry and psychoanalysis have two deep roots—one in the experiences people have through living together in social groups, the other in the experiences people have through interacting with the material world. Both kinds of experience are sifted through private reflection and integration. Many centuries of systematic experimentation and synthesis have fostered the growth of bodies of knowledge about these experiences that comprise the social and natural sciences. Health practitioners draw inferences from this knowledge to offer treatment regimens for individuals who are experiencing distress and disorder beyond their competence for achieving or restoring desired comfort in their lives. The regimens that can be inferred from these distinctive bodies of knowledge are inherently disjointed and may often be in opposition. Physicians and analysts have particular difficulty in adjudicating conflicting claims for the efficacy of particular regimens deriving from these alternative sources. For example, until the early nineteenth century, physicians held with Hippocrates that mental disorders stemmed from imbalances in the four humors of the body, while priests preached the wages of sin and astrologers looked to malign stars. If personal income was any measure, those who cast horoscopes and sold indulgences were far more successful in mental health care than were the physicians and surgeons of those millennia.

These standings began to change in the middle of the nineteenth century with the explosive growth in physics, chemistry, and biology. Psychiatrists, preeminently Bleuler and Charcot, increasingly looked for material causes of mental disorders such as schizophrenia and hysteria. Biologists were spectacularly successful in identifying Treponema pallidum as the cause of general paresis and salvarsan as the therapeutic "magic bullet," thereby creating a compelling biological model of mental disorders for a new generation of practitioners (Maurer and Maurer 2002). What remained after other successes in assigning material causes of aberrant behavior to viruses (rabies, polio, measles), environmental toxins (lead, mercury, ergot), vitamin and mineral deficiencies (cretinism, pellagra, beri beri), hormonal deficits (hypothyroidism, diabetic coma, lack of dopamine in postencephalitic and idiopathic Parkinson's disease), and genetic abnormalities (phenylketonuria, Tourette's syndrome, Huntingdon's chorea) came to be known as "functional disorders," which opened the door to brain theory and the concepts of what Geschwind called "deconnection" disorders (Geschwind and Kaplan 1962) and Glass and Mackey (1988) called "dynamic diseases."

The core concept of brain theory in the nineteenth century was nerve energy, and the parent science was thermodynamics. The flow of nerve energy was conceived to follow hierarchies of reflexes along axonal pathways and through "contact barriers" between neurons that offered resistance. Giving due priority to the first law of thermodynamics, nerve energy was conceived to be conserved, so that if blocked by high resistance in one path, the energy would take another. Freud (1895), in his attempt to lay a scientific foundation for psychoanalysis, later abandoned as "premature," labeled nerve energy as "Q" and wrote:

> This line of approach is derived directly from pathological clinical observations, especially those concerned with excessively intense ideas. These occur in hysteria and obsessional neurosis, where, as we shall see, the quantitative characteristic emerges more plainly than in the normal. . . . What I have in mind is the principle of neuronic inertia, which asserts that neurones tend to divest themselves of quantity (Q). . . . We arrive at the idea of a "cathected" neurone (N) filled with a certain quantity. . . . The principle of inertia finds expression in the hypothesis of a current, passing from the cell-processes or dendrites to the axone. . . . The secondary function [memory] is made possible by supposing that there are resistances, which oppose discharge . . . in the contacts [between the neurones], which thus function as barriers. The hypothesis of "contact-barriers" is fruitful in many directions. (356–59)

Indeed, that was an understatement, in that the greater part of biological psychiatry is now based on the chemistry of synaptic transmission and modulation.

In the twentieth century, the core concept of nerve energy was replaced by "information," which was carried by action potentials and processed in networks of neurons in accordance with the parent science of information theory (Freeman 1997). This model has not been well received by psychiatrists because the basis in logic neglects the emotional, irrational, and chaotic formants of thinking and behavior. The limitations of information processing have become ever more apparent with the growth of neural networks, which require that the dynamics of neurons and networks be frozen into frames, discretized into rational numbers, and linearized in order to use matrix algebra to describe operations on input vectors. Moreover, in the same century the growth of empirical neurochemistry and neuropharmacology has given psychiatrists an array of powerful neuroactive and psychoactive drugs with which to treat mental diseases. Unfortunately, these empirical remedies are accompanied neither by sound theoretical explanations of their actions nor by optimal schedules of administration. Practitioners are currently making do by trial and error under heavy pressures from health maintenance organizations to get the patients out the door, while differences between diverse accounts of the social and biological origins and dimensions of the pathogenesis and treatment of functional mental disorders remain unresolved.

Brain theory continues to grow explosively, fed by new data from the basic sciences and clinical uses of brain imaging, and by the parent sciences of complexity and nonlinear dynamics. These sciences are quite new entries into the situation, so it is premature to evaluate their utility for clinical judgment and selection of treatment regimens. They can provide valuable insights into the nature of brain function, how information theory can be applied, and the ways in which nonlinear dynamics may be used to construct new and more powerful brain theory.

My approach in this chapter is to review the platforms on which the cognitive sciences are based, to explain briefly some new observations on brain function that have been guided by nonlinear dynamics, to describe some implications for brain theory, and from these insights to offer some suggestions regarding how the relations between psychiatrists and psychoanalysts and their patients or clients might be reinterpreted and clarified to the benefit of all.

An Overview of the Cognitive Sciences

The cognitive sciences are broadly concerned with deriving the rules by which information from the world is gathered through the senses, processed in the brain, integrated, stored, retrieved, and deployed through muscular actions. There are many pathways that are being followed in this research. Neurologists observe and treat the disorders of thinking and of behavior in patients with brain damage, disease, and unusual developmental outcomes such as autism. Neurobiologists examine the brains and behaviors of animals using electrophysiological and imaging techniques. Psychologists investigate the stages by which infants and children develop competence in dealing with their unfolding worlds. Philosophers sift through the great systems of thought that have been distilled from human experience. Computer scientists model logic and language. Mathematicians design systems and computer-based dynamical devices that simulate and emulate thought processes, as we experience them through logic, introspection, and phenomenology. Owing to my predominant concern for the relations between cognition and behavior, I emphasize those aspects that are described as "embodied cognition," in which the body serves as the principal tool of the brain for cognitive development and the acquisition of knowledge, and as "situated cognition," in which the structure of the environment determines, and is determined by, the actions of individuals seeking knowledge.

A truism for most experimental scientists is that knowledge of the material world comes through the interface provided by the senses between the world and the brain. This view stands in opposition to alternative views that knowledge is implanted in the genome by evolution and is revealed in the course of ontogenesis to the individual and others, or that knowledge is received through immaterial intervention that is experienced by the individual as inspiration or revelation. I state this truism at the outset to clarify my premise that all knowledge gained by individuals is earned by their actions into the world, from which they suffer the due consequences. The goal of the *neuro*cognitive scientist is to describe, in terms of brain dynamics, how these actions are conceived, planned, and executed in the brains of individuals.

Since the ancient Greeks, scientists have held two conceptions about how our brains work to understand their environments. Scientists working in the tradition of Plato conceive perception as passive. The classic metaphor is Plato's cave, in which light coming from outside cast shadows on the walls and entered the eyes bearing indistinct and incomplete forms. These forms were compared by reason with a store of ideal forms for identification in an operation we now call "pattern recognition." Actions were selected by ethical judgment using the moral faculty, now being replaced by game theory.

In modern terms, this view is described as information processing by the brain using hierarchies of reflex arcs and neural networks. Action begins with the senses, particularly the eyes and skin, when neurons respond to patterns of energy, such as textures of light and dark, of smoothness and edges, and generate patterns of action potentials that carry the forms of objects. The sense organs extract and encode the forms' input as information. The information is carried from the sense organs by action potentials through relays into the upper levels of the brain. There the information is refined in the sensory cortices, stored in the frontal lobes, retrieved, and compared with new information so as to classify fresh stimuli and select appropriate emotions and courses of action. Actions and emotions are selected from menus of algorithms stored in the amygdala and basal ganglia. Movements are initiated by motor commands that descend into the brain stem and spinal cord to contract the muscles in response to the inputs. Behaviorism to the extent that it concerns brains at all (Skinner 1969), "strict AI" (artificial intelligence), industrial robotics, and feedforward neural networks using supervised learning are all based on this Platonic model.

The alternative classic view, propounded by the Aristotelians, is that perception is active. It requires movement into the world by probing, cutting, and burning in order to learn by manipulation the forms, textures, weights, and appearances of objects. Behavior is proactive, not reactive. This model is central to a variety of cognitive systems such as pragmatism, existentialism, Piagetian developmental psychology, Gestaltism, its derivative Gibsonian ecological psychology, and embodied cognition. In these modern views, information is implicit in the objects that the brain is seeking. The search is initiated when the brain creates a goal with a need for information to realize that goal, and the brain directs the sense organs to find the information in the world, using the cognitive map in the medial temporal lobe to direct the search.

At the same time the brain prepares the sensory circuits by tuning them with copies of the motor commands called "corollary discharges" (Freeman 2001; Sperry 1950) that selectively sensitize the cortices to the desired input. The information carried by objects is detected by the senses. They send it to the sensory cortices where it is extracted by resonances in the neural circuits that are tuned just before the search takes place. These actions and the prior tuning constitute the exercise of foresight and selective attention. They limit the entry to the desired information, not whatever forms or energies from irrelevant objects happen to enter the sense organs or be put there by a naive experimenter. A key type of information selected by the resonances corresponds to the uses to which the objects are to be put, their "affordances" (Gibson 1979). This also is the domain of recurrent neural networks using unsupervised learning, which is the blind probing for structure that extracts information by gradient descent in high-dimensional measurement spaces.

A third view differs from both these classic views. This approach was pioneered by Saint Thomas Aquinas (1272) in his effort to bring Aristotelian doctrine into conformance with Christianity. The basic Thomist premise is the unity and inviolability of the self that is inherent in the soul, brain, and body. This unity does not allow the entry of forms (information) into the self. The impact of the world onto the senses gives rise to states of activity he called "phantasms," which are ephemeral and unique to each impact and therefore cannot be known. The function of the brain is to exercise the faculty of the imagination, which is not present in the Aristotelian view, in order to abstract and generalize over the phantasms that are triggered by unique events. These processes of abstraction and generalization create information that assimilates the body and brain to the world. Assimilation is not adaptation by passive information processing, nor is it an accumulation of representations by resonances. It is the shaping of the self to bring it into optimal interaction with desired aspects of the world. The goal of an action is a state of competence that Maurice Merleau-Ponty (1945) called "maximum grip." An example is the intaglio shaping of the hand in grasping a cup, by which neither the cup nor its molecules penetrate the skin or brain. Assimilation is the beginning for all knowledge.

Thus the manner of acquisition of knowledge is by thrusting the body into the world, from which our word "intention" has come from the Latin *intendere*, or "stretching forth." The thrust initiates the action–perception cycle, which is followed by the changes through which the self learns about the world by assimilation (from the Latin *assimulatio*, comparison, to "make like") or the adequation of the self to the world. There is no transfer of information across the senses into the brain, but instead the creation of meaning that can be reexpressed as information within the brain under the existing constraints of the brain and body. In this respect, cognition is related to digestion, which protects the integrity of the immunological self by breaking all forms of foodstuffs into elementary ions and molecules that are absorbed and built into complex macromolecules, each now bearing the immunological signature of the individual self.

Similarly, events and objects in the world are broken into sheets of action potentials like pinpoints of light, the "raw sense data" of analytic philosophers and the phantasms of Thomists, and new forms emerge through constructions by the chaotic dynamics in sensory cortices. The explanation for this manner of function of both the neural and the digestive systems is essentially the same: The world is infinitely complex, and the self can only know and incorporate what the brain makes within itself. This is why neurobiologists using passive neural networks cannot solve the figure-ground problem, why linguists cannot do machine translation, why philosophers cannot solve the symbol grounding problem, why cognitive scientists cannot surmount the limitations of expert systems, and why engineers cannot yet build autonomous robots capable of operating in unstructured environments. The unbounded complexity of the world defeats those classic Platonic and Aristotelian approaches (Kozma, Freeman, and Érdi 2003).

The Neural Dynamics of the Construction of Individual Experience

The Thomist concept of intentionality offers a way to solve these intractable problems, because they stem largely from the attempt by Descartes to make mathematics the foundation of the natural sciences instead of their principal tool for quantitative analysis. Thomist philosophy in the thirteenth century provided the basis for the explosive growth of medieval science, medicine, law, industry, and navigation that nurtured the worldwide expansion of Western culture and the Renaissance, but Thomist philosophy was replaced by the Cartesian revolution in the seventeenth century, giving rise to modern science. If the current impasse is owing to Cartesian philosophy, then its predecessor, Descartes' target of opportunity, gives a well-documented starting place for an anti-Cartesian revolution. In particular, the process of intentionality offers a firm base for interpreting recent neurobiological data that can explain how and why all knowledge is constructed within brains and is not imported through the senses as the forms of objects and events or as information or representations about them.

The evidence on which I base this assertion has come from my experiments on animals that have been trained to respond to conditioned stimuli (Freeman 2000, 2001, 2003, 2004). I record the neural responses to the stimuli at various stages of transmission in the olfactory, visual, auditory, and somatomotor systems as the action potentials elicited by the stimuli course through the brain to the sensory cortices and beyond. The essential finding, alike in all the sensory systems, is that the neural activity directly evoked by a stimulus, the raw sense data, the phantasm, that is observed in bursts of input-driven action potentials, serves to select a pattern of activity to be created in and by that sensory cortex to which the stimulus is directed. The pattern generated by the cortex is not a "representation" of the stimulus, but is instead a briefly sustained neural discharge that constitutes the significance and value of the stimulus for the animal. Such patterns depend on past learning about the stimulus that has been embedded in the modified synapses in cortical networks, so the patterns are unique to each individual and not specific for the stimuli by which their construction is triggered. The sensory cortices broadcast these spatial patterns, while the raw sense data, the phantasms, having done their work, are deleted—attenuated by spatial filtering. The broadcasts overlap in the medial temporal lobe where the patterns interact to form global multisensory percepts. The combined patterns are integrated into recent memory and located in environmental space by passage through the hippocampus with the cognitive map, and at this stage they are finally accessible to awareness as Gestalts.

Each cortical pattern resembles a visual picture in gray tones, in having a common carrier wave (like light) that is modulated in amplitude (light and dark). Each pattern holds briefly and dissolves, making way for the next in a sequence like frames in a movie film (Sacks 2004). Every local pattern is a frame created as a "wave packet" by a phase transition in neuron populations that resembles the transformation of a gas into a liquid, like water vapor into a raindrop. Clouds of action potentials like water molecules in steam condense into scintillating disks in the cortex about the size of a toenail. The origin of the spatial pattern carried by a wave packet lies in the remote past as well as the recent involvement of the animal with its environment. The events leading to the formation of a wave packet in sensory cortex begin with the emergence in the whole brain of a conception of a future state, whether desired or feared, that is embodied in a collection of wave packets. This collection evolves into a neural motor command, which is intended to move the animal in search of the sensory input that is needed to facilitate realization of the desired future state. That command is accompanied by its copies, the corollary discharges that are sent to all of the sensory systems where they selectively sensitize the cortical networks for the modality-specific sensory consequences of the intended action. This preparation involves attention as well as intention, which together yield the state of expectancy, which simultaneously is impending action and the tuning of the sensory cortices to what the animal is seeking by looking, listening, sniffing, and probing.

The response to an expected stimulus can be said to preexist the arrival of the stimulus by the creation of a hypothesis that is to be tested by an act of observation and perception. The hypothesis is the state of selective sensitivity that has the potential for creating one or more types of wave packet. The dynamic process of creating a spatial pattern of the wave packet is a form of generalization that identifies the class to which the stimulus belongs, including its meaning. Abstraction takes place when the sensory-driven activity—the raw sense data—is removed during transmission of the wave packet.

The formation of ever-changing goal states and perceptual hypotheses requires the repeated construction of wave packets with novel spatial patterns.

This construction is done by neural circuits that generate carrier waves, which continually vary in form and confer the property that each construction is never twice identical to those preceding (Freeman 2000). The capability for such novelty resides in brain chaos. Chaotic dynamics has the property of creating information, which is essential for the construction of new goals that precede action, and new categories that precede perception. Chaos also has the capacity for destroying information, which is necessary for generalization and abstraction, and which is done by spatial and temporal filtering.

Every sensory cortex maintains a landscape of chaotic attractors that correspond to the perceptual categories that the subject is capable of discriminating (Ohl, Scheich, and Freeman 2001). When the subject attends to an expected event, the landscape is created, and a known stimulus gives access to the proper basin. After the dynamics converges to the selected attractor, the specific details of the stimulus are removed. The raw sense data by which category selection is performed are discarded after they are no longer useful. These properties of chaos are most evident when testing disproves a hypothesis, because the resulting stimulus is novel. The generalized reaction is known as the orienting reflex. Upon this failure, the prediction is changed by creative activity in the limbic system and disseminated by corollary discharges, so that a new hypothesis is tested. The process is repeated by the creation of new attractors by trial and error, until a reward is forthcoming and a hypothesis is proved.

The changes generated by chaotic dynamics are in the form of the modification of numerous synapses that interconnect the neurons in many parts of the brain. When the process finally succeeds, the changes bring about assimilation not by the incorporation of the forms or the information offered by the world, but instead by a creative reshaping of the brain as well as the body that facilitates continuing interactions of the self with its world, insofar as that world is accessible to the brain and body. Learning to dance, to play the violin, or to play tennis (Dreyfus 1979) requires changes in the body as extensive as those among the synapses in the brain.

The completion of the action-perception cycle up to and including assimilation is by incorporation of the new learning into the life history of the individual. Here is the stage where phenomena are experienced and consciousness appears in the cycle, long after the raw sense data, the phantasms, the flashing pinpoints of light, are gone. To be useful, each new experience must be integrated into the cumulative personal life history, by which actions are judged, new goals created, and new actions planned. In this view, consciousness comes only *after* an action has been initiated, *not before*, so that the action is perceived by the actor as a cause, and the sensory consequences as effects. This self-awareness of the intent-action-perception-assimilation cycle is the basis for the concept of causation and for the critical importance of the time lag between effect and its necessarily prior cause. Studies by Piaget (1930) have shown that this association of cause and effect is laid down in the somatomotor phase of development, when an infant is learning to control its body. How and why the experience of awareness then emerges with early cognitive development in the way that it does are matters for speculation, but its phenomenology gives clear indication of both the powers and the limitations of this remarkable process. Its temporal range is enormous, but its momentary content is sparse. Our actions are influenced by our entire life history, but we are conscious of only minute, intermittent fragments in sequential moments of thought. There is compelling clinical and physiological evidence that the medial temporal lobe is essential for the construction of life history, which gives the wholeness of intentional structure, the self, personhood, or, more popularly, personality. However, that brain part is not necessary for consciousness, nor is the hippocampus a site of long-term memory storage. On the contrary, the dynamic processes that comprise intentionality in action are widely distributed, and likewise the personality to which it gives rise. Furthermore, most of intention is inaccessible to consciousness at any one moment, not so much that access is forbidden, rather that the sheer massiveness of the dynamic state space (the stage of the vast range of conscious and unconscious processes that elaborate all intentional actions) precludes squeezing the entire past through the eye of a needle. Reification of intentionality as "the unconscious" appears to reduce this living body of experience inappropriately to a static warehouse of latent memories, often with locked doors.

In Platonic, Aristotelian, and Thomist doctrines, a separation is made between the material and spiritual domains with identification of a spiritual agency, the soul, that moves the body. In the Cartesian metaphor, the soul is to the body as a pilot is to a ship. Most scientists today have adopted monist views that give no place to soul. Those adhering to a passive view of cognition find the source of agency instead in the genetic and environmental determinants of behavior and debate the relative primacy of "nature" versus "nurture." Those practicing an active view propound the primacy of self-determination but find themselves uncomfortably skewered on the horns of the unresolved antinomy between "free will" and "determinism." New developments in the sciences of nonlinear dynamics, complexity, and chaos indicate that this conflict is a pseudo problem (Freeman 2001). Human action is not wholly determined by genes, world, or self alone, but instead by an ever-shifting balance of interactions among the three formants. The challenge for neuroscientists is to analyze the brain dynamics by which goals emerge in the form of imagined future states, which lead to neural patterns of selective attention, prediction of expected input, and actions that are intended to bring into conformance the flow of sensory input with the desired state. How do we come to dream of that which should be but is not, and then act to realize the dream? In principle, the material mechanisms through which novel patterns are created through nonlinear dynamics can explain the process, without resort to spiritual causes, though speculations are not thereby excluded that spiritual events may parallel material processes.

The Neural Basis for the Construction of Knowledge through Culture

Learning leads to assimilation, but assimilation by itself does not lead to knowledge because knowledge is intrinsically social. It is embedded in the particular culture in and by which a group of humans live. Yet assimilation is by the chaotic constructions within each individual of unique forms and contents from private experience. This process leads to a question of profound importance for neuroscientists and philosophers to answer. How can there be shared assimilation between any two individuals and among many individuals? The world is infinitely complex, offering a different face to each individual. No one can fully grasp any part in its fullness owing to the finite scope of our skills in comprehension. This is the reason we live our lives by continually posing hypotheses and asking questions that by their nature already contain the answers we get and nothing more. This is the reason that knowledge comes primarily by framing questions and only secondarily by finding the answers. The natural tendency of the individual in this ongoing dialectic through learning is to become specialized and grow progressively away from humanity, ever deeper into an arcane discipline that can be shared with fewer and fewer aspirants to like understanding. Such is the loneliness of isolated graduate students and professionals in the humanities, which is comparable to the anomie of rootless urban drones and the angst of intellectual dilettantes.

The natural sciences differ from the humanities in the respect that knowledge comes more overtly through joint action in the field and laboratory. Other groups before acceptance communicate results of experiments from teams of scientists in scholarly conferences and publications with the intent of replication. The most compelling agreement comes with useful application of new knowledge in the development of instruments, chemicals, procedures, and operations that change our ways of living, often dramatically, for better or worse. The more far-reaching developments lead to the institution of new courses of instruction, undergraduate majors, text books and monographs, academic departments, and entirely new industries with enormous economic and industrial investments involving the concerted actions of thousands, even millions, of workers. In brief, shared knowledge comes through shared action.

Assimilation through Hebbian learning is not enough to explain the neurobiological mechanisms by which understanding develops that bonds individuals by the process of socialization. Synaptic learning unchecked leads to isolation, lack of empathy, and inability to act in concert. Examples of extreme failures of socialization may include some autistic children and psychopaths who may have astonishing cognitive skills but stunted emotional development. The neural mechanisms of learning with their tendency to isolation of the individual must be countered by opposing mechanisms. In the context of brain dynamics, the changes in brains that occur during learning under reinforcement are by the growth of self-organized intentional structure, which is progressively elaborated and differentiated. Learning new structure that is logically inconsistent with existing structure in dynamical systems such as brains requires mechanisms for dissolution (also called "unlearning," regression, devolution, or dedifferentiation; Freeman 2001), which occurs by the induction of chaos prior to the emergence of new order.

There is abundant evidence for the existence and operation in the extremes of such destructive mechanisms of chaotic dynamics in the widespread application of social technologies for behavioral modification involved in religious conversions, inculcation of political ideals and allegiances, indoctrination of recruits into military and paramilitary troops and teenage gangs, and the group bonding that occurs in fraternities, sororities, and large corporations. The changes in individuals brought about by use of these techniques do not involve forgetting or loss of memory, but instead occur by restructuring their personalities. Dissolution presages new learning with deep, often dramatic, but rarely catastrophic changes in values and points of view that typically are lifelong. Coercive uses of the techniques are widely known as "brain washing" and "reeducation." These uses have had the unfortunate effect of obscuring the ubiquity and necessity of these techniques in normal socialization. A more felicitous appellation might be "the Scrooge Effect," to emphasize the beneficial aspect of a night of terror. The dissolution prepares for new learning by self-organization, whereby the preexisting life history of an individual is transiently weakened, even melted down, so that new structure can grow that is not logically consistent with all that has come before. The ubiquity of the process provides strong evidence, if any further is needed, that brains are dynamical systems and not logical devices.

The biological techniques for inducing dissolution are well known. Individuals separate themselves or are isolated from their normal social surroundings and support systems. They engage in or are subjected to severe physical exercise as in dancing, sports, and military drills; lack of sleep; chemical stresses of their brains through purgatives and fasting; and the induction of powerful emotional states of love, hate, fear, or anger. At some threshold the customary structure of the individual begins to crumble, and a collapse may occur that was described by Ivan Pavlov as "transmarginal inhibition," the stage of physiological arousal beyond which further excitation leads to paradoxical depression. The experience may range from ecstatic visions of angels and blinding illumination through degrees of elation or discomfort to the stark terror of psychic free fall (Sargant 1957). There is regression to successively earlier levels of assimilation as the structure of intentionality dissolves, particularly with resurfacing old patterns of relations to parental care. There is a loss of normal constraints on behavior and, in extreme instances, of language, locomotion, posture, and even consciousness as the individual collapses. Recovery from collapse is followed by a state of extreme suggestibility, in which the skills of language and the competencies of daily living are regained, yet new values and habits can be established. This is done in a social setting of succor and loving care by attendants who induce by example and exhortation the cooperative behaviors that lead to shared beliefs and, above all, to blind trust in the new companions and the social organization they embody and provide. This is a two-way process, because the caregivers get strong feelings of satisfaction from their supportive actions, and the recipients have strong sensitivity to peer pressures experienced as feelings of need for approval. The process is frequently referred to as being reborn (Verger 1954). In the absence of support there is reestablishment of the status quo ante, meaning that the opportunity for change can be lost, attesting to the high degree of dynamic stability that characterizes intentional structures in normal circumstances.

Little is known about the neurophysiology of these personal and social interactions and even less about the neurochemistry of the changes in brains that occur in and are induced by dissolution. The evolutionary antecedents of the techniques for socialization are likely to be found in the processes by which bonding occurs in altricial mammals as a necessary basis for reproduction (Freeman 1995). The most likely candidate for a leading role in dissolution is a chemical neuromodulator named oxytocin (Pedersen et al. 1992). This neuropeptide has been known for many years as the agent in the female body that induces labor in parturition and subsequently lactation in nourishment of the young. More recently, oxytocin has been found to be released by the brain into itself during sexual intercourse, particularly during orgasm in both men and women, and to be implicated in pair bonding not only of the parents to the child but also of parents to each other. The neurochemical actions of oxytocin in the brain are widespread, extremely complex, and difficult to study, so that much remains to be explored, but present knowledge shows that this neuropeptide is capable of inducing the meltdown of past learning that enables new learning.

A simple example is the release of oxytocin flooding the brain of the multiparous ewe during delivery of her second and later litters, following which the dam refuses to nurse her earlier litters, having expunged the olfactory imprint required for maternal recognition of them as her offspring (Kendrick et al. 1992). This primitive but well documented instance of dissolution serves also to explain its biological utility. Oxytocin is not likely to act alone, rather in concert with other neuropeptides, the neuroamines, and an array of amino acids from the brain stem nuclei and periaqueductal gray matter, all known to mediate states of emotion and levels of affect and disposition (Panksepp 1998; Pert 1997). However, existing data and theory are alike inadequate to the task of modeling neurochemical systems of this complexity.

I postulate that affiliation (Carter et al. 1997) is realized through new learning by cooperative behaviors driven by brains that have been prepared by the neurochemical changes precipitating dissolution, a chaotic state of transition that leads to dissolution and regression, clearing the way to formation of new brain circuits. Cooperative action is the bedrock of social bonding for the same reason that brains work by creating and testing hypotheses as their means for information processing. The reason is that each individual in a social group is infinitely complex and can never be known completely by any other individual. The limitation is ever more severe as the size of groups grows larger than the nuclear family. Inadequacy of knowledge is compensated by the development of blind trust, which transcends language and provides unquestioning lifelong bonds and allegiances. The social technology of bonding is well known, having been explored by anthropologists in studies of tribal rites of passage, ordeals, and ceremonies (e.g., Sargant 1957; Verger 1954), usually accompanied by music, drumming, dance, and other forms of predictable repetitive actions, and by symbols such as flags, icons, totems, and, in modern times, corporate logos, military insignias, and the colored armbands of teenage gangs. I suggest further that the examples from the conversions cited above may be extremes, and that dissolution may be occurring episodically throughout infancy and childhood, and perhaps in minimal degree every night during sleep and dreaming. The process clearly deserves more attention and study than it has yet received.

Inferences Regarding Psychiatric Practice

The human brain is finite, whereas the world is infinite in complexity and variety. We learn what we need and what we can by assimilation, which is more than adaptation by acquiescence. Assimilation follows active intrusion into the parts of the world that are accessible to us, shaping our bodies and brains and the world to meet our expectations, projections, desires, and dreams. Our cumulative experience, when shared with others of our kind through joint actions, supports the growth of knowledge. In the sciences, which comprise a vast transnational social enterprise, knowledge takes the form of "laws." These laws are not eternal truths: they are tools we use to predict, plan, act, and test hypotheses. An example is the law of causality by which we build chains of cause and effect through time. The concept is essential for the assignment by parents, teachers, courts, and tribunals of credit and blame, reward and punishment. This same tool is also widely used in science and technology for constructing linear chains of causes in search of convincing evidence, often referred to as "the smoking gun." This approach gives a feeling of necessary connection, but it is out of place in therapeutic situations, where the task is to determine risk factors, predictors, and relationships in order to fix the problem and not the blame. A prominent example of misuse was the claim by cigarette makers that there was no proof of a causal connection between smoking and lung cancer. That claim impeded efforts of public health officials to educate the public on the dangers of smoking seen as a risk factor irrespective of "cause."

Mental health workers are charged with the responsibility for assisting those who are distressed or who afflict others with their unacceptable experiences and behaviors. Their aim is to bring about changes in attitudes and behaviors through learning. Not surprisingly, their therapeutic approaches, as they have evolved over many centuries, have relied on the well-known techniques of both individual and social assimilation in varying degree and emphasis. Many Western psychiatrists invest heavily in cognitive methods of behavioral modification of individuals by teaching, analyzing, explaining, exhorting, and in extreme cases, coercing conformity within accepted standards of the community. Others rely heavily on mobilization of community support, especially from family and friends (Frankl 1973). Drugs are admissible, even required by practice or law, usually though not always with the consent of the subject. The use of electroconvulsive therapy (ECT) may be likened to the use of drugs in providing a shortcut to force dissolution and regression physically so as to induce a state of malleability and an opportunity for reeducation, though with a heavy price in disruption of memory. We may infer that the desired changes in brain dynamics of learning take place through Hebbian association and anti-Hebbian habituation, extinction, and normalization, which are enacted and supported by neurohumoral agents, including the biogenic amines and neuropeptides in collaboration with nerve growth factors that operate by mobilizing sections of the genome (Panksepp 1998; Pert 1997).

Faith healers and shamans in technologically less complex social groupings rely on techniques that many Westerners regard pejoratively, and shortsightedly, as brain washing. There is heavy emphasis on the familial and social contexts to which behaviors are to be adapted, and there is strong reliance on altered states of consciousness involving the induction of strong emotional arousal leading to trance, transmarginal inhibition, and hallucinatory experiences. The use of drugs such as alcohol, nicotine, mescaline, ayahuasca, and peyote might be regarded as shortcuts to avoid requirements for arduous and prolonged practices such as fasting, purging, vigil-keeping, withdrawal through meditation, and the suffering of painful stimuli, with the possibility, often intentional, of mutilation and scarification in rites of passage. As noted already, the neurochemistry and synaptic changes underlying these often dramatic modifications of behaviors are still largely unexplored by neuroscientists, owing to the extreme circumstances in which they come into play.

Psychoanalysis has different mixes of many of these components. In contrast to most other approaches, the relationship is conventionally dyadic between therapist and patient. The use of drugs seems not to be a part of the culture, perhaps because of early adverse experience with cocaine, and ECT is eschewed. The classic approach using free association may be likened to the unsupervised learning used in recurrent neural networks, the blind search for unknown forms using techniques that are described as random walks, Markov processes, and genetic algorithms. These are the techniques used by bacteria and genes that have no brains. Use of the method in psychoanalysis is based on the premise that the structure generated by intentionality is illogical, vast, and dynamically partitioned into loosely interconnected domains. Dynamic barriers may have walled some of this off as an adaptive mechanism for the avoidance of psychic pain. The aim of the analysts is to assist a patient to rove freely through this minefield of adverse associations in hope of detecting signs of emotional arousal that reflect proximity to a guarded domain of traumatic memories—that is, exerting malign influence on rational behavior without the awareness of the patient. If the dynamic barrier can be surmounted, then that forbidden domain might be brought to consciousness for assimilation and resolution of conflict.

Prior to an attempt to use neurodynamics to gain insights into the therapeutic process, let it be acknowledged that the goal of constructing a map or thesaurus between concepts in neurodynamics and psychoanalysis is illusory. For an example in a nearby field, an impasse has been reached in attempting to map "genes" into "DNA sequences." A geneticist, having localized a gene for a trait like eye color, cannot get a straight answer from a molecular biologist as to which particular sequence of the four base pairs of nucleic acids constitutes the gene. The intellectual structures of the knowledge bases in classical and molecular genetics have deep roots in cultural domains that are too far apart to allow any simple translation between them. Yet the disciplines address the same phenomena from differing perspectives and can be expected to complement one another. Similarly, the neuroscientific structure of "microscopic-mesoscopic-macroscopic-neurodynamics" is comparable to the philosophical structure of "intent-action-perception-assimilation" and to the psychoanalytic structure of "id-ego-superego-transference." The problem at issue is not how to map each term into the others, but how to extract insights in each domain from distinctions that are obvious, even inevitable, in the others, and to use theory to create new therapeutic procedures or more readily adapt those we now have.

Neurodynamics, intentionality, and psychodynamics are descriptions of processes by which structures are created in brain state space, character, and personality. The systems all postulate an imbalance of some kind as the genesis of action, variously described as a nonequilibrium chemical process like a deficit of glucose, as a need like thirst, curiosity, or hunger for power ("drive"), as an intent constituting the prediction of a future state ("stretching forth"), and as the id ("it"). They all postulate goal-orientation, but with differences such that with intent the goals are internally derived in each subject, whereas with drive the goals are externally and universally defined by observers, and with id there is an appeal to genetic transmission of urges in mythic proportions. Cognitive structures are founded on these bases. Reasons, purposes, and motives are the explanations given for actions intended or taken and observed. Wishes, desires, and dreams are the phenomenological experiences of intentional actions contemplated or engaged. Hormone, will, eros, and libido are causal agencies we attribute to actions directed toward homeostasis, sexual pleasure, reproduction, love, companionship, hatred, and power. Such lists do little more than sketch the complexity of human affairs. Where the problem comes into focus is in the application of theory to understand the dynamics of mental disorders, with the intent of changing the intentional structures of disturbed individuals. Of many possible insights and perspectives, my immediate concern is with the phenomena of assimilation, dissolution, and new learning that is possible, after the process of chaotic destabilization has led to regression (unlearning) and a clean slate, or some degree thereof.

The process may appear in psychoanalysis in the form of the core concept of transference (Pincus, Freeman and Modell, in press), which clearly relates to the dynamics of assimilation, whether to objects, events, situations, or other persons, technically between patient and therapist. Neurodynamics may illuminate the process by enabling the distinction between structural advancement by conventional, constructive learning in Hebbian association, habituation, and normalization, versus advancement through discontinuous and illogical modification by chaotic dissolution and rebuilding in new directions. The distinction is more than a matter of degree of change. At one pole is the cool detachment of cognitive therapy, which is appropriate, for example, in depression owing to chemical imbalance, bereavement, guilt, or shame. At the other pole is fierce emotional involvement in abreactive techniques, which are appropriate, for example, in posttraumatic stress disorder, dissociative identity disorders, and various types of neurotic maladaptation. Neurodynamics helps to show that assimilation and dissolution may be active at both extremes and in varying degrees between the poles, while emphasizing that two very different kinds of chemistry, neural processing, and therapeutic methodologies are at work, whether simultaneously or, more likely, sequentially.

An essential element for breaching the resistance in a patient to confrontation of buried material is postulated to be an intense emotional reaction that may be comparable to the prerequisite for a conversion experience. This insight implies that an approach to understanding the biology of abreaction and the malleability that follows may require the same neuroscientific exploration of brain dynamics that is needed to understand the neural mechanisms of social group formation. However, strong emotion by itself is insufficient. Every patient comes to a therapist after making an intentional decision, which carries an expectation and hope of relief to be found through guidance and benefaction. Likewise, the therapist accepts a new patient with the hope of a perfect match. Both are inevitably disappointed in varying degrees as analysis progresses, arousing perhaps quite strong hope, joy, frustration, anger, nostalgia, and fear—indeed, at different times the entire array of human emotions. What may yet be lacking is perception by the patient of his or her own conflicts and inconsistencies in intentional structure. Perception of them may be the key to destabilization as prelude to dissolution. Clearly, this perception carries the weight of danger to the patient and to the therapeutic relationship. The analyst may also experience fear and back away from the prospect of the collapse of intentionality, which may be strong medicine indeed.

Here is the cusp of choice. Many analyses, perhaps most, career through misunderstandings, false leads, open wounds, short-term insights, and small triumphs, but peter out with no clear resolution or, even more disheartening, with the patients' children turning up on the analyst's couch, bringing the same complaints as their parents. There may be no ignition of an intense encounter, no warning sign of incipient destabilization to alert the analyst to a weakness in the intentional structure that has been jangled, no manifestation in tremors of the hands and lips, evasiveness of the eyes, breaks in the voice and train of thought, restless changes in posture, or indecisive pacing. If and when these signs appear, the analyst needs a sure grasp of personality dynamics to decide whether to cut and run or to seek confrontation and precipitate collapse—and be ready to solicit change in a new direction, having already thought through what that direction might best be, based on deep knowledge of the history, family, physiological status, and intentional structure of the patient, and be ready to give handsomely of time, energy, and emotional support during the transition that culminates and justifies transference.

Conclusion

The convenience, utility, and attractiveness of concepts from nonlinear dynamics in advancing further studies of brain functions and therapeutic relationships is obvious, so that some words of caution may be in order. Dynamics in engineering is well-grounded in the science of measurement, so that the numbers coming from observations on physical and economic systems can be used to test theories that are expressed in probability distributions and differential equations. Without the numbers, the theories are metaphors. Without suitable yardsticks and spaces, there are no numbers.

The Shannon-Weaver theory provides a superb yardstick for the measurement of information, but does so by divorcing information from meaning. There is no yardstick for meaning, nor is it likely that there ever can be. The use of metaphors from dynamics for heuristic purposes in psychiatry and psychoanalysis to complement and inform the classical concepts and myths is to be commended, provided that they are not taken too literally. The only existing yardstick of a proposed brain theory is the extent to which theory improves the statistics of the numbers of people who have been compromised in their social and personal lives by mental disorders, the numbers of clients who have been restored to competency by treatment regimens, and the economic and social costs of doing so. Even these numbers are hard to come by, but they constitute the best yardstick we now have, and if brain theory suffices to emphasize this aspect, in addition to explaining the necessity for unlearning of intentional structure prior to the creation of fundamentally new structure, theory will have paid its way.

Summary

I have described the history of brain theory in terms of three kinds of theories of perception. The most widely used sees perception as dependent on passive inflow from the environment of information that is used to make and process representations of objects and events. A second kind views perception as an active search for information that is inherent in the environment and is extracted by tuned resonances in brain circuits. A third kind holds that perception works by the creation of meaning through chaotic dynamics that forms hypotheses about the environment and that promotes adaptation by learning. I also briefly sketched out experimental evidence for creative dynamics in brains. Brains, as finite systems, work this way in order to cope with the infinite complexity of the world. All that brains can know is the hypotheses they construct and the results of testing them by acting into the environment, and learning by assimilation from the sensory consequences of their actions. The process is intentionality. It works through the intent-action-perception-assimilation cycle.

The cost of this solution to the problem of infinite complexity by hypothesis testing is the progressive isolation of individuals as they accumulate their unique experiences through which their personalities form. Socialization and the acquisition of shared knowledge require the emergence of new personality structure by self-organization through chaotic dissolution of existing structure, as prelude to creation of new traits, habits, and values. Dissolution is most clearly detected in a crisis situation as regression to earlier stages of development from which a fresh start can be made. A state of malleability emerges in the depth of crisis, in which compassionate companions through loving care can invite cooperative actions. Joint actions support the growth of a new lifestyle based in trust. Socialization requires neurochemical mechanisms of affiliation and bonding that evolved through the requirements of parental care of altricial offspring in mammalian reproduction. These mechanisms are invoked by means of behavioral techniques from cultural evolution and may underlie effective transference. Therapists should know the dynamics, neural mechanisms, behavioral signs, methods of induction, and therapeutic utility of dissolution. Lack of understanding may cause the failure to seize windows of opportunity for long-term relief by restructuring intentionality in distressed patients.

Acknowledgments

This research was supported by grant MH 06686 from the National Institute of Mental Health. Helpful commentaries on earlier drafts were received from Arnold J. Modell, David Pincus, and David Tresan.

References

Aquinas, St. Thomas. 1272/1952. *The Summa Theologica*, trans. Fathers of the English Dominican Province. Rev. Daniel J. Sullivan. Published by William Benton as Vol. 19, Great Books Series. Chicago: Encyclopedia Britannica, Inc.

Carter C. S., Lederhendler, I. I., and Kirkpatrick, B. 1997. "The Integrative Neurobiology of Affiliation." *Annals of the New York Academy of Sciences* 807: 501–3.

Dreyfus, H. L. 1979. *What Computers Can't Do: The Limits of Artificial Intelligence*. New York: Harper Colophon.

Frankl, V. 1973. *The Doctor and the Soul*. New York: Random House.

Freeman, W. J. 1995. *Societies of Brains*. Mahwah, NJ: Lawrence Erlbaum Associates.

Freeman, W. J. 1997. "Three Centuries of Category Errors in Studies of the Neural Basis of Consciousness and Intentionality." *Neural Networks* 10: 1175–83.

Freeman, W. J. 2000. *Neurodynamics: An Exploration of Mesoscopic Brain Dynamics*. London, UK: Springer-Verlag.

Freeman, W. J. 2001. *How Brains Make Up Their Minds*. New York: Columbia University Press.

Freeman, W. J. 2003. "A Neurobiological Theory of Meaning in Perception. Part 1. Information and Meaning in Nonconvergent and Nonlocal Brain Dynamics." *International Journal of Bifurcation Chaos* 13: 2493–511.

Freeman, W. J. 2004. "Origin, Structure, and Role of Background EEG Activity. Part 1. Analytic Phase." *Clinical Neurophysiology* 115: 2077–88.

Freud, S. 1895. "The Project of a Scientific Psychology." In *The Origins of Psychoanalysis*, trans. E. Mosbacher and J. Strachey, ed. M. Bonaparte, A. Freud, and E. Kris, 347–446. New York: Basic Books, 1954.

Geschwind, N. and Kaplan, E. 1962. "A Human Cerebral Deconnection Syndrome: A Preliminary Report." *Neurology* 12: 675–85.

Gibson, J. J. 1979. *The Ecological Approach to Visual Perception*. Boston: Houghton Mifflin.

Glass, L. and Mackey, M. C. 1988. *From Clocks to Chaos: The Rhythms of Life*. Princeton, NJ: Princeton University Press.

Kendrick, K. M., Levy, F., and Keverne, E. W. B. 1992. "Changes in the Sensory Processing of Olfactory Signals Induced by Birth in Sheep." *Science* 256: 833–36.

Kozma, R., Freeman, W. J., and Érdi, P. 2003. "The KIV Model—Nonlinear Spatio-Temporal Dynamics of the Primordial Vertebrate Forebrain." *Neurocomputing* 52: 819–26.

Maurer, K. and Maurer, U. 2002. *Alzheimer: The Life of a Physician and the Career of a Disease*, trans. N. Levi and A. Burns. New York: Columbia University Press.

Merleau-Ponty, M. 1945/1962. *Phenomenology of Perception*, trans. C. Smith. New York: Humanities Press.

Panksepp, J. 1998. *Affective Neuroscience: The Foundations of Human and Animal Emotions*. Oxford, UK: Oxford University Press.

Pert, C. B. 1997. *Molecules of Emotion: Why You Feel the Way You Feel*. New York: Scribner.

Pedersen, C. A., Caldwell, J. D., Jirikowski, G. F., and Insel, T. R., eds. 1992. "Oxytocin in Maternal, Sexual, and Social Behaviors." *Annals of the New York Academy of Sciences* 652: 194–211.

Piaget, J. 1930. *The Child's Conception of Physical Causality*. New York: Harcourt, Brace.

Pincus, D., Freeman, W. J., and Modell, A. (in press). "Perception in the Clinical Hour: A Proposed Neurobiology of Transference." *Psychoanalytic Psychology*, 2007.

Ohl, F. W., Scheich, H., and Freeman, W. J. 2001. "Change in Pattern of Ongoing Cortical Activity with Auditory Category Learning." *Nature* 412: 733–36.

Sacks, O. 2004. "In the River of Consciousness." *New York Review* 51: No. 1, January 15.

Sargant, W. W. 1957. *Battle for the Mind*. Westport, CT: Greenwood.

Skinner, B. F. 1969. *Contingencies of Reinforcement: A Theoretical Analysis*. New York: Appleton-Century-Crofts.

Sperry, R. W. 1950. "Neural Basis of the Spontaneous Optokinetic Response." *Journal of Comparative Physiology* 43: 482–89.

Verger, P. 1954. *Dieux d'Afrique*. Paris: P. Hartmann.

~

CHAPTER THREE

Neurodynamics, State, Agency, and Psychological Functioning

Jim Grigsby, Ph.D., and Elizabeth Osuch, M.D.

People are consistent in their behavior. When you get to know someone well, you can predict with a fair degree of accuracy what he or she will do in a given situation. The regularities in people's behavior—the recurring patterns of activity, thinking, and attitude that make them knowable—are in large part what we mean when we talk about the idea of *personality*. Yet people do not always do exactly the same things, and from time to time an individual is likely to engage in behavior that seems quite out of character. Moreover, it seems that people sometimes deliberately alter certain habitual behaviors after having spent considerable time engaging in a behavioral pattern. Changing a habit is much more difficult for some people than it is for others. In this chapter, we will investigate some of the neural underpinnings of both stability and change in personality.

The stability of personality, its variability from time to time, and its capacity for enduring change are probabilistic phenomena, with probabilities in part determined by the environment, and in part by the patterns of the individual's constantly shifting physiologic state. The limits and likelihood of personality change and stability, both within and between individuals, are themselves variable over time, a function of hard-wired neural networks and of neural ensembles manifesting plasticity on scales ranging from milliseconds to decades. As is true for other aspects of personality, the capacity for initiating and sustaining changes in behavior that are directed toward a goal, a capacity which we call "agency," is similarly dependent upon state.

The concept of *environment* is relatively straightforward, and in this context we intend it to mean all stimuli, events, and transactions occurring outside the individual, as well as the internal biochemical milieu. The individual is inextricably embedded in his or her environment. The concept of *state*, however, requires definition and description. A person's *physiologic state* is a process that changes from moment to moment. State is the self-organizing emotional and physiological background against which an individual lives his or her life. It is the expression of the activity of neural and endocrine systems affecting mood, emotionality, arousal, activity level, attention, and a number of other factors; it is influenced also by the environment, and by one's own activity. State is continually in flux, and its mercurial nature is of great importance because one's state determines the likelihood that one will engage in any particular behavior, including behavior that is intended to alter either the environment or one's own state. The ability to act on the environment or on oneself in new ways (by altering one's behavior) with intention toward a goal is what we call *agency* or *being an agent* in one's own life. Agency is a complex psychological (and neural) phenomenon, comprising both this capacity for deliberate action as well as the *sense* of agency, or the *feeling* that one is able to behave as an autonomous agent. In this chapter, we address the regulatory influence of state in psychological functioning, and consider the phenomenon of state as a means to understanding how to enhance agency. First, we will examine certain characteristics of brain functioning and some of their psychological manifestations.

Psychological functioning is an *emergent property* of the continual and ever-changing activity of neural networks. A corollary to this assumption is that the relationships among brain processes and psychological processes can be better understood in terms of orderly patterns of brain activity, also known as *neurodynamics* (Arbib, Érdi, and Szentágothai 1998).

Definition of Terms

We begin by defining some terms that are important in this discussion, and with a general consideration of dynamics and neurodynamics. Next, we will discuss the functional organization of the brain, the activity of which reflects the spontaneous operation of a complex, nonlinear, self-organizing system. A fundamental component of this system is the individual's moment-to-moment physiological state, which plays an essential role in determining the probability of various kinds of psychological activity. Finally, we will examine several examples of psychological phenomena that might be considered the manifestations of both normal and pathological neurodynamic functioning.

The brain and the environment mutually influence and are shaped by one another. Neurons are extremely sensitive to ongoing experience, which alters their microscopic structure. This change in structure, which is the cellular basis of learning, is a manifestation of *synaptic plasticity*. Not only is the brain altered—both transiently and permanently—by experience, but it is in turn capable of modifying the environment via resultant behavior. These microscopic changes take place at the synapse—the junction between neurons— and their lasting effect is to change the architecture of, and hence to alter the activation probability of, arrays of neurons that are linked to one another in parallel and in series. These neuronal arrays are also referred to as *cell assemblies*, or *neural networks*.

Another basic concept is that of *emergence*. Psychological activity is an *emergent property* of the brain, associated with (or emergent from) the activation of neural systems. The brain's activity mediates the psychological processes in which humans engage, so that at each instant the total constellation of an individual's perception, cognition, and behavior (in other words, one's unified experience of self and world) is an emergent property of the brain's overall dynamical functioning at that moment. The experience of hunger, for example, is an emergent property of the activity of a number of systems including those monitoring stomach distention and blood sugar levels, and neural assemblies that mediate sensations of pleasure associated with eating.

Systems characterized by complex emergent activity typically have a roughly hierarchical, modular architecture (Globus and Scheibel 1967, Scheibel and Scheibel 1958). That is, they are composed of one or more roughly similar types of elementary building blocks. Biological systems, for example, consist of cells as their fundamental components, while cells themselves contain various subcellular organelles: mitochondria, ribosomes, phospholipid membranes, and so on. The nervous system's modular building blocks are the many types of neurons and glial cells. These are connected with one another in a way that permits neurons and groups of neurons to interact with one another in spontaneously arising *patterns* of activity. The self-organizing patterns of activity observed within different local regions of the brain interact with one another, and from these transactions arise complex and coordinated patterns of regional and global neuronal activity. The occurrence of regular (that is, highly probable) system behaviors (or patterns) and the interactions between building blocks are essential features of emergence. The development of a capacity for adaptation (or learning) permits such emergent systems to manifest increasingly complex activity (Holland 1998).

Most biological systems are inherently *nonlinear*. Linearity refers to a type of relationship between variables in which change in one variable is associated with a directly proportional change in another variable. The momentum of an object, for example, is proportional to its velocity. If velocity doubles, momentum also increases by a factor of two. In contrast, the brain is nonlinear, which means that the activity of a neuron or set of neurons may be related to activity in other neurons, or to psychological functioning, in ways that are discontinuous or disproportional. When the relationship between two systems is nonlinear, it often is impossible to predict the behavior of one system, despite having knowledge of the activity of the other system.

One type of nonlinearity is the discontinuity observed in association with physical state changes, such as when ice melts and turns to liquid water, or when water evaporates and turns to a gas. For example, when water is heated, the temperature steadily increases until it reaches the boiling point, at which time the hydrogen bonds between water molecules are overcome by the increased energy of the molecules that results from heating. Instead of simply continuing to increase in temperature, the water boils, turning to gas. If water didn't change state in this way, heating it would be a relatively linear process. This change from a liquid state to a gas is called a *phase transition*. Complex systems, such as biological organisms, and certain physical–chemical systems, show significant nonlinearities in their behavior, and may show surprising discontinuities analogous to physical phase transitions.

Self-organization is another characteristic of complex systems (e.g., Prigogine and Stengers 1984) closely related to emergence. While organisms are arguably the most complex self-organizing systems, it has been argued that nature itself is a massive self-organizing system (e.g., Bak 1996). A self-organizing system such as an organism has no internal or external executive center that directs its functioning. Instead, the complex set of biochemical processes that represent the activity of the organism occurs spontaneously, and the organism as a whole pulls itself up by the bootstraps, demonstrating emergence. Organisms do not supervise their own conception, development, or growth, nor do they direct the continual process of renewal of cellular components. Given that this is the case, it is particularly interesting that complex organisms like humans manifest the emergent property of agency, wherein we experience ourselves as making choices, as acting in novel ways with intention, and as working toward an imagined goal.

The science of dynamics is the study of processes occurring within and among the components of a system, and of the transactions among the system, its component parts, and a constantly changing environment. The study of dynamics thus is concerned with the orderly ways in which physical, chemical, biological, and other processes occur over time; that is, it deals with change. *Neurodynamics* refers to systematic patterns of neural processing, to "the spatiotemporal operation of the nervous system" (Arbib, Érdi, and Szentágothai 1998)—the patterned, ongoing activity of the brain in its environment. Neuroanatomic structure and its emergent psychological functions can be fully understood only in the context of the simultaneous and sequential activity (i.e., the neurodynamics) of many widely distributed, interconnected regions of the brain. Neurodynamic processes may be examined at levels of organization ranging from the subcellular level, through simple neural networks, to complex aggregates of interacting cells, and to the brain as a whole.

The neurodynamic model of personality is a theoretical perspective in which all psychological phenomena are considered to be associated with complex patterns of neural activity. Personality is viewed as a probabilistic set of properties—behavioral, perceptual, emotional, and cognitive patterns—that are emergent from the activity of many modular, distributed neural networks. The neurodynamic approach emphasizes processes taking place at different levels of organization within the brain, but a primary focus is on the level of neural networks (Grigsby and Hartlaub 1994; Grigsby and Schneiders 1991; Grigsby, Schneiders, and Kaye 1991; Grigsby and Stevens 2000).

This chapter is concerned first with the dynamics of *instantaneous physiologic state* and with the involvement of state in the emergence of the regular, roughly predictable, phenomena of personality. The term "instantaneous" reflects the fact that a person's state differs from moment to moment as a function of the activity of a large number of neural and endocrine systems, of the environment, and of the individual's own activity. Imagine taking a snapshot of state at each instant, lining them up in sequence, and examining the photographs across time. Each will differ slightly from those that precede or follow it, and over long periods of time striking differences (as well as certain recurring similar patterns) would be apparent. Yet no two photographs would ever be exactly the same. State changes constantly, sometimes in subtle ways that are nearly undetectable, and sometimes grossly. The changes may be abrupt or so gradual as to be almost imperceptible.

State is roughly equivalent to the basic physiological/psychological tone of the individual, the medium in which behavior, cognition, and perception unfold. The specific factors that contribute to state are not established, and the contribution of any single variable is likely to be nonlinear and characterized by discontinuities and threshold effects. Although we can only hypothesize about their precise roles in determining state, a number of factors are likely to be important. Some operate at the cellular level, such as electrolyte balance, hydration, membrane permeability and ion channel conductance, blood glucose level, and concentration of neuromodulators or neurotransmitters. Others, although they may be more psychological in nature, are nevertheless emergent properties of neurophysiological activity. These include mood, current emotional status (e.g., anger, euphoria), current motivational status (e.g., thirst, sexual desire), pain or discomfort, level of energy/fatigue, level of arousal, basal activity level, and speed and capacity of information processing. Some subcomponents of state are periodic, such as the sleep–wake cycle or neuroendocrine influences (e.g., periodically varying level of estrogen, progesterone, testosterone, cortisol). Still others reflect such environmental factors as ambient temperature, level and type of sensory stimulation, and the presence or absence of certain people (e.g., parents, spouses, enemies).

Agency, or the act of being an agent in one's own life, is the second concern of this chapter. Agency is the process of choosing, either consciously or nonconsciously, to engage in some action or activity, carrying through that action by one's own effort (with or without the help of others) with the result of a particular outcome that one has envisioned in whole, in part, or in modified form (and sometimes with a result unlike anything that was imagined). This is an especially interesting emergent property of certain organisms, like humans, because the capacity to sustain effort toward a goal is nonexistent on the cellular level, not present in relatively simple organisms, and seems to occur only as a result of the complex, hierarchical activity of a fairly sophisticated brain. The capacity for agency, at any given moment in time, is dependent on the state of the organism. Some states facilitate agency and others prevent it. Thus, the understanding of agency is dependent upon our understanding of physiological state.

Personality: An Emergent Property of
Brain and Environment

The brain is a self-organizing system, so its activity arises spontaneously—without the controlling influence of an internal or external executive. At the cellular and biochemical level there is no agency, no single neural structure or set of structures within us that controls or organizes our behavior. There is no unitary "ego" or "self" that directs what we do. Instead, the spontaneous activity of neurons and groups of neurons, in continual transaction with the environment, is associated with the complex emergent activity we call personality. A complete description of personality therefore should involve neuroanatomy, neurodynamics, environment, and functioning.

Although it is common for people to speak of personality *structure*, in reality personality has no structure per se. Rather, the term *personality* is an abstraction, a way of referring to a set of regularly occurring activities in which people and other animals engage. Neurodynamically, personality "is most accurately conceptualized as reflecting nothing but processes—a set of emergent properties associated with the brain's self-organizing activity. Mind and behavior are the emergent properties of self-organizing processes operating in the here-and-now" (Grigsby and Stevens 2000, 105).

It is important to keep in mind that even the brain's structure—neurons, glia, blood vessels, membranes, and other constituents of the nervous system—is impermanent. Cells continuously recycle their component parts, so that a continuous process of gene expression, protein translation, and molecular remodeling is necessary for maintenance of the organization of the brain's myriad interrelated networks and the functional integrity of those networks. In other words, a biological system can be thought of as "a set of coherent, evolving, interactive processes which temporarily manifest in globally stable structures that have nothing to do with the equilibrium and solidity of technological structures. Caterpillar and butterfly, for example, are two temporarily stabilized structures in the coherent evolution of one and the same system" (Jantsch 1980, 7). The brain, like a caterpillar, is *temporarily* stabilized, but it changes over time as a result of aging, learning, nutritional status, hormonal milieu, neurological insult, pharmacologic intervention, cellular recycling, and other factors.

The Cellular Basis of Memory: Synaptic Plasticity

Experience produces microstructural changes at the junctions between neurons, a phenomenon referred to as *synaptic plasticity*. A good deal of evidence supports the notion that this plasticity is the cellular basis of learning and memory. The basic concept is that repeated, nearly simultaneous "firing" within connected assemblies of neurons produces structural changes that lead to an enhancement of the efficiency with which cells are able to cause one another to fire (Hebb 1949). This process leads to the development and change of neural networks in response to experience, altering the probability of activation of neurons in response to input from presynaptic neuronal arrays. Modification of the nervous system as a result of experience may be transient (e.g., neurochemical processes of brief duration involved in working or short-term memory; Fisher, Fisher, and Carew 1997), or relatively permanent (e.g., structural changes at the synapse mediating long-term memory). The changes characteristic of long-term memory involve the expression of genes and translation of proteins in response to the activation of neural networks in association with experience (Rose 1993).

The dominant theoretical models of long-term memory are referred to as *long-term potentiation*, or LTP (Bliss and Lømo 1973) and *long-term depression*, or LTD. Although not definitively established as the physiological bases of learning, considerable data suggest that both LTP and LTD may be similar or identical to the neural mechanisms involved in learning in vivo. LTP refers to a persistent *increase* in the probability that a presynaptic neuron's action potential (i.e., its firing) will produce an action potential in a postsynaptic neuron (in other words, the result is an increase in *synaptic efficacy*). LTP seems to involve several pre- and postsynaptic mechanisms (Artola and Singer 1993; Bear and Abraham 1996; Linden and Connor 1995; Siegelbaum and Kandel 1991). In contrast, LTD involves persistent, experience-dependent *decreases* in synaptic efficacy.

At the network level, the *functional* outcome of synaptic plasticity is a change in the probability that a network of postsynaptic neurons will respond to a given level and type of neural input. At the level of behavior or cognition, this means that with practice (represented at the neural level by the repeated activation of neurons within a network), the probability of a certain behavioral or cognitive activity changes (that is, the likelihood of the future activation of that network mediating that activity is modified). Learning leads to either an increased or decreased likelihood that an individual will engage in a particular cognitive, perceptual, or motor activity. The occurrence of a learned behavior is hence a *probabilistic* phenomenon; learning changes *probabilities*. The behavior that takes place may have a high probability of occurrence, but whether or not it actually occurs is a function of the specific neural pathways involved, and of the constantly changing status of the internal milieu (i.e., state) and external environment of the organism (Globus 1992; Grigsby and Hartlaub 1994).

Neural Networks:
Functional Implications of Synaptic Plasticity

Most changes in neural structure and function associated with learning involve *networks* of many neurons. A *neural network* is an array of neurons, transiently organized into dynamic assemblies both in parallel (i.e., operating simultaneously) and in series (operating sequentially), and distributed throughout the brain. The precise neurons that are active in such a network may vary from one moment to the next, but they function in a coordinated manner to yield specific emergent psychological properties. In fact, across performances of even a simple activity (e.g., throwing a ball at a target), some very different individual neurons may be activated, although the overall neural network of which they are components remains more or less the same.

Hence, it is the pattern of activity across populations of neurons, and not the specific neurons involved, that is of primary importance in learning. Different neuronal assemblies may be activated in the performance of any given task as a function of a number of variables, especially of the predominant state of the individual and salient characteristics of the environment.

For example, consider a simple and highly overlearned motor activity like shooting free throws in basketball. A player may have taken thousands of practice shots, yet each time he or she shoots a free throw, a different set of neurons is active. Moreover, factors such as fatigue, motivation, pain, the score, the pressure of a close game, and the noise of the crowd all affect the player's state (and hence the specific neurons and network nodes that are activated) to some degree. In addition to variability in muscle activation and perception of the basket (with associated variability in the specific neurons activated), these factors ensure that the precise configuration of neurons firing will always differ from one shot to the next.

This basic idea—that *networks,* and not specific neurons, mediate behavior—holds true even for something as simple as perception of the same object on different occasions. For example, every time you look at your hands, your perception of them is somewhat different. There is always some variability in the angle of perception, the level of illumination, saccadic eye movements (which cause the image of the hands to fall on different regions of your retinas), your attention to visual detail, the direction and speed of movement of your hands, and your current affective state insofar as it may influence perception of your hands. One time you may notice the curvature of the fingers, and on another the veins in the back of the hand, the wrinkles on your knuckles, a crease on one palm, or a hangnail on your thumb. Consequently, it is highly improbable that the exact same sets of neurons would ever be active more than once.

The way neural networks mediate perception is illustrated by Freeman's (1995; see also chapter 2) research into what he calls the *neuroactivity* of cells in the brain's olfactory bulb (a structure involved in the basic, early processing of information concerning smells) in response to specific odors. This neuroactivity involves the response of entire populations of neurons to odor stimuli. Freeman's findings suggest that "sniffing an odorant activates a spatial pattern of firing like a constellation of twinkling stars, though it is never twice identical" (1995, 58). These patterns of activation are distributed over the entire olfactory bulb, so that "by inference, every neuron participates in every discrimination" (1995, 59). By their inactivity, even those cells that remain silent in response to a smell may play a role in representing an odor.

Structural Organization of the Brain:
Modularity and Hierarchy

The brain is a modular, distributed system organized in a complex hierarchical manner. "Lower" levels typically handle very limited, stereotyped, and automatic aspects of processing, such as visual discrimination of line orientation or the detection of pressure on the skin. These lower levels are integrated with one another and with higher levels, both within a functional system such as vision (e.g., contrast, color, and line orientation are integrated to yield a visual representation of some object) and across systems (e.g., vision is integrated with language, so that one knows the name of the objects one sees). Lower levels of the hierarchy generally perform rapid and automatic processing of routine tasks that do not require deliberate, conscious, or effortful processing. This eliminates the need for higher levels of the hierarchy to be involved in behavior that can be automatized, allowing deliberate conscious attention to be focused on more complex tasks, such as planning, that may require effort and consideration of the novel aspects of a situation. Speech and movement, for example, would require considerable effort and attention if they did not become automatic early in childhood.

The distributed processing of speech and language is also illustrated by the fact that, although we can exercise some deliberate control over our speech (for example, when we carefully choose our words), it is not unusual to find ourselves saying something unexpected. Seldom do we have in mind the details of what we say before we say it. When an individual has sustained a neurologic insult affecting language, the automaticity of language may be lost and a great deal of effort may be necessary to express oneself. In the same way, one must struggle in the early stages of learning to speak or understand a foreign language. When any specific activity can be performed nonconsciously, effortlessly, and automatically, one's relatively limited processing capacity may be directed to higher-level cognitive activities like planning, organization, and self-monitoring.

The higher levels of a biological hierarchy have relatively limited top-down direct control over lower levels. For example, it probably is not possible for most people to perceive a blue sky as red. Higher levels do, however, receive constant feedback about the status of the organism's overall functioning, and may effect changes in functioning at relatively complex levels of integration (e.g., change in the *meaning* of perceptual stimuli, or change in state through psychotherapy, hypnosis, or the practice of meditation). Higher levels of brain functioning are, indeed, required to engage robustly for acts of agency—that is, when identifying a goal and then initiating and sustaining new behaviors over time to achieve that goal. This type of behavior demands departing from the automaticity of lower level neuronal functioning.

Neural hierarchies are *reentrant*—that is, they are characterized by a nonlinear architecture by means of which neurons at one level of a hierarchy may influence their own functioning, or the functioning of a different level of the hierarchy. This may occur, for example, through *feedback,* which serves a regulatory, inhibitory function. Reentry also may be manifested in *feedforward,* which can lead to rapid escalation of neural and psychological activity (Goldman and Nauta 1977; Goldman-Rakic and Schwartz 1982). Through reentrant signaling, the brain's many relatively independent modules are closely integrated with other neuronal groups. The integrated nonlinear activity of widely distributed networks produces the synthetic, coherent functioning characteristic of brains and minds, providing the organism with a unified experience of the world and the capacity to behave in an organized, adaptive fashion.

Modularity of Functioning

Depending on the level of organization at which it operates, any given neural module mediates either a specific function, component of a function, or complex of functions. Hence, there is no such thing as a "speech area" or "motor area," but rather there are a large number of self-organizing modules distributed throughout the brain, each representing a node in a network, operating both in parallel and sequentially to accomplish a given task. Each module is relatively autonomous, yet each is woven dynamically into the structural-functional fabric of the whole brain by means of reciprocal and reentrant neural pathways. Any given structural-functional system or subsystem (e.g., language, the understanding of speech, or the recognition of consonant sounds) consists of large numbers of excitatory and inhibitory neurons that are capable of connecting subcomponent modules with one another at different levels of integration as needed. In this way, a complex functional system such as language is mediated not by a single localized brain region (e.g., Broca's area), or even two regions (e.g., Broca's area *and* Wernicke's area), but by processing nodes distributed through multiple cortical and subcortical structures in the brain.

Modular structures, or groups of structures, are in a sense nested within even more complex modular structures. A module at one level may be composed of subcomponent modules at several other, different levels, and may itself be a subcomponent of higher level modules. For example, the basal ganglia could be considered a module, as could the caudate nucleus or putamen (both of which are structures within the basal ganglia), as could groups of cells within the putamen itself. At the same time, the caudate nucleus is a part of a distributed network that, along with prefrontal cortex and other areas, mediates many of the so-called *executive cognitive functions*, such as planning, organization, and the capacity for behavioral self-regulation (Fuster 1997). Simpler cortical modules are organized into large fields of neurons, the degree of complexity of which appears to increase with the complexity of the organism (Kaas 1987).

Modularity of Function: Vision

This is all rather abstract, and perhaps a somewhat more concrete illustration would be helpful. Consider the primate visual system, which provides a good illustration of the nature and complexity of modular architecture. Primates have at least four major visual systems—one cortical and three subcortical— that mediate control of ocular reflexes, detection of movement and location of objects in visual space, regulation of the body's biological pacemaker, and conscious awareness of visual stimuli. For example, the macaque monkey has a visual system similar to that of humans (Kaas 1992), and its modular and hierarchical architecture of vision has been extensively studied. According to Felleman and Van Essen (1991), the macaque has at least twenty-five cortical areas which are "predominantly or exclusively visual in function." The precise function of each of these areas in the visual system is relatively discrete, with each playing a distinctive role in the construction of visual experience. In addition to these twenty-five visual areas, there are at least seven cortical visual association areas that integrate visual stimuli.

Nine of these 32 regions are in the occipital cortex, eleven in the temporal cortex, ten in the parietal lobe, and two in the frontal lobes. By 1990, researchers had identified 305 pathways connecting these regions, 242 of which transmit information bidirectionally. Each of the 32 areas has an average of 19 connections with other visual areas. For example, V1, the primary visual area in the rear of the brain, has at least 16 connections to nine different areas, while V4 (which contains many color-sensitive cells) is linked with 21 different visual areas by at least 39 distinct neural pathways (Felleman and Van Essen 1991).

Felleman and Van Essen estimated that these cortical visual areas are distributed across about ten hierarchical levels. Lower levels of the hierarchy handle circumscribed aspects of visual processing, such as the detection of line stimuli at specific angles, while increasingly higher levels play a greater role in integrating the various aspects of visual stimulation, and in integrating visual experience with the stimuli perceived through other sensory modalities. Most pathways link areas that are one or two levels above or below one another, but some cross as many as seven or even eight levels. This crossing of several levels of the hierarchy permits lower-level neural activity to influence higher-level processing, and vice versa. The visual system also has extensive links with most other cortical areas, and with several subcortical structures, including the thalamus, amygdala, claustrum, caudate nucleus, superior colliculus, pons, and hypothalamus (Iwai and Yukie 1987; Kaas and Huerta 1988; Tigges and Tigges 1985; Yeterian and Pandya 1985).

The brain's modular organization differs significantly from older concepts of localization of function that assumed there was a specific area for each function, the extreme form of which was represented in Gall's phrenology (Gall and Spurzheim 1809/1969). The areas that compose various functional systems are more widely distributed and more highly specialized than the phrenologists ever imagined. They are also, in many cases, more plastic, showing considerable capacity for reorganization as a result of functional and dynamic influences (e.g., Merzenich et al. 1983, 1990). Other functional systems (e.g., language, movement, memory) have a qualitatively similar, complex modular distributed architecture (Cohen 1984; Felleman and Van Essen 1991; Knowlton et al. 1996). Personality itself is an emergent property of the activity of a modular, self-organizing architecture (Grigsby and Stevens 2000).

Integrating the Pieces of a Modular Brain

Neural systems and subsystems must be integrated with one another, a process that involves transmission of large amounts of information between and among systems at various hierarchical levels. For example, the visual system does not simply create a seamless visual scene and then weave it into the fabric of experience along with fully elaborated representations for language, physical perception, or hearing. Instead, information from other systems is fed into the visual system on an ongoing basis while we engage in even the simplest activity. Visual processing in turn affects ongoing activity in other functional systems, each modifying the other continually. The process is highly nonlinear.

For example, the constant flow of feedback from proprioceptors regarding the physical location of our bodies in space, and from the visual system, facilitates fine control of movement and accurate visual tracking of the objects around us. Our functioning is an emergent property of the activity of a large number of widely distributed neuronal arrays, and their activity must somehow be processed to ensure a coherent, accurate, and rapidly refreshed representation of the world and of our selves, as our experience changes from one instant to the next. The system's nonlinearity poses formidable problems insofar as these various neuronal activities must be bound together to produce an unbroken, fluid stream of experience, and the way in which this is done is referred to as *binding*.

Binding must occur across sensory modalities, and there are neurophysiologic data suggesting that synchronous, oscillatory activity—characteristic of several subsystems, including vision, olfaction, and physical sensation such as touch (Bouyer et al. 1981, 1987; Freeman 1995; Kelso 1995)—may be an essential component of this process. One widely held theory is that the integration of modular processing may be accomplished by means of large-scale, time-locked forty Hertz (i.e., forty cycles per second) oscillatory activity involving very large populations of neurons (Llinás and Paré 1996; Singer 1996; Singer and Gray 1995; von der Malsburg and Schneider 1986). In other words, large groups of neurons, distributed throughout the brain, synchronize their activity to produce a unitary representation of the world. The same sort of process— the binding of the activity of widely distributed neural modules—must mediate those neural processes associated with what we call personality.

The coordination of this neural activity is not a trivial problem. Singer (1996) has suggested that in response to a specific pattern of stimuli:

> A self-organizing process is initiated by which subsets of responses are bound together according to the joint probabilities imposed by the specific input pattern, the functional architecture of the coupling network, and the signals arriving through reentry loops from higher processing stages. The essential advantage of such a dynamic, self-organizing binding process is that individual cells can bind at different times, for example, when input constellations change, with different partners. (104)

Such self-organized, correlated firing is associated with both local and global patterns of oscillatory neuronal activity. Sensory stimuli presented for a period of less than twenty-five milliseconds are typically below the threshold required for conscious perception (although nonconscious reactions may be observed to stimuli of such short duration). Some investigators have suggested that stimuli perceived by the brain during these very brief intervals of time may be bound together as a single cognitive event (Llinás and Paré 1996).

Self-Organization of Neuronal Activity

Although the dynamics of binding are not well understood, we do have a picture of some of the ways in which interconnected neurons function to produce emergent neurophysiological activity, ultimately yielding adaptive functioning. One way to approach the question is by analyzing some simple illustrative cases.

Let us assume a hypothetical system of three neurons that we will call A, B, and C. Neuron A forms an excitatory synapse with the cell body of B. B forms an excitatory synapse with the body of C, while C forms an *inhibitory* synapse with the body of A. The three thus form a closed triangular circuit that is capable of oscillatory activity. How might oscillation arise? First, all neurons demonstrate a certain background level of spontaneous activity. If monitored in isolation, a typical neuron would be found to fire a mean of about 5 Hertz in what appears to be a statistically random manner (Skarda and Freeman 1987). This means that there are fluctuations in the frequency of action potentials generated within any specific neuron.

Suppose neuron A spontaneously generates a burst of firing at a frequency sufficient to induce an action potential in neuron B. The synapse between A and B ($A \rightarrow B$) is excitatory, and therefore this burst of activity by neuron A excites neuron B, causing it to fire. If a sufficient frequency of firing is induced in neuron B, it will have an excitatory influence on neuron C through the synapse $B \rightarrow C$. Now, because the synapse $C \rightarrow A$ is inhibitory, increased levels of activity in neuron C will inhibit neuron A, causing a decrease in the frequency its firing. As a result, neuron A fires with a frequency below its baseline level of spontaneous activity. The result is a decreased number of action potentials generated in neuron B, which had previously been *exciting* neuron C. Now receiving less input from B, neuron C will fire less frequently, so its inhibitory influence on neuron A will decrease. This will cause A to return to its previous, higher level of spontaneous activity. With the resulting *disinhibition* of neuron A, the cycle then repeats itself. The outcome is a spontaneous oscillation in this simplified, idealized system. The network's activity oscillates, alternately slowing and accelerating. The inclusion of an inhibitory synapse ($C \rightarrow A$) in this group of three neurons ensures that the system cannot run away in a cycle of feedforward activity. The network activity is dampened on a periodic, or quasi-periodic, basis.

Many systems in the brain demonstrate variations on this theme of oscillatory activity (e.g., Buzsáki et al. 1992; Steriade, McCormick, and Sejnowski 1993; Traub, Miles, and Wong 1989). Different populations of neurons—nodes in a neural network—are interconnected with one another, and the activity of each influences the activity of the others. These interacting, oscillating systems are considered to be *coupled*. The result: large-scale patterns of periodic or quasi-periodic activation.

Now envision a second system consisting of neurons D, E, and F, connected by synapses like those in our first make-believe scenario, but this time all the connections are excitatory (in this case, $D \rightarrow E$, $E \rightarrow F$, and $F \rightarrow D$). This time assume that neuron D, in addition to forming a junction with E, also has an axon that feeds back on itself ($D \rightarrow D$). In this network, spontaneously generated activity in neuron D excites neuron E, while simultaneously increasing the rate of firing in D via the recurrent feedback axon that synapses on itself. Neuron E in turn excites F, while both neuron F and the recurrent axon of neuron D further increase the rate of firing in D. A loop like this quickly creates *feedforward* activity that increases the rate of firing in the circuit until it reaches a physiologic limit set by the time needed to produce and conduct action impulses, to effect synaptic transmission, and to allow each neuron to return to a state in which it is capable of conducting another action impulse (a frequency perhaps as high as 100 action potentials per second, or one every 10 milliseconds). A circuit like this one will not oscillate. Instead, it will rapidly reach a steady state of activity restricted only by the physiological limits of the component neurons, and eventually slowing due to "fatigue."

Neural networks mediating complex psychological activity are more complicated than the cartoon-like networks described here, but similar relationships exist between populations of inhibitory and excitatory neurons. The dynamical patterns of interaction may be extraordinarily complex, considering that there are approximately 50 billion neurons in the human brain. Moreover, depending on its type and location, each neuron receives input from, and conducts signals to, somewhere between 1,000 and 10,000 other neurons, and in turn it projects to a similar number of neurons. The density of connections between neurons in any given area of the cortex is described as "sparse," however, since any given neuron typically connects with less than 1 percent of its neighbors (Freeman 1995). Because each cortical neuron may form a synapse with up to 20,000 other neurons, the density of synapses has been estimated to be somewhere around 800 million to 1 billion per cubic millimeter of cortex (Abeles 1991; Douglas and Martin 1991). Hence, it is not surprising that many variants of network activity may be produced by even relatively simple combinations of oscillating, periodically bursting, or aperiodic neurons. For example, Manor and Nadim (2001) reported on their study of a network that demonstrated two distinct modes of stable oscillatory activity. Transient changes in the dynamics of the network could shift the network activity from one mode to the other, although in the absence of some perturbing influence, the type of oscillation in which the network engaged was determined only by the initial conditions.

Excitation and Inhibition

Abeles (1991) estimated that about 10 percent of the brain's synapses are inhibitory and the remaining 90 percent are excitatory. This means that an average cortical neuron may receive inhibitory input at about 100 to 1,000 synapses. It also receives excitatory input from neighboring (local) and more remote neurons at thousands of synapses. Computer simulations of neural activity suggest that stable neurologic functioning requires a fine balance between these excitatory and inhibitory connections (Abeles 1991). Too much excitation could produce uncontrolled escalation of cortical activation, perhaps resulting in such neurologic phenomena as seizures or seizure-like episodes. Appropriate inhibitory synaptic activity therefore serves to dampen a potentially runaway nervous system. An excess of inhibition, however, could theoretically result in a diminution of overall cortical activity, perhaps producing other pathological conditions.

The importance of the relationship between excitation and inhibition is apparent when we consider oscillatory activity, like that discussed above. Oscillating rhythms may be important neurodynamic mechanisms for the organization, synchronization, and integration of a wide range of neuronal processes. Since neural activity exists in order to support adaptive behavior of all sorts, oscillation, feedback, feedforward, and other large-scale neurodynamic processes are important insofar as they facilitate the emergence of adaptive behavioral, cognitive, emotional, and perceptual activity.

Dynamic Patterns in Natural Processes: Attractors

Most natural processes can be characterized by the patterns of activity they manifest across time. Some processes or events, like the background activity seen on an EEG tracing, appear random. Others, such as the sleep–wake cycle in nearly all animals, the menstrual or estrus cycle in females, and seasonal variability in testosterone levels in males, seem to occur with a relatively regular period. Others are quasiperiodic, occurring at somewhat irregular intervals, while others are simply recurrent. Finally, some may simply represent the endpoint of a complex process. Many of these temporal patterns can be described mathematically, and can be classified into patterns known as *attractors* and *repellors*, concepts that are useful in describing both neural and behavioral activity.

A *periodic* process repeats itself at regular time intervals. For example, a pendulum-driven clock, properly adjusted and wound regularly, will oscillate at a predictable, regular rate of one cycle per second. The activity of such a clock is characteristic of what is called a *periodic attractor*, also known as a *limit cycle attractor*. If one allows such a system to run for a while, without interference, there is a very high probability that its behavior will evolve to a regular and predictable state of activity.

In contrast, a free-swinging pendulum to which no external force is applied (such as that of a mainspring) will eventually come to rest as a result of gravitational and frictional forces. After a while, the pendulum will hang motionless. Such behavior is characteristic of a *point attractor*, which represents a system at static equilibrium, or in a steady state. In the case of both point and limit cycle attractors, every pattern of activity, irrespective of the system's starting point, will evolve over time to the attractor (Abraham and Shaw 1992). For this reason, both limit cycle and point attractors are said to be *invariant with respect to initial conditions*. In other words, if the system is allowed to operate for a long enough period of time, it will settle into a predictable pattern of behavior, regardless of where it started.

A *chaotic* attractor is characterized by behavior markedly different from that of the point and limit cycle attractors. The activity of such a system may at times appear to be regular, or sometimes may appear essentially random. Whatever the case, the behavior of a chaotic system is essentially unpredictable, except perhaps in a probabilistic sense, or under certain clearly specified conditions over a short time interval. Chaotic systems are extremely sensitive to even apparently trivial changes in environmental or system conditions. As a consequence, they may be perturbed by a number of different factors, with effects on the trajectory of their activity that may be quite variable. They are said to show *sensitive dependence on initial conditions*, meaning that even slight changes in their initial status and activity can have profound effects on the course of subsequent activity.

In the case of the clock discussed above with a pendulum driven by a mainspring, no matter where the pendulum starts out, its motion will quickly settle into a predictable limit cycle attractor. A chaotic system, in contrast, may show apparent regularity under certain conditions. Yet despite the fact that its behavior is determined by causal relationships, one cannot make accurate predictions regarding the long-term behavior of a chaotic system, and changes that may occur in the activity of such systems (referred to as *bifurcations*) can make even short-term prediction impossible. Indeed, for a chaotic system, the error inherent in any prediction increases with the passage of time (Abraham and Shaw 1992; Mandelbrot 1982).

In biological systems, periodic processes cannot match the regularity of the pendulum. Yet we can speak of point and periodic attractors as ways of describing spatiotemporal patterns of activity in organisms. The sleep–wake cycle, for example, occurs roughly every twenty-five hours, with a certain amount of variability in the specific timing of the cycle from one person to another. It is entrained to a twenty-four-hour day by exposure to the level of light in the day–night cycle. This sleep–wake cycle is relatively reliable and predictable in this modern era of electric lighting, although one may stay up late some nights and go to bed early on others. If a "normal" individual collected data on her sleep–wake cycle over an extended period of time, it would appear to be very regular, with times of rising, sleep onset, and duration of sleep that are probably normally distributed. The sleep–wake cycle thus can be considered to represent a biological limit cycle attractor. Many other processes are essentially unpredictable, except in a probabilistic sense. The background electrical activity of the brain as measured by EEG, for example, appears essentially random, and may be thought of as representing a biological chaotic attractor. The same may hold true for the rhythm of the heart (Glass and Mackey 1988).

Freeman (1995) argues that the brain dwells in a chaotic but stable state that is perturbed by familiar, meaningful stimuli under the right conditions. These stimuli drive the brain's activity into coherent attractors. The nonlinearity of the brain, and its sensitive dependence on the environment, allow even slight alterations of the internal or external milieu to produce major effects on the brain's activity when it is in certain states. When an individual is in other states, or in different environments, the same stimuli, or even similar stimuli of greater intensity, may have a less marked effect on the brain's functioning. For example, a state of hyperarousal associated with posttraumatic stress disorder will be associated with reactions to certain stimuli that may be qualitatively and quantitatively different from the reactions observed when the individual is in a different state. The brain's ability to shift rapidly from a globally chaotic state into a limit cycle attractor facilitates the maintenance of adaptive functioning in stable environments, while permitting the organism to adapt quickly to novel or rapidly changing conditions. Adaptive functioning by individual organisms may be enhanced—and perhaps even made possible—by these neurodynamic processes.

Repellors: States with a Low Probability of Occurrence

An attractor is a state of relatively stable functioning toward which the activity of a system tends to gravitate. In contrast, a *repellor* is a highly unstable configuration of a system. One might say the system "avoids" the kinds of activity characteristic of a repellor. For example, a person who is frequently hypomanic could be thought of as having a "hypomania attractor," which might represent a neural network with a high probability of activation that mediates an expansive, very energetic state. When such an individual is hypomanic, depression with psychomotor retardation is highly unlikely, and might be thought of as representing a repellor. If such an individual has bipolar mood states, however, repellor and attractor will switch over time.

Neurodynamics and Probability

Neurodynamics is in large part concerned with probability. In chemical and biological systems, the probability of an event is related to the energy required to bring about that event. Thus, those networks with the greatest probability of activation in any given situation are also those networks that require the smallest expenditure of energy for their activation. Networks that are likely to be activated are attractors, patterns of activity with a relatively high probability of occurrence (at least in certain states). A "strong" attractor is one that emerges with little expenditure of energy, while a "weak" attractor requires a system to expend more energy for its development and maintenance. Changes in the state of the organism may affect these probabilities of activation significantly, so that a network that might be described as a strong and stable attractor when an individual is in one state could become a weak attractor, or even a repellor if the state changes in certain ways.

The brain tends to favor "relaxed" states involving lower energy configurations (Abeles 1991). Therefore, neural networks requiring high levels of energy for their activation have a low probability of occurrence, and are inherently unstable. These states requiring inordinately large energy expenditure for their maintenance may be thought of as repellors. Neural networks that require such large expenditures of energy for their activation are ordinarily active only transiently, unless synaptic plasticity (learning) effects a change in the probability of activation (i.e., by reducing the amount of neuronal input required for activation or by increasing the amount of input available) of those networks.

A metaphorical way to describe this is to say that neural activity tends to be drawn into energy "valleys," which may be thought of as stable *basins of attraction* toward which the system tends to gravitate, just as a ball will roll freely downhill, but requires an input of energy to roll up a hill. For someone in a manic state, behavior characteristic of depression is mediated by neural networks with a very low probability of activation at that moment. At the level of neural networks, for someone who is manic to behave in a depressed manner would require a large expenditure of cellular energy in the brain in order to activate depression-associated networks. The probability of that occurring at that moment is very low, and may in fact be zero.

This may appear paradoxical, since a manic state would seem to require a greater overall use of organismic energy than would a depressed state. After all, the manic state is associated with a greatly accelerated level of motor and cognitive activity, thereby making a greater overall metabolic demand on the individual. But consider the dynamic organization of neural networks (attractors) for a person in a manic state. Her activity level is greatly increased, her self-representations are characterized by expansive grandiosity, and she demonstrates flight of ideas and pressured speech. The thoughts, perceptions, and behaviors that have the highest probability of occurrence (i.e., those mediated by neural networks with the highest likelihood of activation) are those associated with the basin of attraction of mania. Thoughts, feelings, and behaviors inconsistent with a sense of grandiose invulnerability—such as a sense of self-doubt, sadness, or humility—have an extremely low probability of occurrence, and in the manic state they are extremely unlikely to be manifested. In essence, they become repellors.

On the level of neural networks, however, the networks with the greatest probability of activation (i.e., requiring the smallest expenditure of energy) are those consistent with one's current physiological state. In a manic state, the networks most likely to continue to be activated are those that mediate increased level of motor activity and accelerated information processing, even though mania may involve a greater expenditure of energy for the organism as a whole. In the same way, it is more difficult for a child with ADHD to sit quietly than to careen out of control, because for such a child, the networks mediating hyperactive behavior are more readily activated than those that might mediate relaxed contemplation. Only a significant change in physiological state will alter the probabilities that these specific kinds of behavior will occur.

The Dynamics of Neural Networks

Neurophysiological studies of olfaction suggested to Freeman and his associates that upon perception of a *familiar* stimulus, neural activity undergoes a sudden shift from a chaotic baseline pattern to one that is organized and coherent (e.g., more characteristic of a limit cycle attractor). A shift of this sort may represent a bifurcation like those that occur when a system "undergoes a major transition in its dynamics, equivalent to, for example, the transition from sleep to waking, or from normal to seizure activity" (Skarda and Freeman 1987, 165).

In contrast, following presentation of a *novel* stimulus, neural activity does not converge to an attractor, but remains chaotic. Freeman argues that this is because the object is unfamiliar, and because there is no established neural network to mediate the meaning of that object (or in the terms of dynamics, there is no learned attractor), the animal cannot recognize the object. In other words, recognizing a perceptual pattern (e.g., a friend's voice, the smell of lilacs, an object used in everyday life) involves the activation of a specific neural network. The neurophysiological manifestation of object recognition is that brain activity temporarily loses its chaotic quality and settles transiently into a basin of attraction. Freeman contends that the background of "random" or chaotic activity allows the brain to remain in a state of maximum responsiveness, so that it is "poised on the brink of instability where it can switch flexibly and quickly" (Kelso 1995, 26) as demanded by novel or potentially threatening situations. Bak (1996) made a similar point when he argued that random noise such as this neural background activity "prevents the network from locking into wrong patterns, with too deep riverbeds, from which it cannot escape" (181).

Neural networks (viz., attractors) are hierarchically organized. Thus, at every instant a global neural network is activated, the emergent property is one's total experience and behavior at that moment. That global network (one's complete representation and consciousness of the moment, awareness of one's self in that representation, and one's associated behavior) in turn is composed of many subcomponent modular networks mediating various perceptions, thoughts, memories, fantasies, behaviors, and so on (Bressler and Kelso 2001). For example, a person's physiological state constantly interacts with the environment to yield the activation of other ancillary attractors, to which one has access when one is in a particular global attractor (Freeman 1995).

Environment–state interactions may change rapidly in response to external and internal stimuli, as illustrated by findings regarding the relationship between pain, anxiety, and attention. In one study, Tracey and her collaborators (2002) used functional magnetic resonance imaging (fMRI) to study whether activity in the periaqueductal gray (PAG) varied depending on changes in attention during painful stimulation. The PAG is a region deep in the brain that, when stimulated electrically, may produce analgesia. In this study, subjects were administered stimulation that was sometimes pleasantly warm and sometimes moderately painful (hot), and were instructed either to pay full attention to the stimulation (whether hot or warm), or to "think of something else." The PAG was not activated during warm stimulation, but was activated during painful stimulation (suggesting analgesia), possibly in association with the release of endogenous opioids in the PAG. During painful stimulation, PAG activation was significantly greater in the distraction condition than in the attending condition (again suggesting analgesia). For each condition, the subjects were asked to rate both the intensity and aversiveness of pain, and for both these dimensions, they rated the pain as less severe while they were distracting themselves. The results are consistent with other studies—and with everyday human experience—indicating that changes in arousal or attention modulate the experience of pain (e.g., Petrovic et al. 2000).

While the response to painful stimulation may be modulated by changing the focus of attention, the experience of pain also may be exacerbated by anxiety, presumably through activity of a network of neurons in an area called the entorhinal cortex (Ploghaus et al. 2001). Using fMRI, researchers exposed subjects to thermal stimuli ranging from very mild through painful. Subjects also underwent a conditioning protocol in which they were shown different geometric shapes that were associated with either mild or noxious stimulation, so that the shapes themselves came to induce varying degrees of anxiety. Subjects then were presented with either the low anxiety (LA) or high anxiety (HA) conditioned visual stimulus, followed by either the low temperature (LT) or high temperature (HT) thermal stimulus. Painful (HT) stimuli were rated as significantly more intense when preceded by a high anxiety rather than a low anxiety visual stimulus (a square and a triangle, respectively). The greatest pain intensity was reported in response to HA and HT stimuli. The effect of anxiety on pain perception was associated with changes in activation of the entorhinal cortex.

Physiological State

The emergent property of physiologic state is the constantly fluctuating background against which all behavior occurs. State is "an emergent property of the self-organizing activity of the brain, acting as an organizer of experience, and influenced by experience itself in a variety of ways" (Grigsby and Stevens 2000, 164). State thus is a complex, multidimensional *order parameter* (in this case, a set of dynamical variables intrinsic to the system that play the role of macroscopic global parameters; Nowak and Lewenstein 1994), influencing behavior by affecting the probabilities associated with activation of specific neural networks. State is the basic physiological/psychological background tone of the individual at each moment in time, affecting behavior, perception, and cognition. State, in turn, is affected by the neural activity associated with these psychological processes. One's state changes constantly—although most of the time, these changes may not be readily observable. Changes in state may occur gradually or abruptly, depending on many intraindividual and environmental variables (e.g., startle, fatigue, grieving, alcohol intake, or an earthquake). Many state changes are trivial, reflecting only small variations in subcomponents of state over short time intervals. But sometimes even trivial changes may yield unexpected nonlinear outcomes that appear discontinuous with prior psychological activity.

Because of the large number of variables continually influencing state, although the basic organization of a state may remain superficially constant, there is considerable variation over time. The complexity of the phenomenon (the number of subcomponents of state, and their relative independence of one another) makes it likely that an individual's state is never precisely the same on any two occasions. Depression, for example, may vary in quality and intensity during the course of a day, or across a period of many weeks, sometimes involving more agitation, anxiety, anger, slowing of thought, or anhedonia, at other times colored primarily by apathy and feelings of futility. The experience of depression at any moment also may be influenced by fluctuating hormone levels, arousal, and current environmental stimuli. Most of the time, the variability observed is at such a fine-grained level of detail that it is clinically and phenomenologically insignificant, yet on occasion, minor variations in subcomponents of state may have significant consequences.

Some Biological and Dynamic Components of State

State reflects the activity of a widely distributed, self-organizing modular system, the biological substrate of which involves a number of structures. For example, stimulation of the amygdala, hypothalamus, septum, basal ganglia, midbrain, medial forebrain bundle, anterior cingulate gyrus, and orbitofrontal cortex may induce neural activity having significant effects on state. These may include emotions, feelings, and drives, including fear, rage, smothering, or thirst. In some cases, electrical stimulation of certain structures elicits feelings so intensely pleasurable that humans and other animals will stimulate their own brains at high rates to produce them if given the opportunity to do so. Likewise, stimulation of other regions may produce feelings and states that are extremely aversive to the organism, or that may be experienced simply as bizarre and mildly unpleasant, such as the feelings of depersonalization, derealization, or déjà vu that may result from stimulation of certain sites in the temporal lobe.

The subcomponents of state affect the probabilities of activation of various neural networks, and thereby influence behavior, perception, cognition, and, in turn, state itself. Much of the time, one or a small number of variables may be the predominant determinants of state (e.g., the sleep–wake cycle), in which case others may be relatively insignificant—at least under a broad range of circumstances. In other situations, these "minor" variables may contribute significantly to an individual's state, and despite the fact that their contribution is typically subtle, their valence may increase when variables that ordinarily are more dominant are relatively quiescent. For different people—and for the same individual at different times—there are differences in the extent to which any given variable actually contributes to state.

State also may be considered an emergent property of the instantaneous combination of global neuronal activity and the probability field for potential activation, establishing the likelihood of activation of any given neural network at each moment. Another way to put this is to say that state might be an emergent property of the activity of its various subsystems at a specific time t, together with the *probability field* at that specific time for all possible states and behaviors at the next moment in time $t + 1$. That is, in conjunction with input from the internal and external environments at time t, state determines the probability of any given state and behavior at time $t + 1$. It also is determined by state and internal/external inputs at time $t - 1$. This means that when we talk about a state, we are making assertions about probabilities.

State, Behavior, and the Environment

In interaction with the environment, state is a major determinant of an individual's specific thoughts, feelings, perceptions, and memories. For example, if someone says he is depressed, we can conjure up a reasonably good mental image of such a state because we are familiar with certain psychological phenomena that are reliably—but not always necessarily—associated with depression. When someone is depressed, there is a high probability that he will act in ways consistent with our idea of depression, although there is significant intra- and interindividual variability in precisely how depression is expressed. This variability is influenced in large part by ongoing changes in certain basic components of state over time, and by changes in the environment (which have their own effects on state). A pleasant interaction with someone may have a positive, even if transient, effect on depression, for example.

There is a complex recursive relationship between state, behavior, and environment. Thus, while a number of variables may contribute to state, the emergent state provides a set of organizational and behavioral tendencies that affect experience of the multiple factors from which the state has arisen. If one is anxious, one may behave in an erratic manner that is different than how one might behave when relaxed. Hence, the state of which anxiety is one significant component has a marked influence on behavior. A person also may regulate his or her anxiety by engaging in a range of different activities: fighting, exercise, relaxation, meditation, or taking a benzodiazepine, for example. These behaviors affect state, which then influences subsequent behavior. The relationship is inherently nonlinear and reflexive; however, the influence of state on behavior is generally stronger and more direct than the influence of activity on state.

Pathological Neurodynamics and Sensory Stimuli

A large number of neuropathological and psychopathological disorders, as well as many normal variants, may be emergent properties of altered neurodynamics. For example, certain types of seizures, psychological reactions to sensory deprivation or sensory overload, and affective instability might well be considered *dynamical disorders* (Glass and Mackey 1979) resulting from the perturbation of brain activity as a function of anomalous or otherwise remarkable environmental stimulation. The likelihood of occurrence of these phenomena varies with changes in the individual's state, and in turn they may exert their own effects on state in a reflexive, nonlinear manner.

To a certain extent the brain is regulated by the type and intensity of sensory input. The stimulation required by an individual varies across time, and there is significant interindividual variation in the optimal amount and type of stimulation. Severely restricting sensory stimulation, for example, may lead to a marked change in the content and quality of consciousness. Studies of sensory deprivation have shown that most people respond to diminished sensory input with mild alterations of conscious experience, or perhaps with dreamy or trance-like states. A small percentage of people, however, become anxious and disorganized in their thinking as a result of sensory deprivation (Goldberger and Holt 1958; Ruff et al. 1961). Sensory overstimulation, on the other hand, may drive the brain into a state of disordered dynamics associated with impaired information processing. The ease with which this may happen is in part a function of the individual's state at the time of the overstimulation (among other factors). For example, under conditions of fever or sleep deprivation, one's ability to tolerate intense stimulation may be significantly reduced. People also vary in the extent to which sensory stimuli regulate their brains, as a function of temperament, experience, or acquired neurologic disorders (e.g., minor head trauma).

Certain types of sensory input of normal intensity also may perturb neural and psychological functioning in susceptible individuals. Reflex epilepsy, for example, is a condition in which brain functioning is driven into a stereotyped pattern of seizure activity (viz., an attractor) in response to very specific sensory stimuli. The precipitating stimuli are generally the same for an individual, and may be rather idiosyncratic. For example, reflex seizures may be induced by exposure to strobe lights (Jeavons and Harding 1975), specific visual patterns (Brinciotti et al. 1992; Chatrain et al. 1970), an individual's own singing or punning (Herskowitz, Rosman, and Geschwind 1984), or even playing board games (Siegel et al. 1992). One patient had complex partial seizures that were initiated by tying, looking intently at, or thinking about shoestrings (Grigsby and Stevens 2000).

Pathologies of Periodic Dynamics

There is evidence that certain disorders may be associated with dysregulation of the body's biological clock. For example, some individuals develop seasonal affective disorder (SAD) during the winter when they are exposed to less light. Presumably, this affects gene expression in an area of the hypothalamus called the suprachiasmatic nucleus (SCN). The SCN receives input directly from the retina via the retinohypothalamic tract, and it is believed that properly timed exposure to light is essential for regulation of the body's daily circadian rhythms (e.g., as manifested in the sleep–wake cycle). SAD can sometimes be treated by daily exposure to sunlight or full-spectrum artificial light at specific times, apparently effecting an alteration in the timing of specific rhythms. Similarly, among many rotating shift workers and people with jet lag, it has been found that desynchronization of biological rhythms may produce depression, sleep disturbance, and other problems (Monk and Gillin 1984). These are *dynamical disorders,* conditions that might be thought of as having a neurodynamic etiology (Glass and Mackey 1979).

Other psychological phenomena are probably manifestations of normal variability in neural and endocrine dynamics. One interesting finding is that people show significant diurnal variation in speed of processing, working memory, reaction time, and learning (Blake 1967; Ebbinghaus 1885/1964; Folkard 1975, 1982). On tests of immediate recall such as digit span, people as a group perform significantly better in the mid-morning than in the late afternoon and early evening. It also has been found that women's performance on certain cognitive and neuropsychological tests (especially verbal and motor skills) may change as a function of estrogen level across the menstrual cycle (Hampson 1990). Among surgically menopausal women, hormone replacement therapy improves certain aspects of cognitive performance (Sherwin 1988). Analogous findings have been reported among males on tests of spatial perception as a function of seasonal and diurnal variations in testosterone level (Kimura and Hampson 1994). Assuming that psychological activity of all types (i.e., behavior, perception, cognition, emotion, memory) is an emergent property of the neural, endocrine, and related activity of the organism, it is conceivable that most psychological phenomena may someday be understood in terms of neurodynamics.

Agency

In addition to neurodynamics and state, this chapter is concerned with the emergent property of *agency*. An act of agency is the process of choosing, either consciously or nonconsciously, to engage in some action or activity, carrying through that action by one's own effort (with or without the help of others) with the result of a particular outcome that one has (in whole, in part, or in modified form) foreseen. Understood at the level of behavior, an act of agency departs from previous patterns of behavior and is a way in which the organism can alter its own state by engaging in certain actions. Yet the capacity for agency, at any given moment in time, is dependent on the physiological state of the organism. Some states facilitate some aspects of agency and others prevent them. In addition, like other neurological processes, the more one activates the modular dynamic networks involved in agency, the more they become attractors rather than repellors. This means that agency is like other neurobehavioral processes in that it can be learned and can become easier with practice—assuming proper functioning of the involved modular networks.

Examples of Acts of Agency and Impairment in Agency

Examples of acts involving agency are a young child turning on and off a light at a switch to observe the effects, going to the grocery store for a specific food, going on a diet to lose weight, working toward an advanced degree, overcoming the traumatic effects of a car accident by going back to the site of the crash to try to understand what happened, and going to a mental health care provider to try to get help for troubling symptoms. Agency is continuous rather than dichotomous; not all behaviors that involve agency engage this emergent process to the same degree. In general, those acts that require greater alterations from habitual patterns of behaving require more agency (viz., greater deliberate effort) than those that represent repetitive behaviors with strong attractors and a high probability of occurring. Likewise, those acts that require numerous steps and greater delays before gratification involve more agency than simple, one-step acts with immediate gratification.

Developmentally, acts of agency start out as simple, one-step processes with rapid reward. As a person gets older, however, the time between an act and the reward lengthen and the novelty as well as the complexity of steps involved also increases. Thus, while turning on a light may be an act that exercises agency in a young child, in the adult it is usually a wholly habitual, thoughtless action that often involves no agency at all—that is, unless one is in a new setting and does not know where the light switches are, or has some brain insult that affects memory or movement.

All else being equal, acts that involve the neurodynamics of falling into a strong basin of attraction involve little or no agency; acts that involve overcoming strong repellors require considerable agency. Getting up to jog in the morning when one has done so regularly involves little agency, while getting up the first time in an effort to begin a jogging program requires considerable agency. In the former case, synaptic plasticity caused by repetition has made the activity a relatively low brain energy (i.e., habitual) endeavor. In the latter case, the brain must forge new pathways (metaphorically and literally), involving substantially more energy.

The following clinical examples demonstrate how agency—or, more accurately, a lack thereof—is often responsible for dysfunction found in clinical populations. J. C. was a twenty-two-year-old, single, male, Caucasian college student who dropped out of school due to an intractable, two-year depression. He had stopped attending his college classes, moved back into his parents' house, slept most of the day, played computer games from the late afternoon when he would wake up until early in the morning, and rarely left the house. He was also refractory to medications and was later determined, via neurocognitive testing, to have a severe cognitive processing problem in spite of scores in the high 90th percentile on several cognitive measures. He had done relatively well throughout school until he reached college and this was the first time he was ever suspected to have had a learning problem.

On further investigation, J. C.'s father was instrumental in propelling him through his high school classes because he had very severe difficulties initiating homework and completing assignments unless he was under the pressure of an imminent deadline. Even then, it usually was his father who pushed him to get his work done. Because his father was an unusually controlling individual, this dynamic suited the father well, and made it quite rare that the patient actually needed to, or even had an opportunity, to plan and carry out any assignments or other activity in his life independently. At age twenty-two, J. C. had never planned and gone on a trip, vacation, or otherwise left his parents' house overnight without his parents' involvement in planning. He had missed many milestones in the development of a capacity for agency.

Psychotherapy with J. C. was marked by attempts to facilitate his interest in, and ability to engage in, activities such as wake and sleep at approximately the same times every day, take regular exercise, interact socially with peers, and then later take a class or two at college, get a job, and so on. All such acts required prohibitive amounts of effort for J. C. Strikingly, he understood cognitively and emotionally that engaging in these activities would be helpful for him, and he often expressed an honest desire and high motivation to do them, but rarely would he follow through. J. C. clearly demonstrated impaired agency over much of his life at baseline, with severe exacerbation of this problem when he was in depressed states, at which time the major behavioral attractor involved inactivity.

In contrast, S. H. was a forty-four-year-old, married, Caucasian, socially conservative woman with a two-year history of anxiety and depression following the accidental publication of her phone number as an "adult entertainer" in a local telephone directory. She received many lewd telephone calls as a result and developed agoraphobia without panic. She would not go out of the house "to face what others would think" of her. A severe depressive episode ensued, and she was not getting out of bed or regularly attending to activities of daily living. She developed memory problems and became passively suicidal. Previously, she had experienced several losses including the death of a parent and a "falling out" with a sibling that led to a lawsuit over some property. Nevertheless, she had been working full time and had been an active stepmother and wife. In psychotherapy, she wanted to accomplish goals, including the regular self-administration of her medications as prescribed, as well as activities that she would decide on in sessions that were intended to challenge her anxieties. When her depression and anxiety lifted somewhat, she would make progress on these goals, but when the depressed or anxious state returned, she would not. Her baseline level of functioning was less problematic than J. C.'s, as evidenced by her previous good level of functioning—that is, her history was characterized by physiological states from which emerged relatively little behavioral disturbance, while J. C. demonstrated some emergent patterns of limited cognitive functioning that presumably reflected anomalous brain physiology, and that may well have been "hardwired" and exacerbated at times by environmental conditions. Consequently, certain physiological states associated with high-level functioning for S. H. had a much lower probability of occurrence for J. C.

Components of Acts of Agency

Although in some ways it creates artificial distinctions in mental processes to do so, it is worth "unpacking" agency to try to grasp its components at several levels of understanding, from the clinical to the neurobiological. This will help clarify what we mean by a person acting as an agent.

Foresight

The first component of agency we will discuss is represented by the last part of our definition. That is, an act of agency is one that has an outcome that the individual has (in whole, in part, or in modified form) foreseen. This refers to the "planning phase" of engaging in a novel activity and it occurs first, before the initiation of the action itself. The "foreseeing" applies as much to the process as to the result of the behavior. If there are multiple steps toward the desired goal, the individual must imagine or foresee (in whole, in part, or in modified form) those steps. This is important in that it is likely critical to initiating such acts and it also distinguishes acts of agency from some pathology.

When one considers starting a new routine—such as jogging every morning—the greatest agency is needed the first morning one jogs. Yet the brain events related to engaging in that single act likely started days, weeks, or months earlier. For the most part, the cognitive functions involved in agency comprise what are referred to by neuropsychologists as *executive cognitive abilities*—such things as planning, organizing, self-monitoring, and the autonomous regulation of behavior (Fuster 1997). First, one must imagine jogging in the morning and develop an investment in both the process and the outcome. There may be several things one imagines, such as what it will be like to get up earlier to jog, how one's knees will take it, what the morning will be like, where one will jog (viz., whether jogging will be both physically and "environmentally" possible), and that the result of jogging will lead to desirable effects such as better aerobic capacity, firmer muscles, weight loss, increased sexual attractiveness, and so on. Both the self and the environment are mentally evaluated in preparation for the act itself and the costs (energy input) versus the benefits, as defined by one's imagined outcome(s), are weighed—though not necessarily in a truly rational manner.

In addition, the reality that jogging in the morning one time will not lead to the desired outcome must be grasped so that the step-by-step process of developing a jogging routine can be realized. This evaluation of costs and benefits is different for different people, and for the same person in different states, and again may rarely be truly rational. In one state, someone may imagine such a wonderful outcome of jogging regularly that she feels eager and ready to start the process as soon as possible. In another state, the same person may imagine that she will never overcome the obstacles to achieve that outcome, and so the act of exerting the effort of starting jogging is a useless waste of energy. The former may occur right before lunch when the individual has lots of energy and ambition and the latter may occur in the early mornings when the alarm clock rings. Being able to establish a relatively positive mental image of the process and the results of one's imagined action, relative to the cost of the action, in the face of fluctuating physiological states (with fluctuating levels of energy, optimism, and mood) is critical to initiating an act that constitutes a repellor, or that has at most a very shallow basin of attraction.

Interestingly, functional brain imaging research indicates that imagining an action involves activity in some of the same brain regions that are involved in carrying out the act itself. This includes the primary motor cortex (Lang et al. 1996; Lotze et al. 1999; Roth et al. 1996; Schnitzler et al. 1997), the supplementary motor cortex (Hyland et al. 1989; Lotze et al. 1999), the premotor cortex (Lotze et al. 1999), the posterior cerebellum (Hanakawa et al. 2003), and even somatosensory regions of the brain (Naito and Sadato 2003). In this way, mental practice is likely to initiate synaptic changes that help lower the energy of activation for engaging in the act. While it is not possible to form a new behavioral habit or break an old one by merely "thinking it through" or imagining doing it, such preparatory mental processing is nevertheless essential. Undoubtedly, it is most important for those acts that require the most agency—like making a life change that will have lifelong repercussions, or by acting in a way that breaks a highly addictive, persistent habit.

Acts requiring greatest agency start with the repetition of an imagining process that seems to prepare the central nervous system for a new behavior. In certain physiological states, it is very difficult to engage this imaginative capacity. Depression is such an example. When severely depressed, neither the patients J. C. nor S. H. could mentally hold the image of engaging in any action, much less any outcome of an action they might engage in. Altering the patient's physiological state is necessary as a first step in such circumstances, to lower the peak of repulsion involved in taking those first mental steps. This can be done with the use of medication(s) or with other interventions. It is futile to expect a depressed or otherwise impaired person to act as an agent when he cannot even undertake and sustain the mental process of imagining his own action or its result.

Alternatively, someone may engage in new behaviors that seem to be great departures from prior habitual behaviors and may look like acts of great agency, but which do not meet this characteristic of having been foreseen. Consider a manic individual, for example. In mania, it is common for people to make many new choices and for activity to be very high. But the actions tend to be quite impulsive and the possible outcomes cannot be imagined realistically. Likewise, people with dementia or delirium may appear to be acting as agents, but often are not doing so because of their diminished capacity to foresee the consequences of their actions. Lack of foresight is a deficit that may compromise agency in a number of other psychiatric conditions as well, including ADHD, impulse control disorders, and psychotic disorders. To act and not think of the effect of one's action is *not* to be an agent in the way we are describing. It is to be subject to the whim of physiological brain states. The loss of functional activity in any number of cortical and subcortical areas may impair foresight and the capacity to engage in the mental activity described here, and can thereby severely limit the ability to engage in acts of agency.

Choice

Choosing (consciously or nonconsciously) to engage in some action—beginning a morning jogging routine, for example—is the next component of agency we will discuss. The word "choosing" is conceptually problematic because of the philosophical dilemma that it raises about free will versus determinism. We will circumvent that concern for the purposes of this discussion by focusing on the *experience* of choice, which involves a *sense* of agency. The experience of choice is an emergent property of the activation of certain neural networks, the exact details of which remain to be delineated precisely, but which seem to involve regions of the prefrontal and medial frontal (e.g., anterior cingulated, supplementary motor) cortex (Grigsby and Stevens 2000).

If one is forced by threat of immediate negative consequences to get out of bed and jog (unlikely as that may be to happen, with the possible exceptions of military basic training), the brain is engaged in a very different set of activities than if one "chooses" the behavior. This is evident in psychiatric patients who are in the hospital setting as opposed to living on their own. When given the structure of the hospital's schedule of waking, eating, sleeping, and other daily activities, the probability that appropriate purposeful acts will be completed is greater than when the patient is at home without the same environmental structure and support. When at home, a depressed person, for example, may find it impossible to decide to act in a particular manner (even if she *can* imagine these actions and the results), particularly if the act involves a departure from habit. Eventually, the patients J. C. and S. H. both "made the choice" to participate in certain activities, such as taking medications, doing something every day that was different from their routine of inactivity, and the like. Initially, however, even making these choices was difficult. This is because emergent properties such as a sense of apathy, futility, and helplessness constituted their physiological states.

To illustrate the behavioral paradigm of choice as it is affected by state, consider the research on learned helplessness (Overmier and Seligman 1967). In early studies of this phenomenon, dogs were assigned to one of two groups: either they were exposed to inescapable electrical shocks or they were not. The inescapable shocks were delivered to the dogs when they were physically restrained and unable to move. Subsequently, both groups of dogs were administered electric shocks from which escape was possible by jumping over a low divider in their cages. Shocks then were administered through the floor of only one side of the cage, shortly after a warning light indicated that the shock was coming. The dogs not previously exposed to inescapable shock quickly learned to jump the barrier to the safe side of the cage, hence avoiding the shock. The dogs that had been exposed to inescapable shock did not learn this means of escape, and often stood passively and simply waited for the shocks to end. Although they did, in fact, have the option of jumping the barrier to be free of the shocks, they previously had learned that there was no way to avoid shock. This effectively reduced the probability of activating the neuronal circuitry of physically moving to escape to the other side of the cage and increased the probability of passively suffering the shocks. The "choice" to jump the barrier to escape the shocks was an option for all dogs in the experiment. But by being taught that their actions had no effect with regard to a shock, the exposed group did not make this choice—most probably because they did not consider (could not foresee) that the choice existed. This example demonstrates an important way in which learning affects decision making: the probabilities of various neurobiological (and thus behavioral) events are strongly affected by the neurobiological (and behavioral) history of the organism.

As with patients like J. C. and S. H., the process of beginning to learn that one's actions can have an effect is a significant step in restoring (or acquiring) agency, and thus a sense of agency, if it can be done. J. C., for example, almost never had been given the choice of any significant action on his own. His father was the author of the majority of the acts of any importance in his life. This greatly interfered with the normal development of agency that occurs in childhood and adolescence. The neural activity involved in deciding on a course of action had a low probability of activation in J. C., so states that involved decision making about actions occurred rarely. Like the dogs in the experiments, J. C.'s ability to choose would seem to "short circuit" and he would passively await the outcome. The passive state was the attractor to which he was drawn when most important decisions were required. For example, when discovering that he was doing poorly in a writing class J. C. worked on several options in therapy. He could withdraw from the class early to avoid a penalty, talk to the instructor, or go to the "disability student services department" at his school and obtain the assistance he needed to compensate for his cognitive processing difficulties. Although he could think through all these options and agreed that there was a need for him to act, he did none of them, but rather waited. He could not rationally explain what he was waiting for; he simply froze. Decision points that involved choices proved to be highly problematic for J. C., as he had gotten extremely little practice with them in his early life. Teaching him to do something active with these states was neither easy nor rapid.

The way to enhance the "choice" component of agency in childhood is to encourage youngsters to make age-appropriate, and increasingly sophisticated choices as they get older. In the therapeutic setting with adults the same may also be true. "Taking charge" of every aspect of a patient's treatment may be necessary at the outset if a patient is floridly psychotic, incapacitatingly depressed or manic, or the like, but as the patient improves, the need to encourage her own choices increases. Ignoring this can lead to prolonged psychopathology and dependence on the treater and/or treatment team.

Self-Initiated Action

The last component of an act of agency we will discuss is the carrying through of the action by one's own effort (with or without the help of others). This aspect of the process is essential because if the desired result comes about due to the action(s) of others, or accidentally, then the neural networks that mediate agency are not appropriately activated. While we may fantasize that it would be wonderful if a robot came and took us out of bed in the morning, carried us out to jog, then moved our legs and body such that we were jogging, this would clearly involve less initiative, less mental effort and energy, and probably fewer synaptic alterations (learning) than if we did it ourselves. It might get part of the job done and move us toward our goals, but it also might prove to be distinctly unpleasant or boring. It certainly would not involve much agency compared with doing it oneself. This is even clearer when we consider the experiment with the dogs. If the experimenter stops the shocks to the floor of the cages, then both groups of dogs receive no shocks and the "helpless" dogs are safe. But the neurobiological consequences of this cessation are not the same as when the dogs jump to escape the shocks. When one set of dogs reliably moves to escape the shocks, they have learned something and have acted on that knowledge. If the other dogs "get lucky" and the shocks stop, they are equally as passive and helpless as if the shocks did not stop.

An interesting series of studies involving rats also may help illuminate the issue of self-initiated action. In 1964, Steiner, Beer, and Shaffer (1969) conducted an experiment in which they implanted electrodes into the ventral tegmental area (or VTA) of rats' brainstems. This area is known to be a region involved in reward and behavioral reinforcement. The rats could press a lever in order to send an electrical stimulus to the electrode implanted in their own VTA. When allowed free access to the lever, the rats spent the majority of their time pressing the lever to receive self-stimulation. The experimenters recorded the pattern of ad libitum self-stimulation, then changed the conditions so the lever no longer stimulated the VTA (*sham* self-stimulation). Instead, without any action by the rats, the experimenters administered the electrical stimulation to the rats' brains, repeating the exact pattern of stimulation the rats had chosen for themselves previously. Under these circumstances, when the rats had no control over stimulation of the VTA, the experience was *aversive* rather than pleasant. In fact, when a lever was provided such that the rats could press it to *stop* the VTA stimulation, they spent considerable time pressing the lever to end it.

The results of these studies are very interesting: when the rats could stimulate the VTA themselves by self-initiated behavior, the outcome was desirable, but the same stimulation became aversive when it was administered by the experimenters and not preceded by self-initiated, goal-directed behavior. Further studies clarified the brain regions and pathways involved in these findings. Specifically, experimenter-delivered stimulation activated the locus ceruleus, dorsal raphe nuclei, lateral septum, the mediodorsal nucleus of the thalamus, and the CA3 region of the hippocampus (a good example of a distributed subcortical neural network). Self-stimulation activated these and many additional areas, including the nucleus accumbens, bed nucleus of the stria terminalis, medial parabrachial nucleus, both the central and basolateral nuclei of the amygdala, and the medial prefrontal cortex (Porrino et al. 1984). While there is more than one interpretation of this behavior in rats, it may be an example of how agency, and perhaps sense of agency, themselves are rewarding experiences. The act of engaging in self-initiated effort toward a goal is fundamentally different and activates more brain regions than non-self-originated stimulation of even highly reward-associated brain regions.

These data also suggest that simply doing good things for people, and no more, may not be the best way to improve their functioning. Children and adolescents demand for the right to "do it themselves" may be a claim for the right to develop their capacity for agency. It is not nearly as satisfying to be given a good result as it is to exert one's own effort for a good result.

The seeming paradox of these self-stimulation experiments raises another interesting parallel in humans. The need to preserve agency at almost any cost can be observed in some cases of children raised under adverse circumstances. It is not uncommon, for example, for children to "bring abuse upon themselves" by triggering an abuser with whom they are inescapably associated, such as a parent or sibling. This can occur in the context of physical, sexual, or verbal abuse. Children living under such circumstances learn that there is no act of agency that will stop the abuse. Consequently, they may learn that by controlling the time, manner, or location of the abuse, they may act as an agent in the only way possible, despite its limitations. By preserving some semblance of agency, the child may actually fare better in the long run than if he behaved as the helpless dog that gives up trying to modify the environment and passively accepts his fate.

The experience of certain states associated with abuse may increase the probability of potentially provocative behavior on the part of the child, frequently resulting in the abuse itself. Initially, these provocative behaviors reflect an attempt to preserve agency, but eventually they become habitual. Such habits are extremely difficult to modify, as the entire process comes to occur entirely outside of awareness.

Understanding the connection between self-initiated effort and the resultant effects is essential to the development of agency. A child may make a choice to act in some way, but the effort involved in initiating that action might be assumed by someone else, or otherwise might be disproportionate to the effort expended by the child. This can lead to confusion regarding the cause and effect of self-initiated actions. J. C., for example, spent his childhood and early adulthood playing sophisticated computer games for as much as fifty to sixty hours per week. As he described it, these highly reinforcing computer games involved the acquisition of imaginary human characters that could be given magical qualities and powers. These magical properties could be acquired only by effort on the part of the player, but the amount of effort was trivial compared with the magical properties that ensued. Within this fantasy world, J. C. could create a character that become a healer by logging on regularly and engaging with the computer for a relatively brief period of time over the course of about a year. Becoming a healer, this character then could heal any illness in any other character in the game. This is in notable contrast to the laws of cause and effect in the real world, where the effort to become a healer is substantially greater (almost a decade of continual effort after undergraduate school), the effort significantly more tedious, and the consequences far more disappointing than acquiring magical powers that allow one to heal everyone.

The process of spending up to sixty hours per week from a young age to adulthood in a "reality" where minimal effort leads to astounding accomplishments entrained J. C.'s brain to expectations that related in no way to the world outside his computer. His capacity for agency (and his *sense* of agency) was impaired by his neurobehaviorally engrained, distorted computer fantasy experiences regarding the results of his efforts and potentially unlimited powers. Indeed, when he imagined various courses of action and the likely results, the possible outcomes seemed so trivial compared with the effort involved that he did not find them appealing, but rather became deeply discouraged. Getting him off the computer and into activities analogous to "cutting wood and hauling water" would go a long way toward helping him readjust to both the disappointments and the accomplishments that are possible from exerting effort in the real world in which we live. This would improve his capacity for acts involving agency.

The challenge for the clinician of promoting self-initiated action is that it is difficult to give patients such opportunities while sitting in one's office with them, or even in contemporary psychiatric hospitals. No longer are there art, music, movement, exercise, writing, work, or other "adjuvant" therapies in most inpatient treatment settings. (Notably, the presence of these sorts of activities is also disappearing from public schools.) Yet they all serve to give patients the experience of exerting their own effort with an observable result—they enhance the understanding of self-initiated cause and effect and thereby promote agency.

From this discussion of agency, it is evident that the capacity for this complex psychological-physiological process is critically important to proper mental functioning. It is a functional system that transcends psychiatric diagnoses and may, in fact, be a common element of the *dysfunction* that occurs in most psychiatric illness. When a human organism is no longer able to act as an agent in his or her own life, something is seriously wrong with the functioning of the central nervous system. In cases such as paralysis from spinal cord injury, the cause is evident, and we anticipate and plan for this difficulty. When impairment of agency occurs in psychiatric illness, however, it usually is not as evident, it involves more complex neural and psychological abnormalities, and we are less well-informed regarding etiology and treatment.

Summary

Personality is an emergent property of neurodynamics. That is, it is a manifestation of complex self-organizing neuronal transactions, which themselves are a function of the brain's modular, distributed architecture. Out of these interactions spontaneously emerges coherent neural activity, the raison d'etre of which is the mediation of adaptive functioning. Associated with various neurodynamic patterns of brain activity are all forms of complex psychological activity. When we examine psychological functioning carefully, we see that it also has a modular organization (e.g., Grigsby and Schneiders 1991; Grigsby et al. 1991). An individual's state therefore is an emergent property of these distributed neural systems. State is of fundamental importance in understanding personality because it determines the probability of activation of neural networks mediating perceptual, cognitive, behavioral, and emotional phenomena. State itself is affected by those emergent properties. Agency, in turn, is the emergent property of a personality in particular states, engaging in specific neurobehavioral processes that may in turn affect both the environment and the state of the individual.

A good deal of the normal variability we observe in psychological functioning is associated with dynamical fluctuations in state across time. In addition, many psychiatric or psychological disorders may be thought of as reflecting disordered neurodynamics (Grigsby and Stevens 2000). Even "learned" forms of psychopathology (e.g., posttraumatic stress disorder) eventually may be more clearly understood as the emergent properties of complex neural processes. An understanding of their anatomic and neurodynamic substrate may facilitate their assessment, explanation, and treatment. It seems reasonable to anticipate a time when neuroscientific contributions to our understanding of the workings of the brain, mind, and psychopathology will lead to a revamping of the diagnostic framework of psychiatry and psychology, significantly improving our ability to diagnose, treat, and prevent the entire spectrum of psychiatric and psychological disorders.

References

Abeles, M. 1991. *Corticonics: Neural Circuits of the Cerebral Cortex.* Cambridge: Cambridge University Press.

Abraham, R. H. and Shaw, C. D. 1992. *Dynamics: The Geometry of Behavior.* Redwood City, CA: Addison-Wesley.

Arbib, M. A., Érdi, P., and Szentágothai, J. 1998. *Neural Organization: Structure, Function, and Dynamics.* Cambridge, MA: MIT Press.

Artola, A. and Singer, W. 1993. "Long-Term Depression of Excitatory Synaptic Transmission and Its Relationship to Long-Term Potentiation." *Trends in Neurosciences* 16: 480–87.

Bak, P. 1996. *How Nature Works*. New York: Springer-Verlag.

Bear, M. F. and Abraham, W. C. 1996. "Long-Term Depression in Hippocampus." *Annual Review of Neuroscience* 19: 437–62.

Blake, M. J. F. 1967. "Time of Day Effects of Performance in a Range of Tasks." *Psychonomic Science* 9: 349–50.

Bliss, T. V. and Lømo, T. 1973. "Long-Lasting Potentiation of Synaptic Transmission in the Dentate Area of the Anaesthetized Rabbit Following Stimulation of the Perforant Path." *Journal of Physiology* (London) 232: 331–56.

Bouyer, J. J., Montaron, M. F., and Rougeul, A. 1981. "Fast Fronto-Parietal Rhythms during Combined Focused Attentive Behaviour and Immobility in Cat: Cortical and Thalamic Localizations." *Electroencephalography and Clinical Neurophysiology* 51: 244–52.

Bouyer, J. J., Montaron, M. F., Vahnee, J. M., Albert, M. P., and Rougeul, A. 1987. "Anatomical Localization of Cortical Beta Rhythms in Cat." *Neuroscience* 22: 863–69.

Bressler, S. L. and Kelso, J. A. S. 2001. "Cortical Coordination Dynamics and Cognition." *Trends in Cognitive Sciences* 5: 26–36.

Brinciotti, M., Trasatti, G., Pelliccia, A., and Matricardi, M. 1992. "Pattern-Sensitive Epilepsy: Genetic Aspects in Two Families." *Epilepsia* 33: 88–92.

Buzsáki, G., Horváth, Z., Urioste, R., Hetke, J., and Wise, K. 1992. "High-Frequency Network Oscillation in the Hippocampus." *Science* 256: 1025–27.

Chatrain, G. E., Lettich, E., Miller, L. H., and Green, J. R. 1970. "Pattern-Sensitive Epilepsy. I. An Electrographic Study of Its Mechanisms." *Epilepsia* 11: 125–49.

Cohen, N. H. 1984. "Preserved Learning Capacity in Amnesia: Evidence for Multiple Memory Systems." In *Neuropsychology of Memory*, ed. L. R. Squire and N. Butters, 83–103. New York: Guilford.

Douglas, R. J. and Martin, K. A. C. 1991. "A Functional Microcircuit for Cat Visual Cortex." *Journal of Physiology* 440: 735–39.

Ebbinghaus, H. 1885/1964. *Memory: A Contribution to Experimental Psychology*. New York: Dover Publications.

Felleman, D. J. and Van Essen, D. C. 1991. "Distributed Hierarchical Processing in the Primate Cerebral Cortex." *Cerebral Cortex* 1: 1–47.

Fisher, S. A., Fischer, T. M., and Carew, T. J. 1997. "Multiple Overlapping Processes Underlying Short-Term Synaptic Enhancement." *Trends in Neurosciences* 20: 170–77.

Folkard, S. 1975. "Diurnal Variation in Logical Reasoning." *British Journal of Psychology* 66: 1–8.

Folkard, S. 1982. "Circadian Rhythms and Human Memory." In *Rhythmic Aspects of Behavior*, ed. F. M. Brown and R. C. Graebner, 241–72. Hillsdale, NJ: Lawrence Erlbaum.

Freeman, W. 1995. *Societies of Brains: A Study in the Neuroscience of Love and Hate*. Hillsdale, NJ: Lawrence Erlbaum Associates.

Fuster, J. M. 1997. *The Prefrontal Cortex*. 3d ed. New York: Raven Press.

Gall, F. J. and Spurzheim, G. 1809/1969. "Research on the Nervous System in General and on That of the Brain in Particular." Ed. F. Schoell. In K. H. Pribram, 20–26. *Brain and Behavior I*. Middlesex, NJ: Penguin Books.

Glass, L. and Mackey, M. C. 1979. "Pathological Conditions Resulting from Instabilities in Physiological Control Systems." *Annals of the New York Academy of Science* 316: 214–35.

Glass, L. and Mackey, M. C. 1988. *From Clocks to Chaos: The Rhythms of Life*. Princeton, NJ: Princeton University Press.

Globus, G. G. 1992. "Toward a Noncomputational Cognitive Neuroscience." *Journal of Cognitive Neuroscience* 4: 299–310.

Globus, A. and Scheibel, A. B. 1967. "Pattern and Field in Cortical Structure: The Rabbit." *Journal of Comparative Neurology* 131: 155–72.

Goldberger, L. and Holt, R. R. 1958. "Experimental Interference with Reality Contact (Perceptual Isolation): Method and Group Results." *Journal of Nervous and Mental Disease* 127: 99.

Goldman, P. S. and Nauta, W. J. H. 1977. "Columnar Distribution of Cortico-Cortical Fibers in the Frontal Association, Limbic, and Motor Cortex of the Developing Rhesus Monkey." *Brain Research* 122: 393–413.

Goldman-Rakic, P. S. and Schwartz, M. L. 1982. "Interdigitation of Contralateral and Ipsilateral Columnar Projections to Frontal Association Cortex in Primates." *Science* 216: 755–57.

Grigsby, J. and Hartlaub, G. 1994. "Procedural Learning and the Development and Stability of Character." *Perceptual and Motor Skills* 79: 355–70.

Grigsby, J., Kaye, K., Kowalsky, J., and Kramer, A. M. 2002. "Relationship between Functional Status and the Capacity to Regulate Behavior among Elderly Persons Following Hip Fracture." *Rehabilitation Psychology* 47: 291–307.

Grigsby, J. and Schneiders, J. L. 1991. "Neuroscience, Modularity, and Personality Theory: Conceptual Foundations of a Model of Complex Human Functioning." *Psychiatry* 54: 21–38.

Grigsby, J., Schneiders, J. L., and Kaye, K. 1991. "Reality Testing: The Self and the Brain as Modular Distributed Systems." *Psychiatry* 54: 39–54.

Grigsby, J. and Stevens, D. 2000. *Neurodynamics of Personality*. New York: Guilford Press.

Grigsby, J. and Stevens, D. 2002. "Memory, Neurodynamics, and Human Relationships." *Psychiatry* 65: 13–34.

Hampson, E. 1990. "Estrogen-Related Variations in Human Spatial and Articulatory-Motor Skills." *Psychoneuroendocrinology* 15: 97–111.

Hanakawa, T., Immisch, I., Toma, K., Dimyan, M. A., Van Gelderen, P., and Hallett, M. 2003. "Functional Properties of Brain Areas Associated with Motor Execution and Imagery." *Journal of Neurophysiology* 89: 989–1002.

Hebb, D. O. 1949. *The Organization of Behavior: A Neuropsychological Theory*. New York: Wiley.

Herskowitz, J., Rosman, N. P., and Geschwind, N. 1984. "Seizures Induced by Singing and Recitation: A Unique Form of Reflex Epilepsy in Childhood." *Archives of Neurology* 41: 1102–103.

Holland, J. H. 1998. *Emergence: From Chaos to Order*. Cambridge, MA: Perseus Books.

Hyland, B., Chen, D. F., Maier, V., Palmeri, A., and Wiesendanger, M. 1989. "What Is the Role of the Supplementary Motor Area in Movement Initiation?" *Progress in Brain Research* 80: 431–36; discussion 427–30.

Iwai, E. and Yukie, M. 1987. "Amygdalofugal and Amygalopetal Connections with Modality-Specific Visual Cortical Areas in Macaques. (*Macaca fuscata, M. mulatta*, and *M. fascicularis*)." *Journal of Comparative Neurology* 261: 362–87.

Jantsch, E. 1980. *The Self-Organizing Universe: Scientific and Human Implications of the Emerging Paradigm of Evolution*. Oxford: Pergamon.

Jeavons, P. M. and Harding, G. F. A. 1975. "Photosensitive Epilepsy: A Review of the Literature and a Study of 460 Patients." *Clinics in Developmental Medicine*, no. 561. Philadelphia: J. B. Lippincott, 121.

Kaas, J. H. 1987. "The Organization of the Neocortex in Mammals: Implications for Theories of Brain Function." *Annual Review of Psychology* 38: 129–51.

Kaas, J. H. 1992. "Do Humans See What Monkeys See?" *Trends in Neurosciences* 15: 1–3.

Kaas, J. H. and Huerta, M. F. 1988. "Subcortical Visual System of Primates." Ed. H. P. Steklis, 327–91. *Comparative Primitive Biology*. Vol. 4, Neuroscience. New York: Liss.

Kelso, J. A. S. 1995. *Dynamic Patterns: The Self-Organization of Brain and Behavior*. Cambridge, MA: MIT Press.

Kimura, D. and Hampson, E. 1994. "Cognitive Pattern in Men and Women Is Influenced by Fluctuations in Sex Hormones." *Current Directions in Psychological Science* 3: 57–61.

Knowlton, B. J., Mangels, J. A., and Squire, L. R. 1996. "A Neostriatal Habit Learning System in Humans." *Science* 273: 1399–402.

Lang, W., Cheyne, D., Hollinger, P., Gerschlager, W., and Lindinger, G. 1996. "Electric and Magnetic Fields of the Brain Accompanying Internal Simulation of Movement." *Cognitive Brain Research* 3: 125–29.

Linden, D. J. and Connor, J. A. 1995. "Long-Term Synaptic Depression." *Annual Review of Neuroscience* 18: 319–57.

Llinás, R. and Paré, D. 1996. "The Brain as a Closed System Modulated by the Senses." In *The Mind-Brain Continuum: Sensory Processes*, ed. R. Llinás and P. S. Churchland, 1–18. Cambridge, MA: MIT Press.

Lotze, M., Montoya, P., Erb, M., Hulsmann, E., Flor, H., Klose, U., Birbaumer, N., and Grodd, W. 1999. "Activation of Cortical and Cerebellar Motor Areas during Executed and Imagined Hand Movements: An fMRI Study." *Journal of Cognitive Neuroscience* 11: 491–501.

Mandelbrot, B. B. 1982. *The Fractal Geometry of Nature*. New York: W. H. Freeman.

Manger, P., Sum, M., Szymanski, M., Ridgway, S., and Krubitzer, L. 1998. "Modular Subdivisions of Dolphin Insular Cortex: Does Evolutionary History Repeat Itself?" *Journal of Cognitive Neuroscience* 10: 153–66.

Manor, Y. and Nadim, F. 2001. "Synaptic Depression Mediates Bistability in Neuronal Networks with Recurrent Inhibitory Connectivity." *Journal of Neuroscience* 21: 9460–70.

Merzenich, M. M., Kaas, J. H., Wall, J., Nelson, R. J., Sur, M., and Felleman, D. 1983. "Topographic Reorganization of Somatosensory Cortical Areas 3b and 1 in Adult Monkeys Following Restricted Deafferentation." *Neuroscience* 8: 33–55.

Merzenich, M. M., Recanzone, G. H., Jenkins, W. M., and Grajski, K. A. 1990. "Adaptive Mechanisms in Cortical Networks Underlying Cortical Contributions to Learning and Nondeclarative Memory." *Cold Spring Harbor Symposium in Quantitative Biology* 55: 873–87.

Monk, T. H. and Gillin, J. C. 1984. "Circadian Lability and Shift Work Intolerance." *Trends in Neurosciences* 7: 459–60.

Mountcastle, V. B. 1979. "An Organizing Principle for Cerebral Function: The Unit Module and the Distributed System." In *The Neurosciences: Fourth Study Program*, ed. F. O. Schmitt and F. G. Worden, 21–42. Cambridge, MA: MIT Press.

Mountcastle, V. B. 1997. "The Columnar Organization of the Neocortex." *Brain* 120: 707–22.

Naito, E. and Sadato, N. 2003. "Internal Simulation of Expected Sensory Experiences before Movements Get Started." *Reviews in the Neurosciences* 14: 387–99.

Nowak, A. and Lewenstein, M. 1994. "Dynamical Systems: A Tool for Social Psychology?" In *Dynamical Systems in Social Psychology*, ed. R. R. Vallacher and A. Nowak, 17–53. San Diego: Academic Press.

Overmier, J. B. and Seligman, M. E. 1967. "Effects of Inescapable Shock upon Subsequent Escape and Avoidance Responding." *Journal of Comparative and Physiological Psychology* 63: 28–33.

Petrovic, P., Petersson, K. M., Ghatan, P. H., Stone, E. S., and Ingvar, M. 2000. "Pain-Related Cerebral Activation Is Altered by a Distracting Cognitive Task." *Pain* 85: 19–30.

Ploghaus, A., Narain, C., Beckmann, C. F., Clare, S., Bantick, S., Wise, R., Matthews, P. M., Rawlins, J. N., and Tracy, I. 2001. "Exacerbation of pain by anxiety is associated with activity in the hippocampal network," *Journal of Neuroscience* 21: 9896–903.

Porrino, L. J., Esposito, R. U., Seeger, T. F., Crane, A. M., Pert, A., and Sokoloff, L. 1984. "Metabolic Mapping of the Brain during Rewarding Self-Stimulation." *Science* 224: 306–9.

Prigogine, I. and Stengers, I. 1984. *Order Out of Chaos: Man's New Dialogue with Nature*. Toronto: Bantam.

Rose, S. P. R. 1993. "Synaptic Plasticity, Learning, and Memory." In *Synaptic Plasticity: Molecular, Cellular, and Functional Aspects*, ed. M. Baudry, R. F. Thompson, and J. L. Davis, 209–29. Cambridge, MA: MIT Press.

Roth, M., Decety, J., Raybaudi, M., Massarelli, R., Delon-Martin, C., Segebarth, C., Morand, S., Gemignani, A., Decorps, M., and Jeannerod, M. 1996. "Possible Involvement of Primary Motor Cortex in Mentally Simulated Movement: A Functional Magnetic Resonance Imaging Study." *Neuroreport* 7: 1280–84.

Ruff, G. E., Levy, E. Z., and Thaler, V. H. 1961. "Factors Influencing Reactions to Reduced Sensory Input." In *Sensory Deprivation*, ed. P. Solomon, P. E. Kubzansky, P. H. Leiderman, J. H. Mendelson, R. Trumbull, and D. Wexler, 72–90. Cambridge, MA: Harvard University Press.

Scheibel, M. E. and Scheibel, A. B. 1958. "Structural Substrates for Integrative Patterns in the Brainstem Reticular Core." In *Reticular Formation of the Brain*, ed. H. H. Jasper, L. D. Proctor, R. S. Knighton, W. C. Noshay, and R. T. Ostello, 31–55. Boston: Little, Brown.

Schnitzler, A., Salenius, S., Salmelin, R., Jousmaki, V., and Hari, R. 1997. "Involvement of Primary Motor Cortex in Motor Imagery: A Neuromagnetic Study." *Neuroimage* 6: 201–8.

Sherwin, B. B. 1988. "Estrogen and/or Androgen Replacement Therapy and Cognitive Functioning in Surgically Menopausal Women." *Psychoneuroendocrinology* 13: 345–57.

Siegel, M., Kurzrok, N., Barr, W. B., and Rowan, A. J. 1992. "Game-Playing Epilepsy." *Epilepsia* 33: 93–97.

Siegelbaum, S. A. and Kandel, E. R. 1991. "Learning-Related Synaptic Plasticity: LTP and LTD." *Current Opinion in Neurobiology* 1: 113–20.

Singer, W. 1996. "Neuronal Synchronization: A Solution to the Binding Problem?" In *The Mind-Brain Continuum: Sensory Processes*, ed. R. Llinás and P. S. Churchland, 101–30. Cambridge, MA: MIT Press.

Singer, W. and Gray, C. M. 1995. "Visual Feature Integration and the Temporal Correlation Hypothesis." *Annual Review of Neuroscience* 18: 555–86.

Skarda, C. A. and Freeman, W. J. 1987. "How Brains Make Chaos in Order to Make Sense of the World." *Behavioral and Brain Sciences* 10: 161–95.

Steiner, S. S., Beer, B., and Shaffer, M. M. 1969. "Escape from Self-Produced Rates of Brain Stimulation." *Science* 163: 90–91.

Steriade, M., McCormick, D. A., and Sejnowski, T. J. 1993. "Thalamocortical Oscillations in the Sleeping and Aroused Brain." *Science* 262: 679–85.

Szentágothai, J. 1967. "The Anatomy of Complex Integrative Units in the Nervous System." In *Recent Developments of Neurobiology in Hungary, Vol. 1: Results in Neuroanatomy, Neurochemistry, Neuropharmacology, and Neurophysiology*, ed. K. Lissak, 9–45. Budapest: Akadémiai Kiadó.

Szentágothai, J. 1975. "The 'Module-Concept' in Cerebral Cortex Architecture." *Brain Research* 95: 475–98.

Szentágothai, J. 1983. "The Modular Architectonic Principle of Neural Centers." *Review of Physiology, Biochemistry, and Pharmacology* 98: 11–61.

Tigges, J. and Tigges, M. 1985. "Subcortical Sources of Direct Projections to Visual Cortex." In *Cerebral Cortex*, vol. 3, ed. A. Peters and E. G. Jones, 351–78. New York: Plenum Press.

Tracey, I., Ploghaus, A., Gati, J. S., Clare, S., Smith, S., Menon, R. S., and Matthews, P. M. 2002. "Imaging Attentional Modulation of Pain in the Periaqueductal Gray in Humans." *Journal of Neuroscience* 22: 2748–52.

Traub, R.D., Miles, R., and Wong, R. K. S. 1989. "Model of the Origin of Rhythmic Population Oscillations in the Hippocampal Slice." *Science* 243: 1319–25.

von der Malsburg, C. and Schneider, W. 1986. "A Neural Cocktail-Party Processor." *Biological Cybernetics* 54: 29–40.

Yeterian, E. H. and Pandya, D. N. 1985. "Corticothalamic Connections of the Posterior Parietal Cortex in the Rhesus Monkey." *Journal of Comparative Neurology* 237: 408–26.

CHAPTER FOUR

~

Emergence: When a Difference in Degree Becomes a Difference in Kind

Craig Piers, Ph.D.

Over the past fifteen years, psychoanalysts have become increasingly interested in the modeling techniques and implications of complexity theory. Complexity theory is based on the findings from several areas of research, including the study of nonlinear dynamic systems, deterministic chaos, self-organization, artificial life, and cellular automata, to name a few. Although these lines of research differ in terms of emphasis and technique, they share an interest in understanding the processes underlying emergence. Emergence describes the development in a dynamic system of collective and coordinated structures, functions, and patterns that are qualitatively different, irreducible, and unpredictable from knowledge of a system's preceding conditions.

Emergence may seem like a relatively uncommon occurrence, but once we begin to look, we see signs of emergence in a wide variety of systems. For instance, there is evidence of emergence in the evolution and extinction of species (Kauffman 1995) and in the history of the Earth's climate and geological changes (Bak 1996). There is also evidence of emergence in predator prey relationships, the spotted or striped patterns of animal coats, and the collective, coordinated patterns of birds in flight, hiving bees, and foraging ants and termites (Goodwin 1994; Resnick 1994). Getting a little closer to home, there is evidence of emergence in organizational dynamics (Goldstein 1994), traffic patterns, the distribution of wealth in society, the spread of disease (Epstein and Axtell 1996; Resnick 1994), patterns of brain activity (Freeman 1995, chapter 2) and human development (Demos, chapter 6; Kelso 1999; Thelen and Smith 1996; Wolff 1996), motivation (Ghent 2002), gender identity

(Harris 2005) and psychic organization or structure (Goldstein, chapter 5). This represents just a partial list of the systems that have been examined through the lens of complexity theory. In this chapter, I suggest that symptoms are emergent, arising from the restrictive unconscious attitudes that characterize the way an individual organizes subjective experience. However, conceptualizing symptoms as emergent will not come for free. On the contrary, it will require revisiting some basic psychoanalytic assumptions about the mind.

Dedicating energy to arriving at yet another new model of the mind is not without its critics. In fact, the difficulties inherent in developing an adequate model of the mind have led some to reasonably conclude that the entire enterprise of modeling should be scrapped and replaced with a purely clinical theory. After all, models can often take on a rather experience-distant quality, even when the findings derived from the models appear to closely approximate the system of interest. This may be especially true of complexity theory with its use of abstract mathematic models. From my perspective, however, an appropriate model of the mind can sharpen and deepen our understanding of a system in unanticipated ways. For this reason, I agree with David Rapaport (1951) who writes, "The disagreements between model makers dwarf all their agreements—except one: that model making is necessary" (407).

As a way of framing much of what will follow, let me cite two ways in which the models used in complexity theory have influenced my thinking. First, they have led me to conclude that much of psychoanalytic theorizing is based on linear dynamics—dynamics that do not provide an account for genuine emergent phenomena. This may seem like a trivial point, but I think it may help explain why aspects of psychoanalytic theory have not been supported by empirical research. Second, and more importantly, the elegant simplicity and robustness of complexity theory's nonlinear models have led me to reconsider some basic psychoanalytic assumptions about the underlying structure, properties, and dynamics of the mind.

In previous work (Piers 2000, 2005), I have focused on chaotic systems and reviewed research that has utilized analytical techniques, such as difference and differential equations. Chaotic systems are a class of nonlinear systems that exhibit staggering variability, sensitivity, and adaptation in response to perturbations (in the form of sensitive dependence on initial conditions), while at the same time, an enduring and distinctive coherence and continuity in their overall organization (in the form of strange attractors). As such, I have found chaotic systems useful in conceptualizing how relatively healthy people remain recognizable, or "in character," in the midst of their variability, adaptation, and change.

Among the findings I found most striking in my study of chaotic systems was that with very little built into the design, nonlinear models generated extremely complicated and unanticipated behavior that resembled real-world systems. It was this observation that ultimately led me to research on cellular automata (CAs) because they are among the most parsimonious, robust, and readily accessible models in complexity theory. In this chapter, I review Stephen Wolfram's one-dimensional CAs, John Conway's well-known, two-dimensional CA known as the "Game of Life," and agent-based modeling techniques used to model social systems (Epstein and Axtell 1996; Resnick 1994). This will be followed by an effort to formulate psychological symptoms as emergent properties of unconscious, restrictive organizing attitudes.

Linear and Nonlinear Systems

Linear systems are systems that evolve in *continuous*, *proportional*, and *predictable* ways. The continuity of change in linear systems means that a system's current state can be readily traced to antecedent conditions. That is, when we observe the changing states of a linear system over time, there is a straight, unbroken line that links one state to the next, even states separated by significant periods of time. Therefore, linear dynamics allow us to arrive at all the possible states of the system through some combination and/or weighting of the identified component parts and forces acting in the system. Continuity of change is related to proportional change or the clear input–output relationship evident in linear systems. Proportional change means that the magnitude of a perturbation is equal to the resulting change we see in the system: minor perturbations having small effects, substantial perturbations having large effects. With all this said, linear systems are predictable. Armed with full knowledge of the current state of the system, we should be able to predict future states of the system at any point in time. None of this can be said of nonlinear systems. Indeed, a telltale sign of a nonlinear system is the presence of abrupt, discontinuous, nonproportional, and unpredictable transformation and change.

It is common for us to assume that there is continuity, proportionality, and predictability between cause and effect. This impression arises from several sources, including perhaps our need to see order and regularity. Among the sources, it should be appreciated that this impression is continuously reinforced by our daily experiences with human-made, mechanical systems, the vast majority of which are based on linear dynamics (Galatzer-Levy 2002). Moreover, we rely on mechanical systems to behave in linear ways. For instance, imagine the trouble that would ensue if we did not reliably know how much pressure to apply to the brake to bring a car to a gradual or sudden stop. While we want our cars to behave in linear ways, complexity theory suggests that linear dynamics fall short of explaining the changing states of many natural and biological systems.

Psychoanalytic Thought

The distinction between linear and nonlinear systems sets the stage for my main thesis. Psychoanalysis, with its emphasis on childhood conflicts of fixed mental content (memories, thoughts, fantasies, and mixtures thereof, along with associated affect), which are carried across time in relatively unmodified form and released under certain conditions, is a model of symptoms founded on linear dynamics. This should not be at all surprising. After all, most areas of science have traditionally turned to linear dynamics to understand systems. In this way, psychoanalysis is in respectable company, formulating its subject matter in ways consistent with the rest of science.

To substantiate my claim, let's return to the beginning with Freud's 1896 paper entitled "The Etiology of Hysteria." In this paper, Freud develops an archeological metaphor to describe the etiology of symptoms and the task of treatment. Freud sees the analyst as an archeological explorer whose "interest is aroused by ruins showing remains of walls, fragments of pillars and of tablets with obliterated and illegible inscriptions." Armed with "picks, shovels and spades" the analyst aims to "clear away the rubbish and, starting from the visible remains, may bring to light what is buried" (184–85). Linking the metaphor back to symptoms, Freud suggests that the analyst must "lead the patient's attention from the symptom back to the scene in and through which it originated; and having thus discovered it, we proceed when the traumatic scene is reproduced to correct the original psychical reaction to it and thus remove the symptom" (185).

Freud's formulation reveals the underlying linear dynamics of his thinking because it indicates that what the analyst is observing in the form of an adult symptom is the reappearance or resurfacing of an anachronistic reaction tied to an enduring traumatic scene embedded in the recesses of the mind. Nothing new or novel is emerging. Consistent with formulations based on linear dynamics, the symptom represents the "unfolding of what has already been enfolded" (Goldstein 2003).

Moving from symptoms to Freud's conceptualization of character, let's turn to his 1915 paper entitled "Some character types met within psychoanalytic work." To reveal the linear dynamics, let's examine Freud's formulation of "those wrecked by success." Freud explains that a person falls ill in the context of success because he is confronted with the fulfillment in reality of an unconscious, forbidden, and anachronistic wish arising from the Oedipus complex. Deeply threatened by the prospect of the wish being gratified, the person defends against its fulfillment by sabotaging his success. Here, the characterological problem—the wrecking of success—is tied directly to the activation of a preexisting and preserved wish in the context of a wish-specific environmental perturbation.

Remaining on the subject of character but following the introduction of structural theory, more evidence for the linearity in Freud's thinking can be seen in his 1931 discussion of "libidinal types." In this paper, Freud derived different character types based on the amount of libido allocated to the id, ego, and superego. The overallocation of the fixed amount of libido in one or two of the psychic agencies to the proportional diminishment of the other agencies served as the explanation of the pure and mixed types he described. In this model, normality was seen as the equal investment of libido in each of the three psychic agencies. This model is a linear one because it suggests that there is a smooth, gradual continuity between the different character types based upon the allocation of a fixed reservoir of libido.

Indeed, there are numerous psychoanalytic formulations founded on linear dynamics.

- The return of the repressed
- Developmental fixation, arrest, and deficit
- Regression
- Psychosis conceived of as the dissolution of defenses and a return to a earlier psychic organization
- Paranoia as an expression of an unconscious homosexual wish
- Anorexic food restriction as the result of an unconscious fantasy of oral impregnation

In each case, the particular adult symptom or psychic organization is tied directly, often in a fairly straightforward manner, to the resurfacing of something preexisting and enfolded in the mind.

Linear dynamics are not absent from contemporary theorizing either. Taking their lead from Freud's archeological metaphor, clinicians often attempt to uncover from the past an as-yet unrevealed trauma to explain a patient's catastrophic symptomatic picture. Such searches, which are often highly selective and biased, invariably turn up memories or fantasies from the patient's life history that bear a thematic affinity to the symptoms and/or the symptomatic relational patterns unfolding in the psychotherapy. This contemporary tendency reveals two linear assumptions. First, to explain a catastrophic picture requires the identification of a cause or perturbation of equal severity, and second, what we see now is simply the reappearance of something already available to the mind.

It is not that psychoanalysis has failed to appreciate the presence of emergent phenomena. As Galatzer-Levy (1978) points out, psychoanalysis has long grappled with discontinuities in both development and treatment. He suggests that in the absence of an adequate model, however, psychoanalysis has attempted to deal with these observations in problematic ways, several of which have already been mentioned. For example, Galatzer-Levy argues that, at times, psychoanalysis has:

- Dismissed emergent phenomena out of hand
- Linked discontinuous change to a perturbation or trauma of equal severity
- Attributed emergent phenomena to an unspecified biological cause outside the scope of psychoanalytic theorizing
- Frontloaded or posited the presence of structures in the initial or starting conditions of the mind, often in post hoc fashion, to account for emergent phenomena while leaving the underlying linear dynamics intact

All of these solutions can be seen as efforts to salvage linear dynamics. None of them are necessary, however, when the mind is conceived of as a nonlinear system with emergent properties.

The frontloading solution is particularly interesting because it may explain, in part, why some psychoanalytic developmental theories see infants and young children as possessing capacities and proclivities that are not supported by well-conducted developmental research (Eagle 1984; Westen 1990). Moreover, frontloading may account for the problematic way psychoanalytic theory has often equated pathological functioning to the way normal infants function, and the related assumption that pathology arises from the persistence of a stage or phase through which all children pass (Mitchell 1988; Wachtel 2003).

Based on findings from complexity theory, Wolff (1996) has raised similar objections about psychoanalytically informed developmental research. Citing research that indicates that nonlinear growth and change abound during the course of development, Wolff suggests that discontinuities are often overlooked because of forced efforts to find continuity between early and later behavioral patterns, structures, and functions through the overemphasis on surface similarities and thematic affinities. As an alternative, Wolff argues that complexity theory demonstrates that interacting, functional, and competent components of a system can organize themselves spontaneously into emergent and task-specific ensembles or collectives, which cannot be reduced or traced back to preceding states. Moreover, he writes that "competent elements are not committed irrevocably to any specific ensemble at the macroscopic level; rather, they are 'soft-assembled' and can enter freely into new coalitions to induce qualitatively different patterns of coordination as the system's initial conditions change" (385). These observations led Wolff to conclude that infant observation was irrelevant to the psychoanalytic effort to understand adult psychopathology.

In my judgment, the effort to find continuity between early and later states is, in part, an outgrowth of understanding the mind in terms of linear dynamics. In fact, to keep the linear dynamics intact, frontloading was both understandable and necessary. Said differently, when our thinking is based on linear dynamics, it is natural to assume that complexity must arise from equally complex initial conditions, components, and processes. It is this linear assumption that has led psychoanalysis to write complexity into the initial conditions of the mind and, in turn, reach conclusions about the mind that are often untenable, unwieldy, and superfluous.

Cellular Automata

As a way of setting the stage for offering an alternative, nonlinear model of symptoms as emergent phenomena, I turn to CAs. John von Neumann and Stanislaw Ulam were the first to introduce the concept of CAs in the 1950s (Peterson 1998). CAs are deterministic computational systems comprised of a number of identical, locally interacting components that evolve in parallel according to fixed rules (Ilachinski 2001; Wolfram 2002a). CAs demonstrate that emergent, complex behavior can arise from very simple underlying dynamics. The simplest CA is comprised of the following:

- A one-dimensional tape of equivalent squares called cells.
- Each cell can take on a finite number of discrete states. For instance, at the simplest level, a cell can assume one of two states: black or white, or in binary terms, 1 or 0.
- Each cell interacts only with cells in its designated neighborhood. The size of the neighborhood determines which of the adjacent cells are to be considered in determining the status of the cell at the next step. For

A. Transition Rules

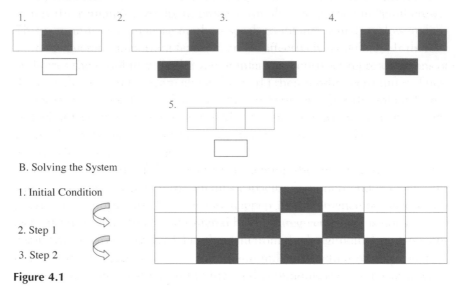

B. Solving the System

1. Initial Condition

2. Step 1

3. Step 2

Figure 4.1

instance, in the case of a simple, one-dimensional CA, the neighborhood is comprised of the neighbor to the left and right of the cell.

At each time step, all the cells update their status in parallel according to fixed transition rules that take into account a cell's current status (as black or white) and the status of its neighboring cells.

Figure 4.1 depicts a set transition rules (A1–5), the system's initial condition consisting of a single black cell (B1), and the changing states of the system through two iterations (B2 and B3). By applying the appropriate rule, the status of each cell at the next iteration is determined. For instance, rule A1 states that when the cell is black and its neighbors to the right and left are white, the cell turns white at the next step. As it turns out, this is the appropriate rule to apply to the black cell of the initial condition of the system as reflected in B1. As such, the cell's status at B2 is white. Taking each cell and its neighbors in turn, the process is then repeated for the all other cells in the initial condition (B1) to arrive at the entire tape shown in B2. To arrive at the status of the system after two iterations (B3), the process is repeated again, and so on for subsequent iterations. It should be noted that while the status of the system changes at each iteration, the transition rules are held constant.

While this is the basic design of a simple CA, researchers often tailor the parts to suit their specific needs. For instance, researchers can:

- Change the dimensions of the CA from one-dimension to two-dimensions (represented as a lattice or X-Y coordinate grid) or three-dimensions (represented as a cube).
- Change the number of discrete states each cell can assume. For instance, the cells can assume a range of colors along a gradient, rather than just black or white.
- Change the type of neighborhood. For instance, with two-dimensional CAs one can use a von Neumann neighborhood (the four neighbors to the north, south, east, and west), a Moore neighborhood (the eight cells surrounding the cell) or a Hexagonal neighborhood (a von Neumann neighborhood plus the neighbor in upper left and lower right corners).
- Change the complexity of the rule by adding constants. For instance, the rule might state that the value of the cell at the next step is equal to the total number of black cells in the neighborhood multiplied by a constant, with the resulting value corresponding to a particular color.
- Change the specificity of the rule. For instance, the rule might state that the value of the cell at the next step is determined by the total number of black cells in the neighborhood (totalistic rules), or state that only specific cells in the neighborhood are to be considered when adding up the total number of black cells (nontotalistic rules).
- Finally, create agents with their own rules, which move along the lattice (which is following its rules) and interact with other agents and the lattice in complicated ways.

From this brief review, one can see that these models offer researchers a range of options. The critical message about CAs is that they generate collective, coordinated patterns and structures with a degree of complexity that is not represented in any one part of the system and could not be predicted from knowledge of the underlying rules and/or the initial conditions of the system. In short, CAs offer a basic, generic model for understanding the dynamics of emergence. In this research, the way these emergent structures are observed is by examining the CA's pattern of activity over time. In this way, the complexity of the pattern serves as an indicator of the complexity of the system's behavior.

Wolfram's One-Dimensional Cellular Automata[1]
Stephen Wolfram (2002a) is one of the central figures in the research on CAs. Among the reasons his work is important is that he has studied in depth the simplest CAs—one-dimensional CAs whose rules are based on the status of the cell and the status of its two neighboring cells (left and right),

and each cell has only two discrete states, either black or white. From this sized neighborhood (a cell and its two neighbors) and with cells only able to assume one of two discrete states, only 256 sets of rules are possible.[2] In his research, Wolfram studied the patterns produced from all 256 sets of rules and found that the patterns broke into four relatively distinct types or classes. This finding led him to devise a classification scheme that could be used to differentiate systems (including many natural and biological systems) based on the complexity of their pattern of behavior.

Importantly, Wolfram has studied more complicated CAs, but among his more interesting conclusions has been that the simplest CAs produce the entire spectrum of conceivable patterns, ranging from repetitive and fractal patterns to complex and random patterns. This means that complex rules and complex initial conditions are not required to arrive at complex patterns of behavior.

Figure 4.2.A depicts a set of transition rules that cover all the possible combinations of a cell and its two neighbors. This set of rules serves essentially as a computational key for determining a cell's status at the next step. For instance, the left-most rule on figure 4.2.A states that when the cell is black and its two neighbors are black, the cell turns black at the next step. The initial condition of the system consists of single black cell (top line of 4.2.B). From this initial condition, figure 4.2.B depicts the pattern that

2A. Transition Rules

2B. Class I system—simple, repeating pattern of behavior

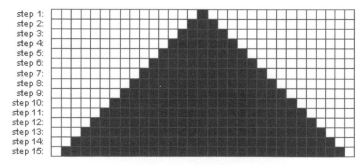

Figure 4.2
Source: Wolfram, 2002b. *A New Kind of Science, Explorer 1.0.*

emerges through fifteen applications of the rules to the changing state of the system. As noted earlier, the pattern that emerges is critically important because it serves as an indicator of the complexity of the system's behavior.

In this particular case, a simple repetitive pattern of black cells has emerged. This pattern, as it turns out, would be repeated regardless of the number of iterations. This is an example of what Wolfram calls a Class I system. Class I systems show a simple homogeneous pattern of behavior that repeats forever. In addition, these systems are insensitive to changes in the initial conditions. That is, changing the initial conditions (for example, from a single black cell to a random array of cells) does not change the overall complexity of the pattern, and the effect of any perturbation is typically stamped out over time. This means that Class I systems are extremely stable and regardless of initial conditions will generate a simple, repeating pattern. A system's sensitivity to initial conditions is also an important issue when thinking about dynamic systems in general because it is an indicator of the system's stability, responsiveness, and capacity to adapt to changing circumstances.

Although the pattern of behavior that emerges in the Class I system depicted in figure 4.2 is itself rather simple, far more complicated patterns of behavior can emerge when slight changes are made to underlying transition rules. For instance, in figure 4.3 a more complicated pattern of behavior emerges when slight changes are made to the underlying rules (figure 4.3.A). It should be noted that the initial conditions for the systems depicted in both figures 4.2 and 4.3 are precisely the same: a single black cell. Figure 4.3.B is a depiction of the pattern of behavior that emerges after 254 iterations.

Figure 4.3.B is an example of what Wolfram refers to as a Class II system. Class II systems are typically comprised of a set of repeating substructures with the whole pattern consisting of nested, scale-invariant, self-similar versions. In short, the pattern of behavior often generated by Class II systems has a fractal organization. While less so than Class I systems, Class II systems are also relatively stable and changes to the initial conditions do not change the overall complexity of the pattern.

Changing the underlying rules slightly again, figure 4.4 depicts the emergence of a pattern of behavior that is in many respects random. In fact, Wolfram (2002a) has demonstrated that the center column of this pattern produces a random string of black and white cells (or 1s and 0s in binary terms). As was the case in previous examples, the system's initial condition consisted of a single black cell. Using Wolfram's scheme, this is an example of a Class III system. Class III systems are chaotic systems, meaning that the patterns that emerge do not develop any regularity. Like all chaotic systems, Class III

3A. Transition Rules

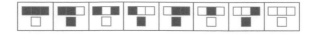

3B. Class II system—nested, fractal pattern of behavior (254 iterations)

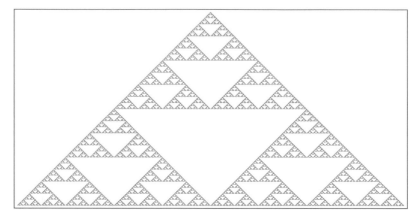

Figure 4.3
Source: Wolfram, 2002b. *A New Kind of Science, Explorer 1.0.*

systems also exhibit sensitive dependence on initial conditions, meaning that these systems are highly unstable and that any change to the initial conditions may result in a radically different pattern of behavior.

Changing the underlying rules a final time and again beginning with a single black cell, figure 4.5 depicts the emergence of a complex pattern of behavior. This is an example of what Wolfram refers to as a Class IV system. Class IV systems are complex systems because they exhibit both regularity and randomness, or aspects of Class II and Class III systems. For example, along the left edge of the pattern (figure 4.5.B), a repeating pattern of different-sized triangles is observed. Toward the middle, however, a far more irregular and apparently random pattern is observed. Class IV systems are responsive to changes in initial conditions, but exhibit greater stability than Class III, chaotic systems. In this way, Class IV systems exhibit order and stability as well as the capacity for adaptation and change.

Class IV systems are systems that Kauffman (1995) and Langton (1992) refer to as on the "edge of chaos." That is, they are neither overly stable and rigid nor fluid and chaotic. Kauffman (1995) contends that living systems evolve "toward a regime that is poised between order and chaos . . . [and that it is] near the edge of chaos—this compromise between order and surprise—

4A. Transition Rules

4B. Class III systems—apparently random pattern of behavior (254 iterations)

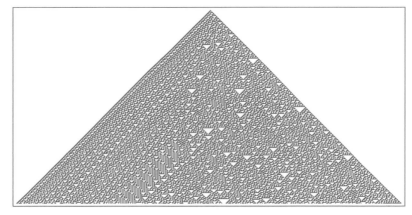

Figure 4.4
Source: Wolfram, 2002b. *A New Kind of Science, Explorer 1.0.*

(that systems) appear best able to coordinate complex activities and best able to evolve as well" (26). Applying these insights to psychoanalytic theory and psychopathology, Palombo (1999; see also chapter 1) spotlights Class IV systems, suggesting that ". . . the ordered realm near the edge of chaos is the optimal condition for human mental activity" (1999, 207). By contrast, Palombo suggests, "pathological mental states can be characterized by their location in the frozen and chaotic regimes far from the optimal level of activity" (1999, 207).

It should be stressed that the patterns produced by Class III and IV systems are emergent because the rules underlying the systems provide no clues as to the complexity of behavior that might emerge. Said differently, Class III and IV systems are "computationally irreducible," meaning that the only way to discover their long-term pattern of behavior is to run the system through several iterations.

Although there is much more to address about Wolfram's important work, in this chapter I will emphasize two points. First, Wolfram's work demonstrates that from simple initial conditions (just one black cell), systems governed by transition rules can generate a wide range of patterns of behavior, from the simplest to most complex. If we generalize from the CAs patterns of

5A. Transition Rules

5B. Class IV system—pattern of behavior containing order and apparent randomness (254 iterations)

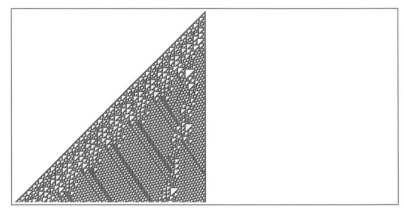

Figure 4.5
Source: Wolfram, 2002b. *A New Kind of Science, Explorer 1.0.*

behavior, we can conclude that we do not need to start with complex initial conditions and complex rules to arrive at complex patterns of behavior. Stated concisely, complexity arises from simplicity. And second, slight changes to the underlying rules can lead to qualitatively different patterns of behavior.

Conway's "Game of Life"

Martin Gardner (1970) first introduced John Conway's "Game of Life" in a column for *Scientific American*. In developing the game, Conway, an Oxford mathematician now at Princeton, wanted to create a computational system that, once started, propelled itself and whose behavior was deterministic, but nevertheless unpredictable (Peterson 1998). In the end, Conway's efforts produced one of the most vivid demonstrations of how a set of simple rules can lead to complex, emergent phenomena.[3]

The Game of Life is played on a two-dimensional grid or lattice. Each cell on the lattice can assume one of two states: alive (black) or dead (white). At each time step, individual cells determine their status at the next iteration and then all the cells update their status in unison. A cell's status at the next step (as alive or dead) is based on simple transition rules pertaining to its current status and the status of its eight surrounding neighbors (a Moore neighborhood). The rules of Life are as follows:

- For a living (black) cell to survive and go to the next round, any two or three of its neighbors have to be alive. Restating the rule in terms of the "life" metaphor, if less than two of a living cell's neighbors are alive, the cell dies (or goes white), as if from loneliness. If more than three of its neighbors are alive, the cell also dies, as if from overcrowding.
- To make this microworld complete, a cell is born (or turns from white to black) if three of its neighbors are alive.

Conway's simple system has proven to be remarkably robust and generative, producing emergent structures that are irreducible and unpredictable from knowledge of the rules and/or initial conditions. In fact, from virtually any set of initial conditions, one is highly likely to observe collective and coordinated emergent structures, patterns, or organizations. Moreover, many of the emergent structures appear so regularly in Life that Life enthusiasts have come to name them. For instance, one particularly common emergent has been dubbed a "glider" because of the way the five-cell emergent structure moves diagonally across the lattice. Figure 4.6 depicts the five phases of a glider's evolution, through which the glider cycles repeatedly as it moves across the lattice. Linking this to the definition of emergence, the glider is emergent because there is nothing written into the underlying rules or initial conditions that would lead us to anticipate its arrival on the scene.

Far more complicated emergent structures also regularly appear in Life. As a modest example, figure 4.7 provides five snapshots of a coordinated ensemble in which a glider moves back and forth between two pentadecatholons (a structure that repeatedly cycles through fifteen states). With figure 4.7.A serving as the initial condition, the glider slides down toward the lower pentadecatholon (figure 4.7.B), and by the thirtieth iteration (figure 4.7.C) has been turned around by the lower pentadecatholon and starts returning toward the upper pentadecatholon (figure 4.7.D). By the sixtieth iteration, it has returned to the initial conditions (figure 4.7.E). Providing the coordinated ensemble is not disturbed by other structures on the lattice, it will continue this period sixty cycle without end.

Wolfram (2002a) has determined that the Game of Life is a Class IV or complex system. Like other Class IV systems, the Game of Life demonstrates the capacity for order and regularity in the form of emergent structures, but also an acute sensitivity to initial conditions. For instance, if just one renegade

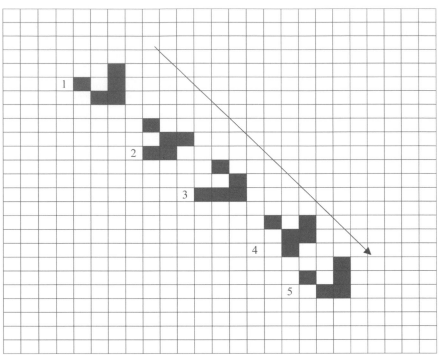

Figure 4.6.   Phases of a "glider"

live (black) cell was inserted into one of the pentadecatholons in figure 4.7, the entire organization would quickly disassemble, ultimately leading to the development of new emergents.

Like the glider, the emergent structure depicted in figure 4.7 could be properly referred to as a first-order emergent. That is, in both cases each cell has unit status and the first-order emergents arise from the interaction of cells. But suppose that first-order emergents could, at some critical point, achieve unit status and maintain their structural integrity, and further, that accompanying their development was the emergence of a new set of rules that were as simple, but were irreducible to the first set of rules. This could lead to a situation wherein first-order emergents could themselves interact to produce second-order emergents. Although the fundamental dynamics would remain the same at all levels—simple transition rules and local interaction—one could begin to imagine a more hierarchically arranged and layered dynamic system. With just such a system, complexity theorists could develop a model that may begin to approach the complexity of the mind.

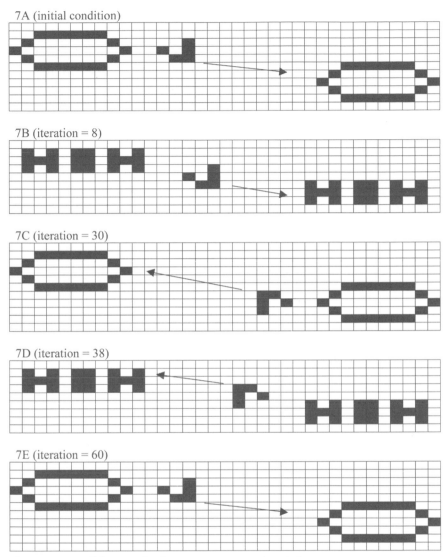

Figure 4.7. "Glider" moving between two pentadecatholons

Agent-Based Modeling

Agent-based modeling is a further elaboration of the CAs reviewed in this chapter so far. In these models, multiple and often heterogeneous "agents" move across the lattice (serving as a "dynamic landscape"), interacting and affecting each other as well as the landscape on which they roam. As is true of the other CAs, each agent's behavior and the evolving landscape are determined strictly by simple rules that take into account the agent-to-agent and agent-to-landscape interactions. Importantly, researchers have demonstrated that these simulated social networks generate emergent phenomena that are often strikingly similar to phenomena observed in real-world social and biological systems.

Epstein and Axtell (1996) are among the leading figures in agent-based modeling. They suggest that among the advantages of agent-based modeling is that the models incorporate elements that are more characteristic of actual human and social systems. For instance, the agents in these models act according to local information, thereby incorporating the "bounded rationality" or imperfect information people have in real-world decision-making. Agent-based modeling is also more in keeping with real systems because the global and collective structures emerge from the "bottom-up," rather than determined by top-down rules or an overarching "invisible hand" guiding the system's evolution.

In Epstein and Axtell's model, agents live, roam, and die on "Sugarscape," a two-dimensional landscape wherein each cell of the landscape holds a different concentration of sugar. The agent has one task: to search out, consume, and store sugar. If an agent finds itself depleted of sugar, it dies. In their pursuit of sugar, agents are endowed with three simple characteristics: locomotion, vision, and metabolism. Taking them in turn, agents are allowed to move in one of four directions (north, south, east, and west) in their pursuit of sugar; agents are able to look various distances across Sugarscape to assist them in determining where to move next; and agents metabolize their sugar stores at various rates as they move across Sugarscape. While Epstein and Axtell typically set locomotion as a fixed variable, in their simulations they usually begin runs by randomly distributing agents across Sugarscape and endowing each agent with varying degrees of vision and metabolism. This allows for a more faithful modeling of the heterogeneity of agents in real-world systems.

Based on this simple model, Epstein and Axtell have observed numerous emergent phenomena that approximate real-world phenomena. For instance, when the population of agents was examined as a whole after a sufficient number of iterations, they found that most of the wealth (defined by each agent's personal sugar store) was held by a small number of agents, paralleling the skewed distribution of wealth found in the United States. A second interesting finding was that under certain circumstances, agents are able to move collectively in ways unavailable to any agent on its own. That is, a direction unavailable to any one agent in isolation (in this instance, moving in a diagonal direction) becomes available to each of the agents when acting in concert with other agents.

This review only scratches the surface of Epstein and Axtell's important work. Indeed, by adding and subtracting simple variables to this basic design they have been able to develop models that faithfully replicate the dynamics of trade, warfare, and disease processes, just to name a few. In each case, they have observed emergent phenomena that in many respects parallel real-world phenomena.

Resnick (1994) has also contributed a great deal to the literature on agent-based modeling. In his work, Resnick has modeled systems ranging from the life cycle of slime mold to the propagation of forest fires. In each case, emergent phenomena derived from deterministic models based on simple rules and local interactions are often observed. For instance, in modeling traffic jams, Resnick replicated the way a collective jam of cars moves in the opposite direction to the forward flow of individual cars. As was the case in Sugarscape, the backward direction of the collective jam is emergent because it moves in ways that are not written into the underlying rules and is qualitatively different from any one car's movement in isolation.

Symptoms as Emergent Phenomena

In what ways are symptoms qualitatively different and irreducible to an individual's preexisting and ongoing state of mind, including conscious and unconscious mental contents? Symptoms are emergent in at least two respects. First, symptoms represent a rupture or qualitative shift in the individual's experience of volitional self-direction or agency. This assertion is based on the observation that people seeking psychotherapy commonly report that they feel compelled to do things they don't want to do; feel things they don't want to feel; think things they don't want to think; say things they don't really mean; are held responsible for actions they didn't really mean to commit; or are "unable" to end relationships they insist are not good for them. In short, to a greater or lesser degree people seeking therapy regularly report feeling impinged upon or controlled by influences (or "impulses") that they experience as foreign or less than fully their own. Indeed, it is often the distress generated by the felt loss of volitional self-direction that first brings people to therapy. In its most extreme form, this quality of symptoms is evident in auditory and visual hallucinations as well as other psychotic experiences (e.g., thought insertion and referential thinking), wherein the individual does not experience himself as the source of the voice, perception, or thought.

The second way symptoms are emergent is that they arise from a psychological context that does not at first glance contain the necessary ingredients to explain their arrival. That is, symptoms often seem inscrutable, peculiar, and nonsensical. I think there would be little disagreement among theorists from even widely divergent orientations that these are two generic characteristics of symptoms and set symptoms apart from other forms of human experience and activity. Furthermore, it is my view that they offer the most compelling evidence that symptoms are indeed emergent.

As reviewed earlier, psychoanalysis has traditionally explained these two characteristics of symptoms with the unconscious, in which anachronistic mental contents are held and can, under the right circumstances, suddenly resurface in the form of compromise formations. In so doing, however, psychoanalysis developed a nonemergence, linear model of symptoms. That is, the symptom was thought to be a linear combination or mixing of mental contents already present in the preceding state of mind, albeit tucked away in the unconscious.

But if we take the models from complexity theory seriously and conceptualize symptoms as truly emergent, we would need to shift our attention away from preserved mental content and zero in on the transition rules that characterize the way an individual organizes subjective experience, including mental contents. This brings me to the mind's attitudes. An attitude describes an individual's unconscious and fairly continuous way of approaching, experiencing, and organizing subjective experience. As such, attitudes can be cast as a set of transition rules that govern the way the flow of subjective experience is organized into subjective states. In this way, unconscious attitudes are akin to the embedded rules of a CA, inasmuch as both govern the complexity of the system's pattern of behavior and are the sources of emergent phenomena.

In cases of psychopathology, the individual's attitudes or ways of organizing subjectivity are based on restrictive transition rules that aim to dispel or forestall anxiety by, one, diminishing the individual's experience of agency, and two, defensively estranging the individual from aspects of his own ongoing subjective experience (tendencies, thoughts, feelings, sensations, and reactions) because those aspects are antithetical and destabilizing to his attitude, and as a consequence, stimulate anxiety. Careful consideration of the self-estranging properties of restrictive organizing attitudes sheds light on the underlying psychodynamics of pathological conditions. Understanding the dynamics is based on appreciating that restrictive attitudes are intrinsically conflict generating. That is, the restrictive nature of an individual's attitudes often puts him at odds or in conflict with himself (or aspects of his own subjective experience). The anxiety stimulated by even the faint awareness of such conflicts leads the individual, in turn, to reflexively tighten, intensify, or increase the restrictiveness of his attitudes. Embodying an even more restrictive set of attitudes, in turn, leads to broader areas of conflict and an increased potential for anxiety. In essence, restrictive organizing attitudes generate self-sustaining and, at times, intensifying positive feedback loops. From this conceptualization of the dynamics, therefore, both conflict and symptoms are seen as emergent properties of underlying restrictive attitudes.

Interestingly, Goldstein (see chapter 5) suggests that feedback loops such as the ones I am describing can be conceived of as functioning as "kernels of redundancy" and become the "seeds" of psychic organization or structure. I find this observation particularly important because when we speak of the mind's organization or structure, we are often referring to the individual's character or personality. Consequently, from this line of reasoning, the individual's character—the organization of his mind—is founded on the restrictive dynamics of unconscious organizing attitudes.

David Shapiro's (1965, 1981, 2000) work on character provides a precedent for conceptualizing symptoms as emerging from restrictive, unconscious attitudes. Among his conclusions, Shapiro (2000) has argued that slight variations in the nature and quality of organizing attitudes can lead to a wide variety of symptoms. For instance, Shapiro sees the obsessive's compulsive rituals, the paranoid's suspiciousness, and the hypomanic's driven spontaneity as emerging from a set of "rule-based attitudes," which differ in their degree of rigidity but are based on the individual organizing subjective experience in relation to ambivalently held rules or standards pertaining to whom he should be, what he should do and what he should feel.[4] In similar fashion, Shapiro contends that the psychopath's recklessness and absence of empathy, as well as, the hysteric's volatile emotionality and impetuousness emerge from a set of "passive-reactive attitudes," which differ in their degree of immediacy of reaction but are based on organizing subjective experience around what is immediately striking or available to the relative exclusion of deliberation, second thoughts, and reflection. In each of these instances, Shapiro is detailing the ways in which a difference in degree can become a difference in kind.

To more fully describe how a specific symptom can emerge from restrictive organizing attitudes, let's turn to compulsive hand washing as a test case. This symptom emerges in people who are relentlessly conscientious (Shapiro 2000). This means that their conscientiousness derives from a felt requirement *to be* conscientious, rather than solely from a set of articulated moral principles or convictions. Moreover, their conscientiousness is often accompanied by a fairly continuous and nonspecific sense that something has been left undone, or if done, has not been done enough or well enough. This unconscious organizing attitude, experienced subjectively as an ongoing tension, often drives such people to do more or to do extra, even more than they themselves think is necessary with regard to the specific activity, just to be sure.

A frame of mind organized around rules, standards, and "shoulds" is particularly well suited for the emergence of compulsive rituals of all kinds. But with regard to compulsive hand washing specifically, it helps explain why such an individual could come to think that, after washing his hands, they were not clean enough, or perhaps, had become sullied by the faucet when he turned the water off. Such a thought may well lead him to wash his hands a second time. He may then feel compelled to repeat this several more times for various other reasons, each time becoming more specific about how the activity should be performed. In order to leave the washroom and return to other activities, at some point the individual will generate a new rule that dictates the manner and frequency with which he should wash his hands. It is at this point we have the emergence of an enclosed symptomatic sequence. I say emergent because understanding the specific features of the symptom—hands, germs, contamination, washing, the frequency, etc., as well as the individual's childhood experiences with such things—is not critical to understanding the source of the symptom. Rather, the symptom emerges anew based on the individual's restrictive way of organizing experience around rules, or a sense that he has never done enough and that things should be done in particular ways. This is precisely where an emergent conception of symptoms departs from a linear conception, because the latter sees the content of the symptom as representing an encrypted linear combination of preexisting mental contents.

Earlier, I mentioned that another emergent aspect of symptomatic behavior is the accompanying, qualitative diminution of the individual's experience of agency. But let me flesh this point out further. Staying with compulsive hand washing, we can see that with the emergence of the symptomatic sequence, more of the individual's actions have become subsumed under a rule. This has the effect of further diminishing the individual's experience of agency, already attenuated by his overarching restrictive attitudes. After all, prior to the closure of the sequence, the individual felt at least some sense of agency prior to executing each step of the sequence. With the emergence of the symptomatic sequence, however, once set in motion, the sequence unfolds according to the rule. That is, more of the individual's actions are *subjectively experienced* as automatic and directed by a rule, rather than by him.

It is worth extending this discussion a bit further to demonstrate how the restrictive organizing attitudes underlying some emergent compulsive rituals—a relentless conscientiousness accompanied by a continuous and nonspecific sense of never having done enough—might shape the individual's way-of-being in psychotherapy. In the psychotherapy of one such patient, this took the form of his frequent attempts to bully and coerce himself into taking some particular action. It is important to note that the particular action changed regularly, but the urgent, persistent nagging remained the same. He often seemed to be severely scolding himself—scoldings that were regularly accompanied by insulting himself mercilessly for his inaction. If the scolding and insults were insufficient to move him to action, he would then generate various disaster scenarios that could conceivably result from his inaction. Importantly, he readily acknowledged when asked that the likelihood of such disasters befalling him was remote. This indicates that his aim in generating a list of conceivable disasters was not to realistically assess the risks of inaction, but to incite himself to action. On many occasions, he would also try to provoke a similar level of urgency and panic in his therapist, hoping to recruit the therapist in his efforts to get himself moving. When the therapist did not respond in kind, he would then scold the therapist for not doing enough to help him take his inaction more seriously and that it was high time that the therapist "take the gloves off." Of course, his nagging and scolding were intended primarily for his own ears. Indeed, the worked-up, exaggerated quality of his scolding was intended to counteract his own lack of interest in taking the action—an action he simultaneously told himself he should take. That is, his lack of interest in taking the particular action was in conflict with his recognition that he *could* take action, and ran afoul of the persistent pressure he placed on himself to do more, or at least, do everything he could. In keeping with this formulation, it is interesting to note that he would often experience a sense of relief at the conclusion of a session, particularly when he spent the majority of the time staying after himself. This was true whether or not he was any closer to taking the action. His relief seemed based on his sense that at least he had done all he could in that day's session.

Again, I provide this brief vignette to demonstrate that restrictive organizing attitudes are not just the sources of emergent symptoms, but can be seen in the way the individual organizes his subjective experience more generally and are present, to one degree or another, in a fairly continuous way.

Attitudes as Procedural Memories

Raising questions about the role of historical mental content in understanding psychopathology requires that I be very clear about what I am proposing. I am not proposing that life events, even early life events, are unimportant in determining the nature of adult psychopathology. Rather, I am proposing that the lasting effect of any life event, as it pertains to psychopathology, is determined by its impact on the nature and quality of the unconscious attitudes that organize subjective experience, rather than that impact taking the form of a pathogenic, unconscious memory of the event. One important implication of this point of view is that what is remembered, how it is remembered, and why it is remembered is not thought to be determined primarily by the characteristics of the event and its corresponding memory, but by the current attitudes that shape the way the past is remembered and determine the significance of particular kinds of memories (Piers 1998). In this way, I am suggesting that what is remembered in a psychotherapy hour has more to do with the restrictive organizing tendencies the individual brings to bear on remembering his past in the here-and-now, rather than the event's emotional significance to him when it occurred in the past.

In response to this conceptualization of attitudes, one could reasonably agree on the central importance of unconscious organizing attitudes and, at the same time, causally link the development of attitudes to specific life events and, in so doing, again stress the therapeutic importance of working through the memories of such events. Such a line of thought would, in essence, be a way of keeping both the baby and the bathwater. While this is conceivable, such a view is reductionistic because it vastly underestimates the impact of subsequent and ongoing life events in developing a causal account for current human activity. As we have seen with nonlinear systems—of which I think the mind is one—it is impossible to isolate, predict, or reconstruct what effect any particular perturbation might have on the evolution of a system. Moreover, emergence in psychic life indicates that what is evident now is often not reducible to what came before. And finally, reducing current activity to a repetition of past events overlooks the self-perpetuating, conflict-generating, and, at times, intensifying dynamics of restrictive organizing attitudes, dynamics that can account for the emergence of symptoms and function autonomously from the myriad and varied past experiences (traumatic and otherwise) that had a hand in setting them in motion.

It is my view that a theory of psychopathology founded on unconscious organizing attitudes offers a more explanatory and parsimonious account of psychopathology than one founded on unconscious memories. I say this because the development of a restrictive attitude toward experience affects the very way ongoing subjective experience is organized into subjective states. By contrast, the effect of unconscious memories of past events would be limited to subsequent events that bear some associative, thematic, or emotional affinity, thereby limiting their explanatory power. Unconscious memories may appear to do a fair job in accounting for a single symptom (or even set of symptoms), but fall far short in accounting for the overarching organizing dynamics responsible for the coherence and continuity of form we see in adult personality, out of which a particular symptom is just one emergent expression.

Although my discussion thus far has focused on unconscious memories, a similar case can be made in relation to models that emphasize unconscious relational scripts or object relations. While models founded on memories, object relations, and organizing attitudes all have ways of accounting for symptoms and the restrictiveness of an individual's functioning, a model of psychopathology based on restrictive organizing attitudes can account for a wider range of the individual's functioning and the distinctive "self-sameness" of his functioning (Piers 2000).

This conceptualization of unconscious attitudes can be situated within current theories of memory. Among contemporary memory theorists, there is general agreement that memory can be broken down into two distinct types: declarative memory and nondeclarative or procedural memory (Squire and Schacter 2002). Declarative memories are memories for specific events (e.g., a birthday, an anniversary, or the death of a loved one), while procedural memories are memories for how something is performed (e.g., solving a math problem, playing the piano, or shooting a basketball). Recently, procedural memory has figured prominently in the work of several theorists in their understanding of psychotherapeutic insight and change (Rosenblatt 2004), personality (Grigsby and Stevens 2000; Grigsby and Osuch, see chapter 3), and transference (Westen and Gabbard 2002). For my part, I suggest that psychopathology arises from unconscious procedural memories in the form of restrictive organizing attitudes, procedures, or rules for organizing subjective experience, rather than from unconscious declarative memories in the form of traumatic childhood events, fantasies, or complex mixtures of the two. As such, treating psychopathology requires therapeutic attention to the restrictiveness of unconscious procedural memory, rather than in excavating early, unconscious declarative memory.

Conclusion

Research on CAs indicates that emergent phenomena—ranging from simple, repeating patterns of behavior to random and complex patterns of behavior—can arise in recursive systems whose evolution is based on rather simple transition rules. In that way, CAs provide a basic, generic model for understanding emergence and demonstrate that complex rules and complex initial conditions are not required to arrive at complex patterns of behavior. This research has led me to reconceptualize the mind's underlying structure, properties, and dynamics and formulate symptoms as emergent phenomena. In my formulation, I link the emergence of symptoms to unconscious restrictive attitudes—attitudes that determine the way an individual organizes the flow of subjective experience into subjective states. In so doing, I draw an analogy between restrictive organizing attitudes and the transition rules of CAs, both of which govern the complexity (or lack thereof) of the system's pattern of behavior and are the sources of emergent phenomena.

Regardless of the fate of my own particular take on this research, I venture to predict that CAs—as well as many other areas of complexity theory—will serve to stimulate new and potentially fruitful ways of thinking about the mind and its pathologies.

Notes

1. I am grateful to Jason Cawley of Wolfram Research for his clarifying comments to earlier drafts of this section.

2. The initial conditions include three cells that are either black or white. This totals 8 (or 2 x 2 x 2) possible combinations of initial conditions. At the next step, a cell can assume one of two states. Therefore the total number of rule sets equals 2^8 or 256.

3. There are several very user-friendly Life programs that can be downloaded for free from the Internet. One of the best I have found is Johan G. Bontes' "Life32." This program as well as a vast library of discovered patterns can be found at: psoup.math.wisc.edu/Life32.html

4. Shapiro's use of the word "rule" in rule-based attitudes is descriptive and far more specific than my description of unconscious attitudes in general as "transition rules," or rules that govern the way subjective experience is organized. A potential confusion arises because the rules that govern the way obsessive, paranoid, and hypomanic individuals organize subjective experience (their attitudes) are characterized by uncompromising "shoulds," standards, and rules.

References

Bak, P. 1996. *How Nature Works: The Science of Self-Organized Criticality.* New York: Springer-Verlag.

Eagle, M. N. 1984. *Recent Developments in Psychoanalysis: A Critical Evaluation.* Cambridge, MA: Harvard University Press.

Epstein, J. M. and Axtell, R. L. 1996. *Growing Artificial Societies: Social Sciences from the Bottom Up.* Washington, DC: Brookings Institution Press.

Freeman, W. J. 1995. *Societies of Brains: A Study in the Neuroscience of Love and Hate*. Hillsdale, NJ: Lawrence Erlbaum Associates.

Freud, S. 1896. "The Aetiology of Hysteria." In *Sigmund Freud: Collected Papers*, vol. 1, trans. J. Riviere, 183–219. New York: Basic Books, 1959.

Freud, S. 1916. "Some Character-Types Met with in Psychoanalytic Work." In *Sigmund Freud: Collected Papers*, vol. 4, trans. J. Riviere, 318–44. New York: Basic Books, 1959.

Freud, S. 1931. "Libidinal Types." In *Sigmund Freud: Collected Papers*, vol. 5, trans. J. Strachey, 247–52. New York: Basic Books, 1959.

Galatzer-Levy, R. M. 1978. "Qualitative Change from Quantitative Change: Mathematical Catastrophe Theory in Relation to Psychoanalysis." *Journal of American Psychoanalytic Association* 26: 921–35.

Galatzer-Levy, R. M. 2002. "Emergence." *Psychoanalytic Inquiry* 22: 708–27.

Gardner, M. 1970. "Mathematical Games: The Fantastic Contribution of John Conway's New Solitaire Game 'Life.'" *Scientific American* 223: 120–23.

Ghent, E. 2002. "Wish, Need, Drive, Motive in Light of Dynamic Systems Theory and Edelman's Selectionist Theory." *Psychoanalytic Dialogues* 12: 763–808.

Goldstein, J. 1994. *The Unshackled Organization: Facing the Challenge of Unpredictability through Spontaneous Reorganization*. Portland, OR: Productivity Press.

Goldstein, J. 2003. "The Construction of Emergent Order, or, How to Resist the Temptation of Hylozoism." *Nonlinear Dynamics, Psychology and the Life Sciences* 4: 295–314.

Goodwin, B. 1994. *How the Leopard Changed Its Spots: The Evolution of Complexity*. New York: Simon & Schuster.

Grigsby, J. and Stevens, D. 2000. *Neurodynamics of Personality*. New York: Guilford Press.

Harris, A. 2005. *Gender as Soft Assembly*. Hillsdale, NJ: Analytic Press.

Ilachinski, A. 2001. *Cellular Automata: A Discrete Universe*. River Edge, NJ: World Scientific Press.

Kauffman, S. 1995. *At Home in the Universe: The Search for the Laws of Self-Organization and Complexity*. New York: Oxford University Press.

Kelso, J. A. S. 1999. *Dynamic Patterns: The Self-Organization of Brain and Behavior*. Cambridge, MA: MIT Press.

Langton, C. G. 1992. "Life at the Edge of Chaos." In *Artificial Life II: Santa Fe Institute Studies in the Sciences of Complexity*, vol. 10, ed. C. G. Langton, J. D. Farmer, S. Rasmussen, and C. Taylor, 41–91. Reading, MA: Addison-Wesley.

Mitchell, S. A. 1988. *Relational Concepts and Psychoanalysis: An Integration*. Cambridge, MA: Harvard University Press.

Palombo, S. R. 1999. *The Emergent Ego: Complexity and Coevolution in the Psychoanalytic Process*. Madison, CT: International Universities Press.

Peterson, I. 1998. *The Mathematical Tourist: New and Updated Snapshots on Modern Mathematics*. New York: W. H. Freeman and Company.

Piers, C. 1998. "Contemporary Trauma Theory and Its Relation to Character." *Psychoanalytic Psychology* 15: 14–33.

Piers, C. 2000. "Character as Self-Organizing Complexity." *Psychoanalysis and Contemporary Thought* 23: 3–34.

Piers, C. 2005. "The Mind's Multiplicity and Continuity." *Psychoanalytic Dialogues* 15: 229–54.

Rapaport, D. 1951. "The Conceptual Model of Psychoanalysis." In *The Collected Papers of David Rapaport*, ed. M. M. Gill, 405–31. New York: Basic Books, 1967.

Resnick, M. 1994. *Turtles, Termites, and Traffic Jams: Exploration in Massively Parallel Microworlds*. Cambridge, MA: MIT Press.

Rosenblatt, A. 2004. "Insight, Working Through, and Practice: The Role of Procedural Knowledge." *Journal of the American Psychoanalytic Association* 52: 190–207.

Shapiro, D. 1965. *Neurotic Styles*. New York: Basic Books.

Shapiro, D. 1981. *Autonomy and Rigid Character*. New York: Basic Books.

Shapiro, D. 2000. *Dynamics of Character: Self-Regulation in Psychopathology*. New York: Basic Books.

Squire, L. and Schacter, D. 2002. *The Neuropsychology of Memory*. 3d ed. New York: Guilford Press.

Thelen, E. and Smith, L. B. 1996. *A Dynamic Systems Approach to the Development of Cognition and Action*. Cambridge, MA: MIT Press.

Wachtel, P. L. 2003. "The Surface and the Depths: The Metaphor of Depth in Psychoanalysis and the Ways in Which It Can Mislead." *Contemporary Psychoanalysis* 39: 5–26.

Westen, D. 1990. "Towards a Revised Theory of Borderline Object Relations: Contributions of Empirical Research." *International Journal of Psychoanalysis* 71: 661–93.

Westen, D. and Gabbard, G. 2002. "Developments in Cognitive Neuroscience: II. Implications for Theories of Transference." *Journal of the American Psychoanalytic Association* 50: 99–134.

Wolff, P. 1996. "The Irrelevance of Infant Observations for Psychoanalysis." *Journal of the American Psychoanalytic Association* 44: 369–92.

Wolfram, S. 2002a. *A New Kind of Science*. Champaign, IL: Wolfram Media, Inc.

Wolfram, S. 2002b. *A New Kind of Science, Explorer 1.0*. Champaign, IL: Wolfram Media, Inc.

C H A P T E R   F I V E

∼

Emergence and Psychological Morphogenesis

Jeffrey Goldstein, Ph.D.

> Every age expresses its state of awareness in its own sense of form, as ev-
> idenced in the arts or in philosophy and science.
>
> —L. L. Whyte

Morphogenesis (or change of structure) has long been a primary concern in evolution as well as embryology. Recently, scientists working within the cross-disciplinary field of complexity theory have reinvigorated the study of morphogenesis through research into the stunning emergence of new order among a great variety of different kinds of systems typically thought of as self-organizing—meaning that the new order appears to arise out of the system's own internal resources when the right conditions are met rather than being imposed by external forces or factors (e.g., Reitman 1993). Even the formation of galaxy clusters is now seen as a self-organizing process in which "morphogenesis is the creation of pattern and form out of a previously random or uniform environment" (Madore and Freeman 1987, 253). This definition points to one of the enigmas surrounding morphogenesis. Where does the novel pattern and form come from if what they come out of is either random (i.e., by definition *lacking in order*) or is uniform (i.e., by definition deficient in the type of order observed)? As the astrophysicists Madore and Freeman put it, "The path from form back to cause is not necessarily . . . simple" (258).

The why's and how's of psychological organization or structure has also been a perennial and dominant issue in psychology with the morphogenesis of *psychological structure* no less in need of explanation than in other complex systems. Various candidates have, of course, been offered, including sundry psychodynamic approaches, personality theoretic constructs, Gestalt psychology, developmental theories, and so forth. Darwinian ideas on morphogenesis, however relevant to the manner in which mental characteristics may have evolved, have not been shown to be directly applicable to the kind of psychological morphogenesis seen in personality development or psychotherapeutic treatment, since the latter are so rapid compared to the slow pace of evolution. What's required, therefore, is a way of conceptualizing the much more rapid change of order seen in psychological development. Since the study of *emergence* in complex systems directly studies the various elements and stages that are found in the arising and changing of the organization of a complex system, research into emergence presents the promise of intriguing hints into psychological morphogenesis as well.

Complexity theory's revitalization of interest in the study of morphogenetic transformation in many ways runs counter to the big achievements in the development of modern science—such as the work of Galileo, Kepler, Descartes, Newton, Faraday, and Maxwell, which was mostly concerned with the action of parts, such as their motion, velocity, acceleration, electrical charge, and so forth, and not their organization or structure per se (Whyte 1954). The complexity physicist James Crutchfield has attributed the lack of progress seen in the study of structure to the dearth of tools for discovering or measuring organization as such (Crutchfield 1993). Complexity theory, however, is overcoming this heritage by peering deeply into the processes involved with the emergence of new order, structure, forms, patterns, properties, and organization in complex systems (Goldstein 1999, 2000). This research is challenging the age-old notion that order or organization is fundamentally the result of an externally imposed force, the latter notion found at least as far back as the pre-Socratic philosophers, then formulated by Aristotle, Stoicism, Neoplatonism, and later disseminated by medieval Scholasticism on into the birth and development of modern science (see Bunge 1979). This is not to say, however, that the study of emergence at the current stage of its maturation can provide a total theory of psychological morphogenesis. But it does offer a novel framework within which to start rethinking what psychological morphogenesis must entail. In order to appreciate how contemporary research into emergence is altering our conceptualization of morphogenesis, it is helpful to briefly look at some historical background first. That will then put us in a position to better understand the insights provided by complexity science.

A Formative Drive

In the pivotal year of 1776, the German biologist J. F. Blumenbach came to the conclusion that the morphogenesis observed in embryo development was not adequately explained as the unfolding of a preexisting *miniature adult* inside the embryo, i.e., the widely held concept of *preformation* (Rousseau 1992). Instead, Blumenbach proposed the existence of a *Bildungstrieb* ("formative drive") specific to each organism that not only gave rise to its determinate structure, but also maintained this structure, repaired it when damaged, and provided a means for its adaptation to the environment (Lenoir 1982). Blumenbach's was certainly not the first such conjecture. William Harvey, the discoverer of the circulation of blood, postulated a similar structure-generative principle a century earlier (Farley 1977), and just twenty years before Blumenbach's own conjecture, the German biologist and *Naturphilosophe* Caspar Friedrich Wolff posited a *vis essentialis* in order to account for growth, change, and development in a manner that did not require the causal intervention of an external power (Farley 1977). Such *epigenetical*, as opposed to preformationist, ideas were brought forward, in part, because preformationism as such did not allow for the introduction of true novelty in order or structure (Richards 1987, 1992). This is a crucial point since morphogenesis by definition is precisely about the exhibition of novelty associated with processes of growth.

Blumenbach's *Bildungstrieb*, which was indeed about the morphogenesis of biological *organization* (i.e., the origin and change of anatomical and physiological structure), was offered to account for the observation that even though the size of animals and plants in the same species could differ markedly from one another, their overall structure or organization was the same. Since for each class of organized beings there was a specific *Bildungstrieb* that gave rise to its determinate structure, the task of the naturalist was to reconstruct that formative drive specific to each class of organism, this drive expressing the general laws unifying the regularities found in reproduction, generation, and nutrition (Lenoir 1982). The formative drive made its organizing influence felt in a manner similar to Harvey's description of his generative principle as a designer or artificial workman ("opifex") who has perfectly planned for the embryo's morphology (Rousseau 1992). Although the ultimate source of this ordering principle may rest in the creative activity of the divine, the *Bildungstrieb* operated as a natural, not *supra*natural drive.

Blumenbach's uneasiness with preformationism was prompted by his research on the polyp, a fresh water aquatic animal with the startling properties of being able to reproduce without sex and, if cut apart, capable of regeneration from a severed part. Although such properties were typically associated with plants, the polyp also had the uniquely animal features of locomotion, a stomach, and patterns of food consumption similar to that of insects. Blumenbach observed that the regenerated structures of the polyp were always smaller than the original, a fact, he believed, that could be adequately accounted for only by the hypothesis of a formative *drive*, since only a drive had the capability of being quantitatively weakened, thus leading to an attenuation of the regenerated part.

Bildungstrieb as a *drive* connoted a force toward the building-up of organization against the counteraction of disintegration. Embryology, of course, would be a natural place in which to postulate a drive for organization since it is the science of morphogenesis par excellence. Although there were materialistic explanations of the polyp's features extant in his intellectual milieu (Laudan 1977), Blumenbach believed a natural but nonmechanical drive was necessary since he believed mechanism by itself was insufficient to explain the apparently goal-directed quality of morphogenesis, an intuition also shared by Harvey in his belief there was more to organic morphogenesis than the simple collocation and alteration of parts (Farley 1977). But, because of the connotation of nonmechanism with an "occult"-type force, the postulation of a *Bildungstrieb* carried the conceptual risk of coming up against the respected Newtonian mechanics of the time (Richards 1987). Newton had repudiated action at a distance and, thereby, indirectly also rejected the possibility of a self-formative power because of its lack of a concrete mechanism for bringing about structure.

Of course, Newton himself was guilty of brashly proposing gravitational force as "action at a distance," a feature of his theory that caused no small amount of conceptual problems. However, the brilliance of his mathematical formulations of gravity did a great deal to mitigate the seeming nonmechanical nature of gravitational attraction. The idea of *Bildungstrieb*, however, did not come with the same measure of mathematical genius, and thus was subject to criticism. For example, the great early biologist Albrecht von Haller, one of Blumenbach's eminent predecessors, espoused preformationism instead, even though he had earlier toyed with epigenetical concepts (Richards 1987). Indeed, in preformationism there was no need for such a self-formative power since it was an actual, material, miniature homonculus in the embryological germ that guided morphogenesis. In addition, the *Bildungstrieb* was not conceived as entirely nonmaterial because it could indeed weaken over time.

In hindsight, of course, the construct of *Bildungstrieb* may seem merely a quaint relic of vitalist biology since modern insights into the dynamics of

DNA and RNA in morphogenetic processes has obviated the need for such nonmaterial drives. Yet, at the time, Blumenbach's work had a profound influence not only on Kant, Schelling, Goethe, and Schiller, but directly shaped the thinking of a majority of prominent German biologists into the nineteenth century (Lenoir 1982). Indeed, Blumenbach's ideas exhibited a striking prescience in their inclusion of a capacity for adaptation: The environment could cause variations, and over generations these variations would take root in the generative fluid and thereby become a permanent structural feature.

Yet, it had to wait for Darwin's theory of evolution to replace talk of a biological morphogenetic "drive" with an appeal to the non-*Trieb*-like concepts of random variations and natural selection. Darwin understood morphogenesis as the result of the slow accumulation of tiny, mostly unrecognizable changes. While it is true that natural selection in specific environmental niches might be displayed as a recognizable discontinuity between varieties or species, Darwin nevertheless held that the processes involved were basically continuous since he believed that any intervening varieties had simply died out from the paleontological record. Indeed, Darwin was fond of quoting the Latin version of "nature has no gaps," a quote repeated in his Linnean Society papers (Richards 1992). I'll return to the issue of discontinuity later, for now it just needs to be emphasized that evolutionary theory in general does not condone the idea of a "drive" or anything like it because variation, sexual recombination, and natural selection are decidedly *not* understood in terms of goal-directness. Since vitalist explanations, however, were decidedly goal-directed, it is important to glean what vitalism was offering theories of morphogenesis.

Vitalist Explanations of Morphogenesis

Goethe, greatly influenced by Blumenbach's *Bildungstrieb*, employed it as the basis for his vitalistic "science" of morphogenesis in which "gestalts" (ideal archetypes of form or order) took the place of the preformationist homonculus as providing the blueprint for morphogenesis (Goodwin 1994). For example, according to Goethe, the visible parts of a flowering plant (the leaves, sepals, petals, nectaries, stamens, and carpels) are all structural transformations of each other. This was possible because a plant's developmental growth amounted to an unfolding of an inherent dynamic unity or wholeness, taking specific shape according to the inner blueprint as well as environmental factors at play (Goodwin 1994). A gestalt possessed an inherent stability that came into manifestation as a whole under the influence of various developmental triggers. In a similar fashion, Kant had interpreted Blumenbach's emphasis on goal directedness in the *Bildungstrieb* as a foundation of his philosophy of organicity (Lenoir 1982). Indeed, without the postulation of some sort of formative drive like Blumenbach's, Kant thought the very fact of life would be contradictory to reason.

Vitalist ideas may have been inspirational in the kind of *Naturphilosophie* taken up by Goethe and others, but they became increasingly discounted as Darwin's theory of evolution took hold of biological science. Yet, around the time of Freud, vitalism was reinvigorated by Hans Driesch's concept of *entelechy*, a gestalt-like, nonmaterial blueprint acting teleologically upon an organism to bring about morphogenesis (Harrington 1996). As in the case of Blumenbach, it was Driesch's experimental research in embryology that led to his vitalist conclusions. In this regard, Driesch destroyed one of the blastomeres of a sea-urchin egg at the two-cell stage of development and observed that, instead of a *half* animal developing out of the remaining egg half, a whole larva developed that was half the normal size. For Driesch, this indicated there was some *form*, specifically termed an "entelechy," that although not perceivable except for its effect was responsible for producing and maintaining the order of the organism, even able to resurrect its primordial wholeness when damaged. Even though Driesch thought he was merely following Aristotle's insistence that sources of form should be investigated with precision and clear explanation, the puzzle of exactly how nonmaterial entelechies interacted with matter generated an even more difficult quandary than the construct was supposed to resolve. Thus, vitalism again found itself in the unenviable situation of resorting to the postulation of a supernatural locus for its core notion of an organization-promoting force.

The positing of a formative drive to explain morphogenetic transformation therefore promised much more than it could deliver. Not only does it come with the need to bring in the supranatural, there is the further issue of how a drive for order conceived as the unfolding of a perfect whole can allow for change as an organism adapts to a changing environment. Be that as it may, what the vitalist perspective did bring to the table was an insistence that the *organization of parts* as such was a critical issue that explanations relying on parts alone were simply unable to address. Today, now that so much progress has been made in laying out the human genome, we find a not dissimilar and onerous challenge in explaining how all of this genetic material interacts to produce the wonderfully whole and adaptable organisms with which nature is replete.

Freud's Drives and Psychological Morphogenesis

Like Blumenbach and Goethe, Freud (1925) followed in the grand Germanic tradition of postulating drives innate in nature, perhaps the most salient example being his notorious *death "Trieb"*—usually translated as "death instinct." In my opinion, it is likely that one of the reasons translators have customarily chosen "instinct" over "drive" as their term for *Trieb* was to avoid associating Freud too closely with the German Romantic, vitalist tradition, since that would presumably have detracted from the supposed scientific soundness of his ideas. But considering the influence of Blumenbach's *Bildungstrieb* in the German life sciences—indeed, considering the whole Germanic tradition of *Trieb* as well as the fact that German already has an exact cognate for the English "instinct" in its *Instinkt*—a more accurate translation of Freud's *Trieb* should be "drive." To be sure, Freud's important essay usually translated "Instincts and Their Vicissitudes" (Freud 1915) has quite a different feel to it when it is more accurately translated as "Drives and Their Fate" (for *Triebe und Triebschicksale*).

Staying true to the heritage of Germanic *Naturphilosophie*, we must consider a *drive* as different than an *instinct*. For example, a drive is not satisfied at the point of satiation but continues to be active as a propulsive tendency toward something. A drive also implies the overcoming of forces recalcitrant to it—such as the death drive pushing against the life drive of eros, or Blumenbach's formative drive against natural tendencies of disorder. Thus, the dual processes of the pleasure principle (eros) and the death drive (thanatos) correspond to the two fundamental activities of construction and dissolution (Sulloway 1979), which was why Freud (1925) chose to describe the death drive as a *Destruktionstrieb*. Moreover, the way that patients would appear to resist getting well in psychoanalysis seemed to indicate there was a *drive* at work in opposition to libido or eros. Nevertheless, neither the pleasure principle nor the death drive were understood as directly responsible for the building-up of psychological organization. Certainly, eros was equivalent to life-giving propensities, but it was not directed at psychological morphogenesis per se, and the death drive, although it might have had the outcome of building repression into psychic structure, was primarily aimed at guiding the organism back into a state of structureless inorganicity. Of course, this dualistic drive scheme has led to no end of conceptual mischief, such as the somewhat torturous reasoning found in Fairbairn's conclusion that the death drive was really a disguised form of the life drive (Fairbairn 1994).

For Freud himself, the origin and change of psychic organization was not directly formulated in terms of mere oppositional drives, but instead as a compromise formation brought about through the distribution, displacement, sublimation, and so on of psychic energy. In fact, in one respect, the Freudian organization of the psyche could be said to be an epiphenomenon, for if he had considered it in terms of a *theoretical given*, his entire metapsychology would not have been in concert with his hypotheses about repression and libidinal energy. In this regard, Freud's (1920) drives were essentially *anti*-change:

> The elementary living entity would from its beginning have had no wish to change. . . . Every modification which is thus imposed upon the course of the organism's life is accepted by the conservative organic instincts and stored up for further repetition. Those instincts are therefore bound to give the deceptive appearance of being forces tending toward change and progress, whilst in fact they are merely seeking to reach an ancient goal by paths alike old and new. (38)

This passage reveals that the maintenance of psychological organization was for Freud primarily an equilibrium-seeking process, since in his scheme of psychological functioning, any build-up of tension, signifying a departure from equilibrium, would seek to be discharged, thereby restoring equilibrium (Goldstein 1990, 1995). Strictly speaking then, within such an equilibrium-based framework, psychological morphogenesis should not be possible at all since any change would lead to the activation of countervailing forces. That's why Freud characterized drives as "elastic" and expressions of "inertia" (Sulloway 1979).

Consequently, in order to account for the morphogenesis in psychological development that he observed in his patients during their analytic treatment, Freud instead appealed to the then prevalent idea that ontogeny recapitulates phylogeny—that is, the individual organism grows by repeating the pattern of phylogenetic evolution (Sulloway 1979). This theory of *recapitulation* was an update of the idea of preformation, but in Freud's case the phylogenetic record took the place of preformationism's homunculus as the blueprint for morphogenesis. Indeed, nineteenth-century embryologists had begun to detect in the development of the fetus a serial unfolding of the forms of the hierarchy of species (Richards 1987). For example, Tiedemann had "observed" that the eye of the human fetus at five months was similar to a fish's eye. Since the gradations of fossil record were supposed to be mirrored in the development of a human fetus, stages of embryonic development that didn't appear to have a counterpart in the animal kingdom merely represented an extinct creature, a strategy akin to Darwin's explanation of apparent discontinuities in evolution as mere lapses in the paleontological record.

Although recapitulation eventually lost much of its sway, the more vital-istically oriented biologists interpreted the putative appearance of primitive life forms in the fetus as a sign of archetypal or ideal types struggling for a more perfect realization. Thus, instead of recapitulation, there was an alter-nate drive for ever greater congruence to the ideal that the early stages of de-velopment were just more imperfect attempts of what was to come (Richards 1987). In fact, one way to interpret Jung's break with Freud is to view Jung as going in the direction of the Romantic, vitalist tradition, with his notion of the archetype of the "Self" operating like a drive for psychological orga-nization, whereas Freud limited his drives to eros and thanatos (Goldstein 1979). Whatever the merits of Jung's approach, the fact remains that one of the serious problems afflicting Freud's account of psychic organization has been the lack of a sufficient explanation for either developmental change or treatment-effectuated psychological morphogenesis (Wilden 1980; Zukier 1985).

The whole notion of "drive," in fact, has assumed something like the char-acter of a putrid odor for most modern psychoanalytic theorists who have spent a great deal of energy in trying to sanitize psychoanalytic theory from it. The major criticism of drive theory has focused on its mechanistic nature and the consequent quantification of psychic energy it assumes. Thus, Roy Schafer tried to throw out the idea of drive altogether, replacing it with his own Wittgensteinian-based "action language" (Schafer 1976). Although Schafer's work provides a brilliant phenomenological redescription of the subjective experience inherent in symptomatology, it is not satisfactory from the point of view of explaining actual change in psychological organization resulting from successful treatment since it pretty much abolishes explana-tion in favor of description.

Despite all of the attempts to banish the notion of drive from psychoana-lytic theorizing, it has proven somewhat resistant to a complete jettisoning. Thus, Bollas (1991) has suggested a psychoanalytically framed "destiny drive" seeking to establish a core self that is waiting to be actualized, not as a hidden script tucked away in the unconscious, but rather as a set of unique person possibilities that is first facilitated in a Winnicottian fashion through proper maternal mirroring. One might ask why Bollas has been intent to bring back the specific word "drive" and not, for example, "urge," "tendency," "preference," or some other less "driven" terminology? Perhaps "drive" carries not only a sense of something natural and innate and therefore something that ultimately cannot be avoided, but also the reassuring aura of a pregiven guiding principle only requiring the proper conditions in which to flourish. Indeed, the *Bildungstrieb* could also not be actualized, for what choice does a polyp have concerning its morphogenesis? Yet, it must be asked if the positing of such drives with their apparently always accompanying puzzles about how they operate on material bodies is really required, or if another more helpful direction can be gained about morphogenesis from studies of emergent complex systems that do not mandate the need for a drive per se.

Morphogenesis and Emergence

The Study of Emergence

The idea of emergence has been around for over a century, although complexity theory has prompted an intense revitalization of the notion. A vigorous earlier movement based on the idea of emergence arose during the 1920s and 1930s in the form of "emergent evolutionism" that, not content with Darwin's commitment to continuity and gradualism in evolution, attempted to reinstate discontinuities into evolutionary theory. The emergent evolutionists conceived evolution as a series of evolutionary jumps, each jump bringing forth novel "emergent levels" (Blitz 1992). The emergent level was considered so novel in organization and properties, it was thought neither predictable from, deducible from, nor reducible to the lower level out of which it emerged. The aforementioned vitalist Driesch himself became a fellow traveler to emergent evolutionism even though proponents of the latter believed they could avoid having to posit any kind of vitalist drive for order and thereby stay within a scientific, albeit nonmechanistic perspective. This movement suffered an untimely demise, in part because although the concept of emergence was put forward as a scientifically founded emendation to the theory of evolution, it was primarily described negatively. Emergents were *not* predictable from, *not* deducible from, and *not* reducible to lower level dynamics (Goldstein 2001). Thus, this earlier study of emergence remained a speculative idea without the benefit of experimental methods, verification, or adequate mathematical formalizations.

The concept of emergence didn't go away, but was taken up by theoretical biologists and neuroscientists in their search for antireductionist constructs (Goldstein 1999; specific papers in Ayala and Dobzhansky 1974; Medawar 1969; Popper 1978; Sperry 1986). This second phase of emergentist thought served to place emergence within the context of both scientific and mathematical formulations of organic wholeness, conceptualizing the latter primarily in terms of self-referential *closure*. For more, see the work of the emergentist process philosopher Alfred North Whitehead, the Cambridge theoretical biologists J. Woodger, J. Needham, and C. Waddington, and the mathematical biologist Robert Rosen (Goldstein, forthcoming). In spite of the rigorous philosophical and mathematical formalisms emerging during this period, this second phase remained fairly within the confines of armchair conjecture.

The big breakthroughs concerning emergence had to wait for the advent of modern complexity theory in which emergence could be researched in actual laboratories as well as in the virtual computational laboratories for artificial emergent phenomena studied in the field of artificial life (Adami 1998; Langton 1996; Reitman 1993). Artificial life is offering an extraordinary opportunity to study the emergence and change of organization because the process of morphogenesis can be examined by tracking emergent and lower levels simultaneously (Wuensche 1998). In such computational emergence, simulations consisting of a network of individual components or "agents" are programmed to interact according to certain rules. Since global behavior is not specified explicitly in the program, the global dynamics that occur emerge "hierarchically—on the 'shoulders' so to speak—of the local behavior" (Langton 1986). Emergent phenomena are typically observed in artificial life simulations in terms of an ongoing updating of the system occurring in discrete steps.

Since the morphogenesis investigated in artificial life obviously does not involve psychological organization per se, why should it be thought that the former can provide insight into the latter? To be sure, the application of artificial life to the field of psychology is in its infancy, but there are several promising avenues. First, just as psychological theory in the past has borrowed ideas on psychological organization from other disciplines, so psychology can now benefit from insight into the emergence of order in many different scientific and mathematical arenas. Indeed, the emergent phenomena of artificial life have been proven to be formal mathematical systems in the sense that they can simulate a universal computer (Turing Machine)—they can be interpreted in terms of purely formal mathematical systems, such as recursive logic (Berlekamp, Conway, and Guy 1982). This means that they offer insight about the origination and change of organization in a most general kind of way, and thus should apply to a whole range of complex systems that can be modeled by way of such formal systems.

Moreover, ground has been prepared by earlier conceptualizations of mentation according to a network of feedback loops among various psychological, neural, and physiological components. Such theorizing has shed light on many previously obscure questions concerning mental functioning (e.g., see Dewan 1976; Rosenblatt and Thickstun 1977). Finally, in this regard, Piers (2000) has discussed the psychodynamic concept of *character* in terms of "self-organized complexity," referring to the way character represents how experience is organized around attentional strategies, and more recently how symptoms can be explicated as emergent (see chapter 7).

Characteristics of Organization and Key Elements of Emergence

To better appreciate how the study of emergence can provide insight into psychological morphogenesis, the concept of organization in general needs to be clarified. Synonyms for "organization" include: *structure, order, pattern,* and *form.* Although psychological "structure" is typically synonymous for what is being referred to here as psychological *organization,* "structure," as in *character structure,* tends to connote a *foundational* edifice as in the super-structure of a building. As Whyte (1954) put it, "structure" inclines toward a regular and ordered arrangement, as in the structure of a crystal. "Organization," though, because of its inclusion of *organ,* tends more to an *organic* interpretation. Also, order in particular doesn't seem exactly fitting because, according to the *Oxford English Dictionary,* its Latin etymology has more to do with series, rank, array, and regularity, so that "to order" implies keeping things in order or putting them in a rank as in a hierarchy, a class, a group, or in a spatial or temporal sequence.

Furthermore, "order" is usually understood in opposition to *disorder* or *chaos,* a connotation that simply doesn't hold when it comes to contemporary findings about the crucial role of randomness in the building up of new organization (see Goldstein 1997). "Pattern" also is not quite appropriate since it connotes an original prototype in the sense of its root in *pater* or father. Moreover, *pattern* is somewhat abstract like a blueprint, whereas *organization* refers to an actual, concrete set of relationships among parts. Finally, whereas "form" is often used today in the sense of *shape* or outer *contour,* Whyte (1954) indicated that "form" has kept its Aristotelian and medieval sense of the qualities that make anything what it is. Like "pattern," "form" doesn't quite capture the coordination and interdependence of parts that *organization* does nor does it have the dynamism that *organization* can have. *Organization* then, is about relationships among parts, a dynamic network holding the parts together in a whole and acting to coordinate their function. Therefore, when I refer to emergence per se, what I have in mind is the *organization* and *reorganization* of parts making up an emergent whole.

To be sure, the concept of emergence has many things in common with other, older notions related to wholes, gestalts, or coherent entities (Goldstein 2000). Yet, emergent phenomena have a set of characteristics that distinguish them from these related ideas (modified from Goldstein 1999):

- *Radically novel organization*: neither predictable from, deducible from, nor reducible to antecedent, lower-level conditions
- *Dynamical*: appearing and changing over time
- *Ostensive*: emergents reveal themselves as a system evolves
- *Cohesive*: emergents are enduring, integrated wholes spanning across system components
- *Macrolevel*: the organization itself is on a "higher" level than the micro-level of the components that are being organized

The study of computational emergence like that found in artificial life is providing unprecedented insight into how emergent phenomena with these characteristics can arise in a self-organizational manner rather than as the result of an imposition on or an importation into a system. Since the new organization observed in such simulation emerges without being programmed in explicitly, the ensuing emergent organization is not best conceived in terms of a "drive" because there is no impulsion to bring it about. Instead, novel organization arises naturally given the right kind of system and the right kind of conditions. It is important to note two caveats about self-organization (see Goldstein 2002, 2003, 2004, 2005). First, it requires the right kind of system and the right kind of conditions; second, it is not to be thought of as a purely spontaneous process because it requires certain *constructional* operations—laboratory constraints and their natural analogues.

The following critical elements involved in the emergence of organization in these computational networks can provide compelling insight into the processes of psychological morphogenesis:

- rules of interaction and the generation of "seeds" of organization
- propagation of these "seeds"
- windows of opportunity
- arising of new attractors
- role of "containers"
- the generation of novelty

We'll now go over how each of these elements may show themselves in psychological morphogenesis.

New Organization and Its Propagation

New organization emerges when the components or "agents" of the network are interacting with each other in certain ways. This means that these components must be connected with each other. Both the "rules" of inter-action and the manner of the connectivity must be such that they are ca-pable of generating what can be called *seeds* of new organization and then be able to *grow* and *propagate* these seeds throughout the system. (For more on rules, see chapter 7.) One could call rules with such a potential *self-triggering* in that, once conditions are satisfied, the rules set up the condi-tions necessary for them "firing" again. It is also possible that several neigh-borhood rules which map to different states get "linked" together so that a repeating *cycle* of states stays fixed in place or propagates across the array (Langton 1986). In Kauffman's (1993) electronic networks, such "seeds" of organization consist of similar self-sustaining feedback loops not unlike what happens in autocatalytic or cross-catalytic chemical reactions. One way to think about these feedback cycles is that they have the capacity for generating *more of the same*, in other words, they function as kernels of *re-dundancy*. This can take place by way of feedback loops in the system serv-ing to stabilize certain patterns of behavior. In the presence of requisite connectivity among the components, a linking-up of these kernels of re-dundancy form "islands" of stability that are propagated and joined into larger entities (for an illuminating and technically accessible study of the formation of a similar kind of order in so-called random graphs, see Barabasi 2002). The production and propagation of *more of the same* is in-deed what Piers (2000) has shown character does with experience in gen-eral, in the sense that character only allows into consciousness that which is congruent with its organizing principles. The implication, however, is that we are faced with the challenge of how to conceptually account for a system undergoing morphogenesis and not simply managing to produce only more of the same.

Research into artificial emergence has demonstrated that there are partic-ularly fertile conditions offering a kind of window of opportunity for the emer-gence and change of organization. This window represents a region that is nei-ther too orderly nor too random: If the parameters governing the system are "tuned" beyond the window, the resulting complexity of structure becomes too disorganized and the propagating emergent phenomena do not have an opportunity to take hold. Furthermore, as Langton (1986) has shown, emer-gent organization on one level can provide the basis for new emergent orga-nization at a higher level, so that the organization becomes a nested hierar-chy. Langton describes this region metaphorically as the "liquid" stage between solids (too orderly) and gases (too chaotic). This window of oppor-tunity for emergence has been termed the "edge of chaos" (Kauffman 1995). It is in this window that novelty can be introduced into the system because a concomitant sensitivity to small changes can lead to either many small or a few large "avalanches" of change. However, since further research has challenged some of what the concept of the "edge of chaos" suggests (Mitchell, Crutchfield, and Hraber 1993), it is better to think of this window of opportunity as fertile ground where seeds of organization can grow and join up with other seeds, rather than something teetering on the verge of disorder.

Attractors and Organization

A powerful way to understand the emergence of new emergent order in artificial life has been through the ideas of bifurcation and attractors, concepts borrowed from dynamical systems theory (Goldstein 1996). In this mathematical theory, complex systems are viewed as evolving patterns that undergo a qualitative change at critical parameter values. This qualitative change is understood in terms of a "bifurcation" or change in the "attractors" of the system. Attractors are an abstract mathematical representation of stable organizing patterns—what's possible for a system's dynamics during particular conditions (or within particular value ranges of parameters).

In a sense, an attractor represents the *sameness* of the aforementioned *more of the same*. In Kauffman's (1995) networks, the relation of the emergence of new organization with new attractors can be seen in how a network with as many as a hundred thousand nodes may settle down and cycle through a mere 317 attractors. Kauffman believes the presence of attractors has important implications for relating his electronic networks to living systems because the attractors may correspond to development pathways—potentials for cell differentiation. A word of caution is needed here, however: attractors are *not* causal agents, they are merely mathematical representations of the qualitative dynamics within certain conditions. Keeping this stipulation in mind, however, the concept of attractors offers considerable help in distinguishing between ordinary and more radical change—whereas ordinary change is a gradual change taking place *within* a particular attractor, radical change corresponds to the emergence of new attractor(s) taking place at bifurcations.

"Containers" and Emergent Organization

One of the sources of the order found in emergent phenomena that has tended to be overlooked is the *containment* field or boundaries within which emergence takes place (Goldstein 2001). In Salthe's (1993) tripartite scheme, for instance, emergence takes place on a level N out of interactions on a lower level $N - 1$, but constrained by boundary conditions of level $N + 1$. The boundary conditions of level $N + 1$ can be conceived as a "container" that shapes the new organization emerging in level N. This can be seen in emergent phenomena in simple physical systems. Berge and his associates (1984) found that in the famous Benard convection cells, the distance separating two neighboring currents is on the order of the vertical height of the container. Thus, the container's specific height influences the resulting order emerging inside it. In addition, the number of convection rolls can be curtailed by reducing the ratio of horizontal dimension to vertical height. In a similar vein, Weiss (1987) found that instabilities in the thermal boundaries of liquid systems similar to the Benard system lead to more complicated kinds of convection.

Kauffman (1995) also points to the role of "containers" in emergent organization by way of the "compartmentalization" found in autocatalytic sets—research into coacervates or membranes that arise when glycerine is mixed with other molecules to form gel-like structures that then concentrate organic molecules inside themselves and exchange them across its boundary. Kauffman suggests that once an autocatalytic set is enclosed within a spatial compartment, the self-sustaining metabolic processes can increase the amount of copies of each type of molecule in the system. Then, when the amount has doubled, the compartment can divide into two. These facts suggest that the actual physical container helps to shape the ensuing emergent phenomena. Emergence, then, is a qualified type of spontaneity, depending on such factors as the "shape" of the "containers" in which emergence takes place.

Novelty Generation and Negation

A survey of the literature on emergence from its first inception reveals that is has been typically defined by way of *negation: not* predictable from, *not* deducible from, and *not* reducible to lower-level dynamics (Goldstein 2001). In fact, this negation can be interpreted as what allows for novelty in morphogenesis because the previous lower-level patterns have to be surpassed, or in more vivid and accurate terms, actually *destroyed* during the process of emergence (see Freeman, chapter 2; and Goldstein, forthcoming). Yet, the new organization that emerges must at the same time follow lower-level patterns or the system couldn't be said to be deterministic. For example, in Holland's (1998) scheme for emergence in artificial life, novelty generation is thought of in terms of the evolutionary mechanisms of random mutations and genetic crossover where "parental" genetic material is recombined in the offspring. The rules for recombination can be said to "negate" the previous combinatory array. Related research into the emergence of organization in artificial life has identified yet other specific procedures whereby novelty is generated in the midst of the redundancy mentioned above.

Elsewhere (Goldstein 2002, 2004, 2005), I have phrased the radical novelty generation found in emergence as a result of the activity of "self-transcending constructions" (STC), pattern-changing operations that simultaneously involve both recursion operations as well as the processes able to introduce novelty to keep the recursion from simply generating more of the same as discussed above (Goldstein 2001, 2002). It is important to note that the recursive sameness seen in graphic portrayals of such amazing features of dynamical systems as fractals (Kaye 1989), which show the same or similar pattern repeated on smaller and smaller scales, is too self-similar to account for real novelty. Hence, STCs must include a more potent form of negation that acts to transcend mere generation of the same, what may be called procedures that introduce self-*dis*similarity (Wolpert and Macready 2000).

Furthermore, novelty generation in emergence is also not adequately understood as some sort of "creative synthesis." Although "synthesis" involves an element of negation in the dialectical sense that the thesis is negated to form the anti-thesis, and then both are superordinately negated at a higher level in the synthesis, the novelty exhibited in emergent morphogenesis is not a synthesis of opposites, but a transcendence of a previous pattern brought about by both following and negating the lower-level pattern (for the logic of following and negating see Goldstein, 2005). That is, morphogenesis in terms of emergence in complex systems is a radically *creative* process that must entail both a following of previous patterns and a simultaneous negation of these same patterns in order for a truly original outcome to be possible. The term "self-transcendence" has been employed to capture this simultaneous operation of following *and* negating.

Negation in Freud's Metapsychology

It is interesting to contrast the creative role of negation in emergence with Freud's (1925) turn to the concept of negation in his theory of repression: "The content of a repressed presentation or thought can thus make its way through to consciousness on the condition that it lets itself be negated. The negation is a way to take cognizance of what is repressed; indeed it is already a 'lifting and conserving' of the repression, but not for all that an acceptance of what is repressed" (239). Freud attributed this power of negation to both the death drive and to the reality principle in the sense that consciousness following the pressure of the reality principle operates according to the repression wrought by negation (Ricoeur 1970). Negation, then, for Freud was *not* a vehicle of psychological health.

The role of negation in Freud's death drive, though, can be interpreted in a more constructive manner. Thus, Ricoeur (1970) discusses the role of negation in Freud's example of a child playing the game of *fort da* (Freud 1920): the "good" little boy plays with a wooden reel making it disappear and reappear while uttering "O-o-o-o," for *fort* ("gone") and *da* ("there"). Freud used the example to explain how the death drive arises from instinctual renunciation and repetition (the reel disappearing) displayed in the "good" behavior of the boy since he has been obeying his parents. Here the reel represents the disappearance and return of the mother. Ricoeur, however, views this play as the child achieving some sense of mastery over the object—that the unpleasure involved is to some extent mastered by way of the negation inherent in the disappearance. In other words, the child is playfully using negation to establish a mastery over the negativity of losing the mother. Ricoeur links this *fort da* type of negation with artistic creation in the sense of a disappearing (negation) of the archaic object as fantasy and its reappearance in the art object.

Indeed, Ricoeur points out that Freud himself gave negation at least the positive role of allowing for a cognizance of what is repressed through his employment of the Hegelian term *Aufhebung* ("lifting up")—that is, a cognizance of what leaks through in spite of repression, though, to be sure, this is decidedly not an acceptance of what is repressed (Freud 1925). Furthermore, negation shows up in repetition compulsion that can be interpreted in a fashion suggested by Piers' (2000) description of character's complexity role of producing simply more of the same. However, in repetition compulsion and character shaping experience we are actually witnessing a failure of negation in the evolutionary/emergent sense. Rather than the previous developmental mode of organization being effectively and successfully negated, the present organization is drawn back to the earlier mode. Therefore, the concept of emergence, interpreted according to the idea of STC, offers a way to include negation into the very processes of change, development, and growth—at least to the extent that somehow or other *what was* must be negated for *what's new* to emerge.

Emergence and Negation in Psychological Morphogenesis

Research into emergence in complex systems shows how operations of negation can be viewed constructively by the way they serve to introduce novelty into redundant patterns. For instance, Holland's novelty generation through random change and genetic recombination serve to negate a mere repetition of the same. Otherwise, emergent morphogenesis would not be able to proceed at all, for all that would result would be an iteration of past structure. Morphogenesis implies a creative emergence of new organization, and that creative emergence necessitates some process whereby past patterns are negated. Furthermore, this research shows that morphogenesis can be explained without the need to postulate a formative drive. Morphogenesis happens innately and naturally when complex systems are in appropriate conditions. The novel order that is seen to emerge at these appropriate conditions is then understood as a consequence of the system creatively transmuting the seeds of organization and order found in its connectivity, rules of interaction, and "containers" (see Goldstein 2004). This means that novel organization, with its novel properties, simply doesn't pop out of the sky, nor is it supernaturally caused. Instead, new organization comes about when appropriate connectivity, rules of interaction, and a surfacing, following, and then negating of previous patterns are established under appropriate therapeutic conditions.

In this way, psychological morphogenesis can be interpreted as novel reorganization of psychic material when natural processes of pattern negation are allowed to proceed. This may be what is happening not only in child's play, or artistic creation, but also in the creative play of successful treatment. Moreover, research into morphogenetic change in emergence is suggesting that we do not need to postulate either a formative *drive* or an external imposition of new structure onto the psychological system. Instead, psychological morphogenesis can be understood as an outcome of the complexity of psychological dynamics undergoing creative emergence, processes that include elements of both spontaneity and active construction. In such a perspective, then, psychological morphogenesis during successful treatment is neither impelled nor imposed, but takes place when novelty generation is allowed to take its natural course and what emerges is appropriately fostered.

Conclusion

This chapter has offered several intimations about how psychological morphogenesis may proceed by applying insights from the study of emergence in complexity theory and its precursors. Certainly, each of these insights requires a great deal of further fleshing-out and also prompts a whole series of new questions:

- What psychological structures or ingredients specifically correspond to "seeds" of order propagating in interconnective networks?
- What conditions of the therapeutic alliance are appropriate for this interconnectivity to transpire?

- What are therapeutically efficacious strategies for both following and negating already-existing attitudes, behaviors, and dynamics?
- How does internal psychological structure parallel the structure of the therapeutic connection?

Of course, a whole host of new questions will arise from the burgeoning application of complexity theory to the study of psychological dynamics. The study of emergence in complex systems offers a very clear conceptual advantage, namely, a way to think about change during therapy that appeals neither to some sort of mysterious *formative drive* nor the need to impose change on a natural process. The sciences making up the study of complex systems are providing us with innovative new findings, methods, and constructs to overcome the conceptual dead end of equilibrium-based theories. It is hoped that further research along these lines will prove beneficial for more deeply understanding psychological morphogenesis.

References

Adami, C. 1998. *An Introduction to Artificial Life*. New York: Springer-Verlag.

Ayala, F. and Dobzhansky, T. 1974. *Studies in the Philosophy of Biology: Reduction and Related Problems*. Berkeley, CA: University of California Press.

Barabasi, A-L. 2002. *Linked: The New Science of Networks*. Cambridge, MA: Perseus.

Bar-Yam, Y. 1997. *Dynamics of Complex Systems*. Reading, MA: Addison-Wesley.

Berge, P., Pomeau, V., and Vidal, C. 1984. *Order within Chaos: Towards a Deterministic Approach to Turbulence*, trans. L. Tuckerman. New York: John Wiley and Sons.

Berlekamp, E., Conway, J., and Guy, R. 1982. *Winning Ways for Your Mathematical Plays*. Vol. 2. New York: Academic Press.

Blitz, D. 1992. *Emergent Evolution: Qualitative Novelty and the Levels of Reality*. Dordrecht: Kluwer.

Bollas, C. 1991. *Forces of Destiny: Psychoanalysis and the Human Idiom*. London: Free Association Books.

Bunge, M. 1979. *Causality and Modern Science*. New York: Dover Publications.

Crutchfield, J. 1993. *The Calculi of Emergence: Computation, Dynamics, and Induction*. Santa Fe Institute Working Paper #94-03-016. Santa Fe, NM: Santa Fe Institute.

Dewan, E. M. 1976. "Consciousness as an Emergent Causal Agent in the Context of Control System Theory." In *Consciousness and the Brain: A Scientific and Philosophical Inquiry*, eds. G. Globus, G. Maxwell, and I. Savodnik, 181–98. New York: Plenum Press.

Fairbairn. W. R. D. 1994. "From Instinct to Self." In *Selected Papers of W. R. D. Fairbairn. Volume II: Applications and Early Contributions*, ed. D. E. Scharff and E. Fairbairn Birtles. Northvale, NJ: Jason Aronson.

Farley, J. 1977. *The Spontaneous Generation Controversy from Descartes to Oparin*. Baltimore: Johns Hopkins University Press.

Freud, S. 1915. "Instincts and their Vicissitudes." *Standard Edition*, Vol. 14, 67–104. London: Hogarth Press, 1957.

Freud, S. 1920. "Beyond the Pleasure Principle." *Standard Edition*, Vol. 18, 1–64. London: Hogarth Press, 1955.

Freud, S. 1925. "Negation." *Standard Edition*, Vol. 19, 235–39. London: Hogarth Press, 1961.

Goldstein, J. 1979. "The Phenomenologies of Jung and Binswanger." Paper presented at *The Conference on Jungian Studies and Creativity*. Oxford, OH: Miami University.

Goldstein, J. 1990. "Freud's Theories in the Light of Far-from-Equilibrium Research." In *System Dynamics '90*, vol. 1, ed. D. Andersen, G. Richardson, and J. Sterman, 440–54. Cambridge, MA: MIT Press.

Goldstein, J. 1995. "Unbalancing Psychoanalytic Thought: Beyond the Equilibrium Model of Freud's Thought." In *Chaos Theory in Psychology and the Life Science*, ed. R. Robertson and A. Combs, 239–52. Hillsdale, NJ: Lawrence Erlbaum Associates.

Goldstein, J. 1996. "Causality and Emergence in Chaos and Complexity Theories." In *Nonlinear Dynamics in Human Behavior*. Studies of Nonlinear Phenomena in Life Sciences, vol. 5, ed. W. Sulis and A. Combs, 161–90. Singapore: World Scientific Publishing.

Goldstein, J. 1997. "Embracing the Random in the Self-Organizing Psyche." *Nonlinear Dynamics, Psychology, and Life Sciences* 1: 181–202.

Goldstein, J. 1999. "Emergence as a Construct: History and Issues." *Emergence* 1 (1): 49–62.

Goldstein, J. 2000. "Emergence: A Construct amid a Thicket of Conceptual Snares." *Emergence* 2: 5–22.

Goldstein, J. 2001. "Emergence, Radical Novelty, and the Philosophy of Mathematics." In *Nonlinear Dynamics in the Life and Social Sciences*, NATO Advanced Studies Institute Series, ed. W. Sulis and I. Trofimova, 133–52. Amsterdam: IOS.

Goldstein, J. 2002. "The Singular Nature of Emergent Levels: Suggestions for a Theory of Emergence." *Nonlinear Dynamics, Psychology, and Life Sciences* 6: 293–309.

Goldstein, J. 2003. "The Construction of Emergence Order, or How to Resist the Temptation of Hylozoism." *Nonlinear Dynamics, Psychology, and Life Sciences* 7: 295–314.

Goldstein, J. 2004. "Flirting with Paradox: Emergence, Creative Process, and Self-Transcending Constructions." *Capital Science 2004 Proceedings*. Washington, DC: Washington Academy of Sciences.

Goldstein, J. 2005. "Emergence, Creative Process, and Self-Transcending Constructions." In *Managing Organizational Complexity: Philosophy, Theory, and Practice*, ed. K. Richardson. Greenwich, CT: Information Age Press.

Goldstein, J. forthcoming. *Flirting with Paradox in Complex Systems: Emergence and the Role of Self-Transcending Constructions*. Mansfield, MA: ISCE Publishing.

Goodwin, B. 1994. *How the Leopard Changed Its Spots: The Evolution of Complexity.* New York: Charles Scribner's Sons.

Harrington, A. 1996. *Reenchanted Science: Holism in German Culture from Wilhelm II to Hitler.* Princeton, NJ: Princeton University Press.

Holland, J. 1998. *Emergence: From Chaos to Order.* Reading, MA: Addison-Wesley.

Humphries, P. 1997. "How Properties Emerge." *Philosophy of Science* 64: 1–17

Kauffman, S. 1993. *The Origins of Order: Self-Organization and Selection in Evolution.* New York: Oxford University Press.

Kauffman, S. 1995. *At Home in the Universe: The Search for Laws of Self-organization and Complexity.* New York: Oxford University Press.

Kaye, B. 1989. *A Random Walk through Fractal Dimensions.* Weinheim, Germany: VCH.

Langton, C. G. 1986. "Studying Artificial Life with Cellular Automata." In *Evolution, Games, and Learning: Models for Adaptation in Machines and Nature.* Proceedings of the Fifth Annual Conference of the Center for Nonlinear Studies, Los Alamos, NM, May 20–24, 1985. Ed. D. Farmer, A. Lapedes, N. Packard, and B. Wendroff, 120–49. Amsterdam: North-Holland.

Langton, C. G. 1996. "Artificial Life." In *The Philosophy of Artificial Life,* ed. M. Boden, 39–94. Oxford: Oxford University Press.

Laudan, L. 1977. *Progress and Its Problems: Toward a Theory of Scientific Growth.* Berkeley, CA: University of California Press.

Lenoir, T. 1982. *The Strategy of Life: Teleology and Mechanics in Nineteenth Century German Biology.* Dordrecht: D. Reidel Publishing.

Madore, B. and Freeman, W. 1987. "Self-Organizing Structures." *American Scientist* 75: 252–59.

Medawar, P. 1969. *Induction and Intuition in Scientific Thought.* Philadelphia: American Philosophical Society Press.

Mitchell, M., Crutchfield, J., and Hraber, P. 1993. *Dynamics, Computation, and the "Edge of Chaos": A Re-examination.* Santa Institute Working Paper 93-06-040. Santa Fe, NM: Santa Fe Institute.

Piers, C. 2000. "Character as Self-Organizing Complexity." *Psychoanalysis and Contemporary Thought* 23: 3–34.

Popper, K. 1978. "Natural Selection and the Emergence of Mind." *Dialectica* 32, 3/4: 339–55.

Reitman, E. 1993. *Creating Artificial Life: Self-Organization.* New York: McGraw-Hill.

Richards, R. 1987. *Darwin and the Emergence of Evolutionary Theories of Mind and Behavior.* Chicago: University of Chicago Press.

Richards, R. 1992. *The Meaning of Evolution: The Morphological Construction and Ideological Reconstruction of Darwin's Theory.* Chicago: University of Chicago Press.

Ricoeur, P. 1970. *Freud and Philosophy: An Essay on Interpretation.* New Haven, CT: Yale University Press.

Rosenblatt, A. D. and Thickstun, J. T. 1977. "Energy, Information, and Motivation: A Revision of Psychoanalytic Theory." *Journal of the American Psychoanalytic Association* 25: 537–58.

Rousseau, G. 1992. "The Perpetual Crisis of Modernism and the Traditions of Enlightenment Vitalism." In *The Crisis in Modernism: Bergson and the Vitalist Controversy*, ed. F. Burwick and P. Douglass, 15–97. Cambridge, UK: Cambridge University Press.

Schafer, R. 1976. *A New Language for Psychoanalysis*. New Haven, CT: Yale University Press.

Salthe, S. 1993. *Development and Evolution: Complexity and Change in Biology*. Cambridge, MA: MIT Press.

Sperry, R. 1986. "Discussion: Macro- versus Micro-Determinism." *Philosophy of Science* 53: 265–70.

Sulloway, F. 1979. *Freud, Biologist of the Mind: Beyond the Psychoanalytic Legend*. New York: Basic Books.

Weiss, N. 1987. "Dynamics of Convection." In *Dynamical Chaos: Proceedings of the Royal Society of London*, ed. M. Berry, I. Percival, and N. Weiss, 71–85. Princeton, NJ: Princeton University Press.

Whyte, L. L. 1954. *Accent on Form: An Anticipation of the Science of Tomorrow*. Westport, CT: Greenwood Press.

Wilden, A. 1980. *System and Structure*. London: Tavistock.

Wolpert, D. and Macready, W. 2000. "Self-Dissimilarity: An Empirically Observable Complexity Measure." In *Unifying Themes in Complex Systems: Proceedings of the International Conference on Complex Systems*, ed. Y. Bar-Yam, 625–43. Cambridge, MA: Perseus Books.

Wuensche, A. 1998. *Classifying Cellular Automata Automatically*. Santa Fe Institute Preprint 98-02-018. Santa Fe, NM: Santa Fe Institute.

Zukier, H. 1985. "Freud and Development: The Developmental Dimensions of Psychoanalytic Theory." *Social Research* 52, 1: 9–45.

~

CHAPTER SIX

The Dynamics of Development

E. Virginia Demos, Ed.D.

My task is to explore development, particularly the development of the psyche, from a dynamic systems perspective. The most general definition of development, taken from the *Oxford Universal Dictionary* is "a gradual unfolding; a fuller working out of the details of anything." If we take the human psyche as our subject and consider its development over the life course, our focus will be on specifying what it is that unfolds, namely what psychic components and capacities does the infant begin life with, and what are the rules and constraints that regulate the details of their unfolding. Approaching psychic development from a dynamic systems perspective changes the rules in several very important ways. But first, perhaps we need to review briefly what the old rules were.

Linear Stage Models of Development

One of the most prevalent conceptual frameworks for thinking about development has been a linear stage theory model, which has appeared in various versions (Klein 1952; Lichtenberg 1983; Mahler, Pine, and Bergman 1975; Piaget 1967; Stern 1985; Werner 1957). There are several common assumptions embedded in stage thinking:

- There is a necessary *invariant order* governed by a master plan laid down in our genes, or in our nervous system, directed toward a predetermined end goal

- The order is linear and invariant, in that each step is seen as necessary for the individual to be able to progress to the next stage
- Progression is then defined by stages, which are assumed to be more or less homogeneous across a wide range of functioning and contexts, and which are roughly correlated with the child's age
- Finally, it is assumed that we start out with capacities and functions that are either global and undifferentiated, or discrete and uninte-grated, and therefore lacking in volitional coherence, organization, and effectiveness

Hence, from the perspective of stage theories, development represents a lin-ear, step-by-step, invariant progression of getting better and better or closer to some optimal, functional end point of organization, control, and effec-tiveness. Thus, for example, Piaget (1967) described the period from age two to six as the presymbolic stage of cognitive development, thereby defining this four-year period of life in terms of deficits—namely, the seeming inabil-ity of children at these ages to reason symbolically when given standard tasks. The focus was not on what the child was doing or on the context of the child's world, but rather on how the child failed to measure up to some pre-determined standard.

In stage theories, *functioning* at all ages is compared against a *yardstick* of optimal adult functioning, so by definition, all earlier stages are deficient. This pejorative lens has prevented stage theorists and researchers from ex-ploring what infants and young children were actually doing, since if the the-ory says the capacities aren't there, then no one looks. Or as Galatzer-Levy (2004) suggests, phenomena that cannot be incorporated into a theory be-come effectively invisible. Further, I would add, the emphasis on progressive movement has tended to trivialize findings that indicate that in some areas of infant functioning (for example, the differentiation of linguistic phonemes), infants move from being generalists to specialists, which entails losing potentialities that were present earlier (see Demos 1992, for a more de-tailed discussion of this point).

The value of a stage-theory approach and its general appeal have been that it has organized vast amounts of data into a few general categories. But it did so by overvaluing homogeneity and treating individual variation as noise, and by overvaluing the end product as represented by performance on defined tasks, thereby ignoring the competence of the organism and the processes by which the organism defines relevant tasks at all ages. Both of these stances obscured the importance of context and the dynamic nature of the match occurring in the transactions between the organism and the context. Finally, it has always been difficult for stage theories to account for the emergence of new behaviors and to articulate the process of change, namely what causes an organism to go from one stage to the next, without recourse to vague notions of maturation or changes in the brain.

Stage theories have been under considerable attack for the last several decades due to a variety of factors. These factors have included advances in video technology allowing slow motion exploration of infant behaviors, which revealed early organization and competence; extensive reexamination of Piaget's tasks and choice of materials; and changing concepts of dynamic processes in other sciences. Piaget's theory has received the most thorough exploration and has been challenged on all fronts. As more and more data have accumulated, the claim for homogeneous functioning across cognitive tasks has not held up (Fisher and Pipp 1984). Moreover, as tasks were redesigned to approximate children's actual experience with the world using materials and situations relevant to their lives, their logical reasoning abilities became evident, thus the claim of early reasoning deficits has not held up (see Donaldson 1979, for young children; Baillargeon 1990, for infants). And finally, as data on infant capacities have accumulated over the last three decades, the assumptions of incompetence in Piaget's (1967) and Mahler and colleagues' (1975) theory, or super competence in Klein's (1952) theory have not held up. But perhaps the most compelling and comprehensive challenge to stage thinking in development has come from the pioneering work of Esther Thelen (1984, 1986) on infant walking and other motor patterns. I will summarize briefly Thelen's work here, in order to use it as a model for a dynamic systems approach to development.

Thelen's Dynamic Systems Approach

Several preorganized motor patterns are widely documented in early infancy, such as the sucking pattern, the walking pattern, the grasping pattern, and the affective expressive patterns on the face. These have often been described as reflexes—thought to be relatively invariant patterns organized at subcortical levels of the brain—that disappeared as the nerves in the cortex gradually became myelinated, while the cortex, with its capacity for reflective conscious control, became more dominant. These behaviors were thought to then reappear later as flexible motor patterns, influenced by learning, organized at this higher cortical level, functioning as an expression of a predetermined genetic timetable.

Thelen demonstrated that the organized walking pattern manifested by newborns does not disappear and argued that its manifestation seems to be controlled by the changing ratio of muscle strength to body fat. In early infancy, body fat accumulates more rapidly than muscle strength increases. Thelen speculates that this may occur because the human infant is not born with a covering of dense hair or fur; thus, temperature regulation has a higher survival priority than locomotion in the early months. Therefore, from roughly one to seven months of age, body fat dominates over muscle strength, and the infant appears to lose the organized walking pattern. However, Thelen showed that when the infant's lower body is submerged in water at those ages and the upper torso is supported, the walking pattern is fully evident. She further demonstrated in a series of ingenious experiments with treadmills that the walking pattern continues to be present, and that the onset of bipedal locomotion occurs only when the infant's muscular strength has increased sufficiently to allow the infant to support his or her body weight on one leg (Thelen 1986; Thelen, Ulrich, and Niles 1987).

Thelen adopts a dynamic systems approach to development that she has articulated more thoroughly in a book she coauthored with Linda Smith called *A Dynamic Systems Approach to the Development of Cognition and Action* (1994). Her work and the work of many others has challenged us to revise our understanding of the processes of developmental change and focuses our attention on exploring the conditions that promote the emergence of new behaviors. Her data on the emergence of bipedal locomotion, for example, suggest that the onset of new behaviors can occur in quite a localized manner, involving changes in the coordination of or the changing ratio between two continuous variables, such as the accumulation of body fat and muscle strength. Variables like these are determined by peripheral and local conditions, and not centrally programmed and controlled by a master plan located somewhere in the cortex. Thelen's model of the controlling factors in the onset of bipedal locomotion can also account for the enormous individual variation actually observed in this phenomenon, which can occur any time between roughly eight and eighteen months.

Nevertheless, we all become bipedal walkers. This fact represents a corollary assumption in dynamic systems models—namely, a dynamic system always operates within certain constraints, or initial conditions, biases, or values (see Edelman 1987, 1992). In terms of locomotion, we are constrained by our evolutionary and biological history, which limits and shapes our skeletal and muscular capacities. For instance, we have two legs, which biases us to learn to walk in an upright position. But even here, it is assumed that dynamic factors, many of which we do not yet understand, were operating in evolutionary time to determine the nature of those constraints and biases. In dynamic systems, constraints and biases function in a general way, setting the initial background conditions within which dynamic transactions can occur. Dynamic transactions are defined as responsive to and governed by local variations both within the organism and in the environment. Therefore, the emergence of any new behavior is conceptualized as the result of a match that can occur in a dynamic exchange between the specific organizational characteristics of the organism (including the organism's intention to do something), and the specific characteristics of the task or context. It follows, then, that lived experience is as powerful a determinant in shaping developmental outcomes as are genetic factors and biological heritage.

It also follows that individual variation and idiosyncratic, creative adaptations are the rule. Thelen's work on infant reaching behaviors illustrates both the methodological and theoretical importance of this rule. Piaget argued that reaching and grasping behaviors in early infancy were dependent on the infant having obtained a certain level of cognitive organization—namely, the coordination of a visual schema with a tactile schema in order to form a schema of a reachable, graspable object. However, with the aid of slow-motion film, researchers have been able to demonstrate that what seem to be random swiping motions of very young infants are in reality quite well-organized reaching and grasping motions directed at objects (Bower 1977). The infant's hand moves through a perfectly executed grasping pattern that reaches its apex just as the hand comes closest to the object. The effort fails not because of the lack of knowledge or cognitive organization, but because the very young infant does not yet have sufficient muscular strength to support and to guide his or her own arm in an accurate path to the object. Piaget argued that knowledge required acting on the environment, thus the infant's muscular weakness became synonymous with a lack of cognitive, perceptual, and motivational organization. In a dynamic systems model, transactions with the environment are conceptualized more broadly than large muscle actions.

Thelen and colleagues (1993) studied the onset of reaching behaviors longitudinally in four young infants. Given the rule of individual variation, longitudinal case studies are the most appropriate methodology for understanding the dynamic processes governing the emergence of new behaviors. The age of first reach ranged from twelve to twenty-two weeks, and each infant used a different strategy, involving the coordination of different muscle groups. For example, the two more active infants had to learn to damp down their movements, while the two quieter infants had to increase the speed and energy of their movements. Reaching emerges when the infant can intentionally adjust the force and direction of the arm. Thelen and her coworkers conclude, "These results suggest that the infant central nervous system does not contain programs that detail hand trajectory, joint coordination, and muscle activation patterns. Rather, these patterns are the consequences of the natural dynamics of the system and the active exploration of the match between these dynamics and the task" (1058). The infant is an active participant in seeking a creative solution to the task of regulating its arm and grasping an object.

I have focused on the emergence of these familiar motor patterns to illustrate some of the principles of a dynamic system's approach to development because they are easier to comprehend than the more abstract models of physics and math, and because they deal with the living human organism, which raises all the issues of the role of motivation, consciousness, and choice, as well as the organization of the human mind and nervous system. But they share the principles of dynamic systems operating in physics and mathematics, namely that a few simple rules operating in the context of defined initial conditions can intrinsically generate complex dynamics and results. Small changes can lead to abrupt changes and shifts in organization, which are emergent and not predictable (see chapter 7). In a dynamic systems model, there is no need to hypothesize the existence of a predetermined goal or outcome.

A Bio-Psycho-Social Approach

If we return now to the development of the human psyche and approach it from a dynamic systems perspective, we must locate the infant within a bio-psycho-social context. I will therefore be trying to integrate current knowledge of the neurosciences, infant capacities, affect, dynamic systems, and relational clinical practice. I will also be drawing on my own formulations based on my participation in longitudinal case studies of infants and caregivers observed in their homes and in a variety of settings.

My view differs from other available conceptualizations of these processes in at least three important respects. First, I emphasize the infant's early competence that is continually elaborated over time in dynamic, creative, and highly idiosyncratic ways. Second, I stress the central role of affect in organizing early experience. Third, I argue against predetermined agendas or stage-like sequences in development. In my view, the infant psyche is not buffeted by imperious instinctual energies of the id, nor guided by a predetermined attachment agenda, nor essentially created or activated by the ministrations of a caregiver. Rather, the infant psyche is guided by what I consider the two most basic human preferences or biases (values in Edelman's theory, 1987) that are the product of our evolutionary history and function by differentially weighting experience in such a way that they are felt to be of the highest priority. These two most basic human biases are: 1) psychic coherence and organization is better than noncoherence, a bias in which the vicissitudes of affects play a central role, and 2) being an active agent in effecting the course of events is better than having no effect on events. In psychoanalytic writings, Ghent (2002) and Greenberg (1991) have also speculated that there may be early and basic tendencies or preferences for coherence and agency, which then dynamically generate "motivational systems" such as attachment. In speaking of coherence, Ghent states: "I think a value or bias of this nature must underlie the tendency of neural networks to categorize and re-categorize successive experiences along the lines suggested by Edelman" (779).

The infant arrives in the world possessing complex psychological functions guided by these two basic psychic biases or values. These biases operate at a general abstract level with a set of other, broader, uniquely human biases and self-organizing capacities. Taken all together, they constitute the initial conditions for adaptation and survival, providing the infant with the ability to engage in dynamic transactions with the animate and inanimate world. The infant's psyche will create its own unique organizations and specificity of patterns that will be contingent on experience. Thus, psychic development will be shaped by the dynamics of these intrinsic self-organizing characteristics, by opportunities for matches between intrinsic dynamics and external conditions and situations, and by the specific dynamics of these transactions with caregivers and with the world. There are no predetermined plans or progressions of psychic development, nor are the outcomes proportionally related to the array of inputs.

Biological Bases of Development

Let me begin with my conception of the biological givens of the human infant, which includes constraints as well as initial capabilities, particularly for psychic experience and organization. First, we need to understand the nature of the human brain. The neurosciences have provided us with a framework for understanding the origin of the mind—category formation, consciousness, memory, and affects. To look to the brain sciences for our baseline is neither to equate mental life with nor to reduce it to biology, but rather to insist that mental life is partially the result of and constrained by the principles governing the anatomy and functional characteristics of neurons.

The adult human brain contains about thirty billion neurons, which are densely overlapping, branching, and interconnected, producing a hyper-astronomical number of synapses: ten followed by at least a million zeros

(Edelman 1998). These synapses are themselves regulated by chemical and electrical processes that operate in variable and complex ways, further magnifying the complexity of connective possibilities and dynamics. Edelman claims "that the human brain is special both as an object and as a system—its connectivity, dynamics, mode of functioning, and relation to the body and the world is like nothing else science has yet encountered" (37). We therefore have to be prepared to accept new concepts and explanatory models to account for the dynamic psychic phenomena observed by developmentalists and clinicians alike.

At birth, the distribution of neurons is complete. There are very few places in the brain where new neurons develop, therefore *development in the brain is the result of lived experience*, which leads to the proliferation of dendrites, axons, and increasingly complex neural networks. Unused neurons die off. The functional unit of mental activity is not what occurs in a single neuron, but rather is the integration of a network of interconnecting neurons all activated at the same moment as a response to changes in local conditions both within and outside the organism, which result in a thought, a memory, a perception, a feeling state, and so on. All information is represented in the brain by temporal configurations of interconnected neurons. The brain operates like a complex dynamic system (see chapter 2).

The nineteenth-century model of physical energy utilized by Freud in the *Project for a Scientific Psychology* (1895/1966) led him to conceptualize the nervous system as designed to keep quantities of excitation from building up, or failing that, to rid itself of excitations through mechanisms such as neuronal contact barriers, screens, and dampeners, and direct neuronal connections that facilitated discharge through motor pathways. By contrast, current neuroscience formulations describe the nervous system as intrinsically active and focus their efforts on understanding the complex organization and dynamics of this system. There is continual activity at all levels of the system, from the microanatomical level of the nerve cell and the synapse, to the synchronized networks level of neuronal action, to the conscious experience of a perception, thought, or feeling. The nervous system is connected through multiple synapses via electrical signals and the release of neural transmitters (chemical signals), all of which contain "information," not psychical energy. These signals are designed to create within milliseconds a complex configuration or pattern of neuronal activity that "represents" a simulation of a sensory or motor event. The brain has evolved to function as a reality simulator, not as a tension reliever as in Freud's model. It does not apprehend the world directly and thus requires ongoing sensory input in order to do its job of creating a simulation of the world. Sensory input modifies ongoing neuronal activity, resulting in momentary temporal patterns of neuronal activity that can be "recognized" or "matched" when they recur, and the more they recur, the stronger the neural connections become. These recurring processes allow the organism to learn from experience and to adapt to and predict change, so as to live in and act on the world as effectively as possible.

As a result of our evolutionary history, the human brain is structured and organized hierarchically beginning from the bottom and moving up from the brainstem, midbrain, limbic, and subcortex to the neocortex and, in some respects, it develops neural networks in this same order. Thus at birth, although the distribution of neurons throughout the brain is complete, the density of dendrites and synapses is more prevalent in the first four regions of the brain than in the neocortex. But these are relative differences, for the right hemisphere of the neocortex quickly begins to develop dense connections in the first year of life, while the left hemisphere of the neocortex is slower to do so. Since the brain depends on lived experience to develop its neural networks, one of the constraints operating is the need to achieve a balance between circuit permanence and circuit plasticity. To put it in psychological terms, this constraint operates as a need to find a balance between relying on past experience and remaining open to new possibilities. One consequence of this constraint seems to be that the subcortical, limbic, emotional circuits that develop in infancy tend to have less plasticity, while the neocortex continues to develop new dendrites and synapses throughout life. Therefore, early emotional learning can have long-lasting effects on psychological functioning, but these effects can be modulated and regulated by continued developments in the neocortex.

Another important consequence of the hierarchical organization of the brain is the difference between implicit and explicit processing of experience, which effects the way learning is represented in memory. Damasio (1994), based on his work with brain damaged patients, has argued that learning derived from these two different modes of processing is stored in separate parts of the brain. All early learning occurring in the neonate and infant is processed through the limbic, subcortical, and right hemisphere regions of the brain, and is called "implicit" or "procedural" knowing. It involves how to do things, and includes sensory-motor and emotional-relational patterns of behaving and interacting that occur implicitly through sensing, feeling, and doing. Thus, early, nonverbal, emotionally patterned communications between infant and caregivers are stored in implicit, procedural memory. Implicit, procedural learning continues throughout life, but by the middle of the second year of life, declarative learning emerges.

The emergence of this second mode of processing coincides with increased neural activity in the left hemisphere, the hippocampus, and the corpus callosum. It involves integrating sensory and emotional information with spatial and temporal sequential information and with semantic associations or images, producing narrative or linguistic re-representations. These two memory systems can remain separate, or through conscious efforts to label and articulate experience, implicit knowledge can become explicit. There is no predetermined necessity or plan for either outcome. Thus, there is enormous individual variation in how integrated these two memory systems are and in what particular content areas. Psychotherapy, as a treatment modality, is designed to enhance this integration by putting words to procedural, implicit knowledge.

Infant Capacities

Given these characteristics of the neonate's brain and nervous system, what basic capacities do neonates possess? Here the data from the neurosciences and from the last three decades of research in developmental psychology on infants converge nicely. I can only list the results here, without supporting evidence, and must refer the interested reader to an earlier, more detailed presentation of these data (Demos 1992).

There is a growing consensus that the infant has the capacity to experience the full range of basic emotions: enjoyment, interest, distress, anger, fear, startle, disgust, and shame; that the infant can recognize recurrent patterns of stimuli, can detect invariance in stimuli, and can detect contingencies between self-generated actions and effects on the environment; that the infant can distinguish between internal and external events; and that the infant possesses perceptual biases inherent in possessing a human nervous system, brain, and body. Thus, for example, the infant can hear sounds only within certain frequencies, can see colors only in certain wavelengths, can perceive motion only at certain rates, and visually prefers light–dark contrasts and contours. Since many of these perceptual biases comprise stimulus characteristics that are routinely produced by other humans, there is no need to postulate the existence of a preformed idea or attachment agenda. In a dynamic systems model, given the match between the dynamics of the infant's emotional, organizational, and perceptual capacities and biases and the dynamics of existing adult faces and voices (and given a usual, expectable environment) it is inevitable that the infant will be drawn to other humans, and as a result of dynamic transactions will quickly construct a representation of the faces and voices seen and heard most frequently.

Finally, infants are capable of coordinating information emanating from affective, perceptual, cognitive, memory, and motor functions in order to try to bring about desired events and to limit or escape from undesired events. In a remarkable experiment reported by DeCasper and Carstens (1981), newborn infants quickly learned to lengthen the pauses between their bursts of sucking in order to turn on a recording of a female voice singing. These same infants became upset twenty-four hours later when, having been placed in the noncontingent phase of the experiment, they discovered that the singing voice was no longer contingent on the length of their pauses, and that they no longer had control over this stimulus. This experiment reveals an amazing amount of mental organization within the one-day-old infant, for in order to succeed in this task the newborn had to coordinate perception (detecting the contingency); emotion (interest in the stimulus); cognition (generating a plan to repeat this interesting event); motor patterns (voluntarily lengthening the pause between sucking bursts); and memory (remembering the plan and comparing the outcome to the goal).

This experiment also highlights another important characteristic of the newborn, namely the newborn's capacity and preference for being an active agent in influencing events. The neonates' ability to imitate facial expressions (Field et al. 1982) and to replace reflex sucking with voluntary sucking (Brunner 1968) are other examples of the infants' preference and intention to do voluntarily what they have experienced involuntarily. Such an intention is not innate. It involves generating the idea that this would be something to do. It is as if the infant thinks "this is nice, but I'd rather do it myself." Where does such an idea come from? Tomkins (1978), in discussing these early phenomena, gave the following answer, which argues for a dynamic systems perspective:

> It represents an extraordinary creative invention conjointly powered by primitive perceptual and cognitive capacities amplified by excitement in the possibility of improving a good actual scene by doing something oneself. These are real phenomena and they appear to be highly probable emergents from the *interaction* of several basic human capacities. This is why I have argued that we have evolved to be born as a human being who will, with a very high probability, very early attempt and succeed in becoming a person. (215)

I will return later to the issue of agency and its importance in psychic development.

In summary, the data we now have indicate that infants arrive in the world with preadapted capacities for feeling, thinking, perceiving, remembering, acting, and coordinating these capacities in consciousness to produce

voluntary acts, and to learn from recent past experience. And while these capacities may be biased or organized in general ways to facilitate transactions
with other humans and with the world, they do not contain preformed contents or goals. This view of a competent infant represents a departure from
earlier formulations of an incompetent infant, both in developmental psychology and in psychoanalysis. As Bower (1974) reminded us, such formulations ignored a basic evolutionary rule, namely that the more capable a
species is in adulthood, the more capable is the newborn of the species. The
infant's competence also represents a departure from our understanding of
the role of the caregiver, which I will discuss later. Finally, implicit in these
data, particularly those involving volition, are assumptions about the infants'
capacity for subjective experience, or consciousness and motivation. To explore this issue, we must turn again to the neurosciences.

Consciousness and Affect

The understanding of consciousness and nonconsciousness emerging in neuroscience is more developed and complicated than in either developmental
psychology or psychoanalysis. There are at least three different phenomena
specified in neuroscience—namely, conscious, nonconscious, and a defensive, dynamic unconscious. There is also a distinction between primary consciousness, involving an awareness or experiential registration of the current,
continual stream of perceptual, emotional, cognitive, and motor events, and
self-reflective consciousness, involving an ability to reflect on mental
processes in a symbolic, re-representational mode, creating a virtual reality
that can be altered. The capacity for primary consciousness is present at
birth, and perhaps earlier (DeCasper and Carstens 1990). In awake states,
the neonate is experiencing events in primary consciousness, including emotional states, all of which are processed in implicit, procedural learning and
memory. The capacity for self-reflective consciousness emerges sometime in
the middle of the second year, and is correlated with explicit, declarative
learning and memory, ushered in by the emergence of an increasing density
of neural connections in the neocortex (particularly in the left hemisphere),
the hippocampus, and the corpus callosum. The capacity for self-reflection
represents the emergence of a new capacity, generated by lived experience
and the intrinsic dynamics of the human brain.

These varieties of consciousness may be unique in humans, but the capacity for primary consciousness is probably present in many other species as
well. Tomkins (1962) argues that consciousness evolved as a necessary evolutionary adaptation when organisms began to move about in space, and thus

needed to be capable of learning and making voluntary choices. Such capabilities require an internal context in which the organism can become aware of new surroundings, actively compare these to previous situations, construct meanings, devise strategies, and monitor responses, just like the neonates in the DeCasper and Carstens experiment described above. The state of consciousness is such a context.

I would suggest further that all new learning has to occur in a conscious state, registered in subjective experience. There is no other entry to the mind. Sensations or events arising from internal or external sources must be subjectively registered in consciousness if they are to become meaningful to the organism. Only there can they be processed, be given meaning, be compared to past, present, or future meanings, and become elements in plans and goals. Such goals may include defensive efforts designed to exclude them from consciousness, becoming unconscious for dynamic reasons. But this is not the unconscious of Freud, filled with predetermined libidinal and aggressive instinctual energies and aims. This unconscious is comprised of experiences that were once conscious but could not be subjectively tolerated and thus cannot now be allowed to recur. They are dynamic potentialities that could be reassembled and reactivated in certain situations or under certain conditions. Defensive activity is necessary and designed to prevent such a reassembly and reactivation in order to protect the coherence of the mind and the capacity to be an active agent.

Consciousness seems to function as a control center for the organism, operating as a dynamic system seeking organizational coherence, therefore limiting its channel capacity. It would quickly become swamped if it had to know everything that was going on in the organism. Many neurological, chemical, and homeostatic processes, as well as many perceptual, cognitive, and motor processes, have evolved to function outside of consciousness, even though they clearly support and affect this realm and are in turn affected by it. But all those phenomena that are in the realm of conscious mental functioning must compete for entrance into the limited channel capacity of consciousness. What are the rules governing this selection process? Although Freud taught us long ago that the motivated wish not to know about painful affects is a major dynamic criterion for excluding entry into consciousness, he was unable to fully appreciate the more comprehensive role of affects in psychic functioning. Not all affects are unbearable, including many negative states.

Tomkins (1962), building on Darwin and Freud and going beyond them, has suggested that the competition for entrance to consciousness is governed by the degree of urgency attached to any particular phenomenon, and that affect has evolved to provide urgency, functioning as an analogue amplifier. Each affect is comprised of a correlated set of bodily responses, that include facial muscles, vocal, respiratory, blood-flow changes, heightened skin receptor sensitivity, and other autonomic responses, which create an analogue of the rate or intensity of stimulation impinging on the organism, thereby combining urgency, abstractness, and generality (e.g., a sense of "too much" or "too fast" or "just right"). This analogue amplification then is experienced as a qualitative affect state able to both capture consciousness, thereby causing the organism to care about what is happening and, with its qualitative valence, shape and facilitate a response. Thus, more urgent affective events will compete with less urgent affective events for entry into consciousness. For example, one affect can override another affect, as when the excitement of an athletic activity can temporarily override the pain and related distress of an injury sustained during the activity. The proposition that affect operates as an amplifying mechanism that "makes bad things worse and good things better" (Tomkins 1978, 203) so that we can become aware of what is happening is in direct opposition to Freud's idea that affect operates as a discharge of tension. Tomkins' formulation allows for many more gradations of negative affective experience and a broader view of their adaptive functions.

Tomkins' theory of affect has received some support from neuroscience, infant research, and research on facial expressions. Neuroscience conceptualizes affect as a complex psychobiological state, composed of correlated autonomic, endocrine, and muscle responses that may or may not involve consciousness and cortical modulation. It also validates the necessary and adaptive function of affect as coordinating the mind and body by documenting the ways in which affect organizes and focuses perception, thought, memory, physiology, and behavior in order to support optimal coping with whatever situations have triggered the affect. Darwin (1872) argued more than a century ago that emotions evolved as preparations for action, priming the organism to respond adaptively to a wide variety of situations, thereby enhancing their capacity to survive. Tomkins (1962) built on this insight, arguing that affects are the primary motivational system. Moreover, he went well beyond it by specifying the correlated sets of responses involved and their functioning as analogue amplifiers. These correlated sets of responses, triggered by different rates and intensities of incoming stimuli, are transformed into distinctive qualitative affective states.

Neuroscience tells us that the amygdala is the hub of incoming and outgoing emotional signals. It receives incoming sensory stimuli and transforms them, via mechanisms that are still unclear, into preprogrammed emotional responses involving the endocrine system, the autonomic nervous system, and the skeletal muscles. LeDoux (1996) has demonstrated the existence of two input pathways to the amygdala. There is a shorter pathway by which sensory stimuli from the thalamus go directly to the amygdala, bypassing the cortex, and set in motion an emotional response. Also, there is a longer pathway that goes from the thalamus to the cortex to the hippocampus and then to the amygdala. The orbitofrontal cortex relates stimuli to past experience with objects, people, and events, while the hippocampus processes episodic features of time and place and helps to modulate emotional arousal by binding cortisol receptors. This latter function of the hippocampus makes it vulnerable to very high rates of cortisol, as occurs in traumatic events, which can damage hippocampal cells, thereby leaving the amygdala unmodulated. All of these brain–body changes are fed back to the brain and compete for consciousness. There are three possibilities. If these brain–body changes become conscious, they will result in a subjective experience of emotion. If they are not urgent enough to win out in the competition for consciousness, they will remain nonconscious. If these brain–body changes are too intense or threatening, they may evoke defenses which will block entry to consciousness.

State Organization and Ideo-Affect Complexes

Data from infant researchers such as Sander (1969) and Wolff (1973) have argued for the centrality of state and state organization as a concept that could connect the biological level and the psychological level. They paid attention to the cyclical states along the sleep–wake continuum and conceptualized state as any well-defined organizational coherence within the organism that can be recognized when it recurs and that determines how the infant will respond. Sander (1982) argued further that the infant's experiences of her own recurrent states represent the focal points around which the infant's inner awareness or consciousness consolidates, and that the ego begins as "a state ego, rather than a body ego" (Sander 1985, 20). Sander went on to say that "the organization of state governs the quality of inner experience" (1985, 26), and described these waking states as alert inactivity, waking activity, alert activity, and crying. I have argued elsewhere (Demos 1986, 1988, 1989b), based on Tomkins' theory of affect (1962, 1963) and on the available evidence on infant affect expressions and behaviors, that these organized waking states of the neonate are distinctive affect states. Thus, for example, the alert states are states of interest, and the crying state is the affect distress or the affect anger, depending on the intensity and pattern of crying.

The newborn infant then, has the capacity to experience affect, but does not yet have past experience to draw on. It follows that a hungry, crying neonate neither knows why she is crying, nor that there is anything that can be done about it. The cry in this initial experience represents a preprogrammed affective response to a continuous level of nonoptimal stimulation (namely hunger), which in Tomkins' formulation triggers the rhythmical cry of distress, consisting of a correlated set of facial-muscle, blood-flow, visceral, respiratory, and skeletal responses, which act to amplify this level of nonoptimal stimulation to produce an inherently negative experience for the infant. This initial experience of distress is as close to pure affect as is possible, but this purity is short lived, for the evolutionary function of such an amplifying mechanism is to make the organism care about what is happening and to organize a response.

If we return to the hungry, crying neonate, this theory would argue that because she is crying, she now cares about what is happening, namely she cares about trying to bring about a cessation of this distressing state. She is therefore motivated to pay attention to what happens next, to remember what these distressing sensations feel like, and to begin to connect them to antecedents (hunger) and consequences (comfort and food). For example, if a caregiver has consistently responded in a timely and helpful way to the infant's crying, within 3 or 4 weeks the infant will stop crying at the sight or the sound of the caregiver's approach. This phenomenon occurs because the infant has already connected the experience of distress with the approach and comfort of the caregiver and thus is able to anticipate that the caregiver's approach means that comfort will soon follow.

This experience represents the construction of what Tomkins (1978) calls an ideo-affect complex, which allows the infant to stop crying and wait. Ideo-affect is an abbreviation for ideo-perceptual-memorial-action-affect complexes, which refers to the involvement of all of the critical subsystems that together constitute a human being. *The construction of ideo-affect complexes is the primary dynamic, creative process by which the infant gradually organizes his/her psychic life.* One of the biases operating here, implicit in much of our thinking about motivation, is that positive affect states feel better than negative affect states, thus the infant is motivated to enhance and prolong positive affect states (interest and enjoyment), and to limit, modulate, escape from, or avoid negative affect states (distress, shame, anger, fear, and disgust). But the infant has limited capacities to bring about such desired outcomes and needs support from a caregiver. I will discuss the role of the caregiver in a later section of this chapter.

There are many factors involved in determining both the ease or difficulty the infant will have in establishing connections between his/her affect state and its antecedents and consequences, as well as the specific content and frequency of these connections. I will focus on two of these factors in more detail below, namely the infant's capacity to modulate negative affect and the infant's capacity to maintain a sense of active agency. But first, I would like to briefly mention other factors involved. Some factors reside in the infant, and involve such characteristics as the infant's irritability, clarity of waking states, intensity of reactions, and so on.

Sander (1975) has argued that the organism has to achieve a basic level of organizational regularity and stability that can provide the background against which changes in coherent unities (states) can be perceived and recognized, both by the infant and by the caregiver. In normal, full-term neonates with a responsive caregiver, this can be achieved in the first week of life. But for premature infants and drug-addicted infants, the process of achieving a basic organizational regularity of coherent states will take longer, and will require more help from an empathic caregiver. Other factors involve the caregiver's role, because the caregiver is not only engaged in responding to the infant's affect states, but is also engaged in expressing affect to the infant and in evoking affects in the infant.

The capacity of the infant to process the connections between affects evoked from all of these sources and their consequences will also be effected by the following variables: the ratio of positive to negative affects; the sequencing of positive and negative affects; the clarity of these states; their predictability; their frequency; and their goodness of fit between the infant's processing rate and the rate of change from one affect to another. The infant will have to cope with all of these variables in trying to sort out what goes with what and what leads to what. For example, an affectively labile parent may make it difficult for an infant and young child to sort out the affective valence of transactional events, as well as the antecedents and consequences of the affect; whereas a parent who frequently evokes intense negative affects will focus the infant's efforts on trying to avoid or to limit the painful quality of these experiences, often, thereby, constricting the potential scope of the positive affects. The interplay of all of these factors underscores both the complexity of the infant's psychological processes involved in establishing these connections and the highly idiosyncratic nature of the ideo-affect organizations that occur as a result. Such a multiplicity of possibilities does not fit easily into three or four general patterns of relating. This brings us directly to the role of the caregiver.

The Social Context: A Reconceptualization

So far, we have explored the biological and psychological context of the infant's psychic development, which has led to a reevaluation of and recognition of the infant's psychological capacities and competence. This represents a new conceptualization of a one-person psychology, which, as Ghent (2002) suggests has "nothing to do with its homonym, but everything to do with the infant's intrinsic capacity to integrate outer experiences with inner constraints and create solutions sui generis" (781).

As we now turn to the social context of the infant's psychological development, namely the role of the caregiver(s), it too will necessarily involve a reconceptualization. Older formulations that saw the mother as creating de novo organization and basic capacities within the infant are no longer viable. These recent data on the infant's capacities have led me to argue elsewhere (Demos 1993) that contrary to Winnicott's (1965) statement that "there is no such thing as a baby," there is indeed a baby with a functioning set of unique social, experiential, and organizational capacities, and there is a mother with her unique history and capacities. The infant clearly needs a mother and she has considerable influence, but her role must now be seen as enhancing, supporting, interfering with, discouraging, or ignoring her infant's ongoing processes and efforts. It is here that the dynamic systems idea of the importance of the particularities of the match between what the infant brings to the situation and what the mother brings comes into play. Thus, our focus is on the goodness of fit between the infant's needs, agenda, state, and so on and the caregiver's needs, agenda, state, and so on at any given moment, and in specifying as precisely as possible the elements and dynamics of these transactions, as well as their longitudinal course.

The context for these transactions is the relationship between the infant and the caregiver in which the unique characteristics of each participant are contributing something essential to the complicated, dynamic processes of getting to know each other and forming a relationship. For each must learn about the other's preferences, tolerances for affective intensity, and pacing of stimuli, limitations, and distinctive modes of behaving. In other words, they have to learn to live together, to understand each other's meanings, to find ways to manage conflict, and to find a balance between helping, hurting, ignoring, enjoying, manipulating, and dreading each other.

Given the capacities of both participants, these transactions also involve the dual processes of intrapsychic and interpsychic activity. For as the infant and mother are involved in learning about each other, each is simultaneously engaged in managing and organizing his or her own inner experiences and constructing idiosyncratic meanings. When things go well, these complex processes can result in an optimal outcome of mutual regulation in which the integrity and value of each partner is respected. But this is not a relationship between equals in terms of physical strength, knowledge, self-reflective capacities, experience, instrumental effectiveness, and emotional regulation. All of these advantages are possessed by the caregiver(s), and yet to be attained by the infant and growing child. Thus, exploitation and a loss of mutuality are possible.

Erikson (1950) has been most eloquent in helping us to appreciate "the basic fact that human childhood provides a most fundamental basis for human exploitation" (418), and to see the larger social implications. He noted that "the polarity Big–Small is the first in the inventory of existential oppositions such as Male and Female, Ruler and Ruled, Owner and Owned, Light Skin and Dark, over all of which emancipatory struggles are now raging both politically and psychologically" (418). Erikson sees the polarity of parent and child (and male and female) as "the divided function of partners, who are equal not because they are essentially alike, but because they are both essential to a common function" (418). He goes on to say that "exploitation exists where a divided function is misused by one of the partners involved, in such a way that for the sake of his pseudo aggrandizement he deprives the other partner of whatever sense of identity he had achieved, of whatever integrity he had approached" (418).

Titrating Stimulation and Modulating Affect
Within this general context of the relationship, we can begin to explore more specifically various caregiver functions from a dynamic systems perspective. Perhaps one of the most basic functions involves titrating stimulus input for the infant. For while neonates possess perceptual, cognitive, affective, memory, and motor capacities to begin to construct representations of the world they live in, they have only modest capacities to regulate exposure to stimuli. Infants can shut their eyes or turn their heads away from intense visual stimuli; they can spit out or regurgitate bad-tasting food, but they cannot turn off their ears (nor can we) except by falling asleep; they cannot rid themselves of excessive tactile stimuli; nor can they use cognitive strategies to deal with information overload. They therefore are dependent on caregivers to maintain their stimulus worlds within an optimal range for processing information, a function which involves regulating variables such as pacing, intensity, clarity, and the optimal mix of redundancy and novelty.

A prime example of the effort of caregivers to regulate their own input to match their infant's capacity to process stimuli is contained in "motherese." This is a universal language mothers speak to infants, which is slow, redundant, exaggerates important features, and is affectively modulated. It thereby optimizes the possibility for the young infant to construct representations of these exchanges and to learn about the world their mother personifies. Thus, it represents a "goodness of fit" or a match between what the infant brings and what the environment can provide. It seems to have been creatively invented by mothers all over the world, emerging from their desire to communicate with their young infants.

The involvement of the caregiver in helping the infant regulate positive affects is essential because the infant's capacity to sustain and elaborate interests and enjoyments does not just happen in the absence of negative affects; it must be nurtured and fostered by the caregiver. There is not space to detail the processes involved, but the data from the longitudinal studies mentioned earlier suggest the more the infant and young child received support in expanding, elaborating, sustaining, and communicating states of interest and enjoyment and their related ideo-affect organizations involving phantasies, plans, and the like, the more they were able to experience themselves as the source of interesting ideas and events, to sustain their interests when alone, to invest in their interests readily and easily, and to find a wide range of objects and activities interesting and enjoyable. By contrast, the more the infant and small child failed to receive support in expanding, elaborating, sustaining, and communicating positive affects and their related ideo-affective organizations, the more they constricted their interests, experienced boredom, and were unable to sustain interests when alone or derive enjoyment or excitement from their activities. In this realm of positive affects, it seems the rich get richer and the poor get poorer, as early patterns spontaneously build on themselves. This phenomenon may partially explain the long-lasting benefits of Headstart.

This caregiver function of modulating stimuli and achieving optimal levels is perhaps most important in the realm of helping the infant regulate negative affect states. Earlier, I had stated that consciousness operates as a dynamic system seeking organizational coherence, and that in order to maintain that coherence it must defend itself against overwhelming, unbearable affects. I distinguished between disregulated affect and more modulated, regulated negative affects that the organism needed in order to mobilize adaptive responses to the world.

Infants have a very limited repertoire of responses for managing experiences of distress and anger, and these work best at relatively low levels of intensity. A fussy infant can suck on fingers, hands, or fists, thereby using a rhythmical pattern of stimulation to override the arhythmical pattern of low-level distress, or they can focus on an interesting object, thereby using one affect (interest) to override another (mild distress). But once the intensity of the negative affect increases, the young infant does not possess the instrumental capacities, the experience, or the knowledge to modulate it. If nobody intervenes to help the infant manage such states and the infant is left to cry, negative affects can escalate in a positive feedback loop, cycling up into higher and higher densities, resulting in a potentially traumatic experience for the infant, setting in motion massive defensive efforts. The caregiver is crucial in helping the infant achieve optimal densities of negative affect that are neither too low, thereby preventing the infant from exercising and developing regulatory capacities, nor too high, thereby overwhelming the infant and evoking defensive responses. It is difficult to specify this optimal level, since it will vary from infant to infant, from moment to moment, and from context to context. Nevertheless, it is recognizable when it occurs because it allows the infant to remain organized and focused on trying to do something about the situation.

There are two aspects to this caregiver function. One involves protecting the infant from traumatic experiences of negative affect that can threaten the coherence and the experience of continuity of the infant's psyche. The second involves enhancing the infant's capacity to endure, tolerate, and persist in the face of moderate intensities of negative affect in order to develop instrumental coping skills. Taken together, these two aspects of the caregiver's modulating function lead to a sense of trust within the infant—a trust in the reliability and manageability of one's own inner experience. For the infant will have learned that the onset of distress or anger does not evoke the need for a retreat or the dread of an escalation, but rather that such experiences can be tolerated, that their causes can be resolved, and that they have a beginning, middle, and an end. The infant will also learn that others are reliable and that the world is trustworthy. Over time, if this optimal regulation of negative affects continues, it will allow the young child to develop a variety of adaptive strategies for managing distressing, maddening, or frightening situations, and will enhance his/her capacities to tolerate and explore the distress, anger, and fear in oneself and in others without excessive worry about being surprised, overwhelmed, or disorganized by these states.

The ability of an infant–mother pair to achieve this goal of optimal regulation of negative affect is influenced by the characteristics of both participants in relation to affect. Since affects operate as an amplifier, expressions of affect will evoke more of the same affect, both within the person expressing the affect and in the observer, or transactional partner. Infants will vary in terms of vigor, irritability, soothability, organizational coherence, and adaptability. But all infant affect is unsocialized, resulting in a more full-voiced, full-faced, and full-bodied display of affect than occurs in adult affect expressions, thereby increasing the likelihood that caregivers will experience a variant of the distress or anger of their infants (see Boukydis 1979; Frodi and Lamb 1980; and Wiesenfeld, Malatesta, and DeLoach 1981, for studies of the variables affecting adult responses to infant cries).

This phenomenon of affective resonance is an important aspect of empathy, which involves not only the current experience of distress or anger in the context of the infant's affective display, but also an activation of the caregiver's own unique history of learning with respect to these evoked affects. The caregiver, then, has to manage this complex state, which will both inform and complicate the task of understanding the infant's experience and of providing an intervention that is attuned to the infant's needs. In other words, the caregiver, in order to be helpful, must hone his/her complex experience into a resonant specificity that will meet the specificity of the infant's experience. Without this subjective meeting (if the caregiver overreacts or underreacts), he/she will be unable to foster the development of tolerance of negative affect within the infant. Furthermore, if caregivers are defended against the pain of their own experiences of distress or anger or fear, they are much more likely to evoke these intense negative affects in the infant or young child, or to abandon the infant or young child in such states. Such parents will thus fail to protect the infant and young child from traumatic experiences of negative affects (the use of fear as a disciplinary technique, or the transmission of unconscious anxiety by one generation to the next as the result of unmetabolized past trauma).

Fostering Agency
I would like to turn now to the caregiver's role in helping develop the infant's capacity to maintain a sense of active agency in relation to the world, to others, and to his or her own internal processes. By a sense of active agency, I am referring to the experience of initiating an action and succeeding in causing something to happen. The DeCasper and Carstens (1981) experiment described earlier, in which newborns learned to alter their sucking pattern in order to hear a female voice singing, demonstrated that the issue of agency is pertinent from the beginning of life and that its future viability is being determined from birth on. Sander (1982) has suggested that when a family can facilitate the infant's own efforts at goal realization and provide opportunities for the infant to initiate goal-organized behaviors, it will provide "the

conditions which establish not only the capacity for self-awareness, but conditions which insure the use of such inner awareness by the infant as a frame of reference in organizing his own adaptive behavior" (17). He goes on to say that "the valence of this inner experience under these conditions of self-initiated goal realization will be felt as the infant's own" (17).

The issue at stake here seems to represent a basic human bias—namely, optimizing the experience that the locus of control of events is within oneself. Shapiro (2000) has presented compelling evidence to support his argument that "abridgments of volition" are at the heart of all mental illnesses. When an infant's efforts at goal realization are not fostered, the infant learns to turn away from or ignore internal cues as a frame of reference for action and becomes skilled at reading the cues of others. Winnicott (1971) has called this the beginnings of a false-self organization. I am arguing here that it is not due to the infant's failure to differentiate self from other, but is the result of a failure of parental fostering of the infant's efforts at goal realization. Thus, the infant learns that one's own wishes, goals, and initiatives are not valued. This issue of the infant's agency and initiatives must be negotiated within the family between infants and caregivers, for it will involve inevitable clashes of agendas between the infant's goals and the goals of other family members. Once again, individual variation is the rule, thus there are many possible scenarios (see Demos 1986, 1988, 1989a, 1989b) that involve both the timing and the content of the caregivers responses as important variables in determining the fate of the infant's sense of agency. I will illustrate brief examples of these variables.

Let us begin with the importance of the timing of caregiver responses. Imagine an infant who is experiencing low-level distress, manifested by whimpering and motor restlessness and who gradually works up into a rhythmical cry and more vigorous motor restlessness. Somewhere in this sequence of events, the infant will become aware of a distressed state (A), of experiencing an intention to end or decrease it (I), and of mobilizing behaviors to achieve that goal (M). I refer to this entire process as AIM. It represents a dynamic coming together within the infant of an optimal level of affective stimulation, with whatever past experience has accrued from connecting the antecedents and consequences of previous similar states, which results in the emergence of a goal and the beginnings of an initiative to achieve that goal. If the caregiver intervenes at that moment and is able to match the specificity of the infant's goal (in this example, offering comfort and/or an appropriate remedy), the infant will experience the caregiver's response as a recognition and a validation of his/her own initiative, as well as a realization of his/her goal.

This entire transactional event will reinforce the infant's use of internal cues as a frame of reference for future action. However, if the caregiver intervenes too early, before AIM has had sufficient time to emerge (e.g., at the first sign of whimpering), the infant will receive a remedy before any awareness of a problem has been experienced, and the caregiver's responses will be experienced by the infant as coming out of nowhere, or not connected to the infant's experience or agenda. Alternatively, if the caregiver intervenes too late, AIM will have been disrupted by the increasing intensity of negative affect, so that the infant's sense of having some control over events will be lost. Here again, the importance of an optimal intensity of affective experience is pertinent, an intensity that is neither too brief nor too weak to evoke AIM, nor too prolonged and intense to overwhelm AIM.

Many variables dynamically active in the caregiver can influence his/her capacity to respond in a matched and optimal way to the infant. First, the caregiver must be able to perceive the infant as an autonomous being capable of experiencing the elements of AIM—namely, affect, intentionality, and mobilizing a response. Second, the caregiver must value the infant's capacity for agency and initiative, while at the same time recognizing the infant's limits and needs for support. There are several potential difficulties here. The issue of initiatives can become a battleground over who is boss in the family, or the caregiver can feel too much gratification in anticipating the infant's every need, thereby becoming indispensable and fostering excessive dependency in the infant. Alternatively, the caregiver can overestimate the infant's capacities, offering too little support and fostering pseudo independence in the infant. A third variable involves the caregiver's capacity to tolerate these optimal levels of affect in the infant in order for AIM to emerge, which raises many of the issues discussed in the previous section on the caregiver's role in helping the infant modulate negative affects. Fourth, since all early learning is characterized by ineptness, the caregiver must be able to tolerate the infant's bumbling or awkward efforts at mobilizing a response.

The difficulties here are that the caregiver can experience too much shame, or fear of potential failure, or experience contempt for or impatience with ineptness. This can lead to either berating the child or taking over the task, thereby robbing the infant of an opportunity to develop his/her own instrumental capacities. Managing all of these variables, including the capacity to judge just the right amount of struggle that will be experienced by the infant and young child as an optimal challenge, and as well as providing just the right amount of assistance that will enhance the infant's and young child's sense of themselves as effective agents, requires judgment, skill, self-awareness, containment, and empathy on the part of caregivers. Such matched responding will also foster growth in the infant's and young child's regulatory and instrumental capacities.

The contents of the caregiver's responses are also important in determining the fate of the infant's sense of agency. Imagine a young infant gazing intently at and reaching toward a nearby object (a manifestation of AIM—the affect of interest, the intention to explore the object further, and the mobilization of a reaching action), but the infant is unable to fully execute this plan and begins to express fussy sounds of frustration and mild anger. If we now focus on the content of the caregiver's response, we can see that it can take on a positive or negative meaning for the infant in the context of the infant's state of AIM. If the caregiver facilitates the infant's efforts at reaching by changing the infant's posture or moving the object closer, the infant is likely to remain interested and persist. However, if the caregiver is irritated by the fussing and reacts punitively, or ignores the fussing and the infant's goal, the infant is likely to become more frustrated and/or distressed. I am suggesting that the infant experiences these events as affective sequences— the former would be a positive-negative-positive sequence, (specifically, interest-frustration-interest) and the latter would be a positive-negative-negative sequence (specifically, interest-frustration-increased frustration and/or distress). In this way, the specific kind of caregiver response helps to determine the motivational meaning of the whole sequence for the infant, namely, what to expect when one experiences a particular affective state and tries to carry out the intentions and actions mobilized by such a state. Clearly positive-negative-positive affective sequences enhance the infant's sense of agency, and the capacity to tolerate moderate levels of negative affect and persist in the face of difficulties. This strengthens the expectation that persistence will lead to a successful realization of one's goal.

While most children experience a variety of affective sequences, a steady diet of positive-negative-negative affective sequences will eventually undermine a child's sense of agency. The affective dynamics involved tend to be the following: positive affects are minimized, negative affects are compounded and intensified by caregiver behaviors, and the child is then left alone to cope with the consequences. In motivational terms, the child learns that his/her affective states and the intentions and actions related to them do not seem important or valuable to caregivers. Thus, the inclination to use one's inner awareness of these states and plans as a frame of reference for organizing adaptive behavior is not supported.

In terms of agency, the child learns that alone he or she is unable to develop skills and solve problems, unable to endure or modulate negative affect states, and unable to reestablish positive affect states. At such times, the child experiences the self as devalued, ineffective, and helpless. In such a state, the need for parents is heightened, which leads the child to shift away from inner states and focus all of his or her efforts on obtaining and sustaining a parent's involvement. While this strategy can help the child retain some semblance of a sense of agency, it substantially constricts the degrees of freedom open to the child by closing off internal sources of vitality and information. Positive-negative-negative affective sequences can occur with many subtle variations involving the relative intensities of the positive and negative elements. For example, parents caught in ambivalent stances toward their children can repeatedly create and then spoil positive experiences for their children, thereby seducing their children into disappointment. These sequences can also vary in terms of the particular negative affects involved, the frequency of their occurrence and in many different mixtures with positive-negative-positive sequences. But regardless of the particular variant, they all tend to work against the infant's and child's goal to maintain a sense of agency, which in Erikson's terms represents a failure of mutuality.

Conclusion

My goal has been to present a dynamic systems perspective on early psychic development. I began with a brief summary of the concepts of dynamic systems most relevant to human beings who possess consciousness, volition, and motivation. I then explored the biological, psychological, and social contexts of early psychic development that were seen as providing both constraints and dynamic potentials for the emergence of various capabilities. My emphasis was on the early competence of the infant, the role of conscious experience, the creative process of constructing ideo-affect complexes as the basic units of psychic experience, and the basic biases of protecting psychic coherence and organization, and of maintaining a sense of agency. In reformulating the role of the caregiver, I stressed the importance of titrating stimulation, fostering the elaboration of positive affects, the optimal regulation of negative affects, and the goodness of fit, involving both timing and content between the infant's needs, state, and agenda, and the caregiver's needs, state, and agenda as variables directly involved in determining the fate of those basic biases.

This represents a bare bones framework, an initial effort toward understanding the complexity and the dynamic processes shaping the beginnings of the human psyche. While much had to be left out, I have tried to illustrate the dynamic, self-organizing, and open-ended nature of developmental processes that result in creative and idiosyncratic adaptations to specific contexts and conditions, and that do not lend themselves to formulations of stages or of predetermined agendas. This complexity and specificity seems to fit rather well with our clinical experience, where the idiosyncratic details of the patient's experience must be discovered and given voice to, and where the goodness of fit between the patient's need, state, and agenda at any given moment and the therapist's capacity to understand and fashion a communicative response is crucial. Sander (1992) states that "moments of meeting" between the therapist and patient occur when "the awareness of the therapist is shared with the patient and meets a kindred specificity being experienced in the patient's awareness. . . . [T]his is a healing moment that sets the conditions for a change in organization by providing a new base from which the patient can act as agent in his own self-recognition" (583–84).

References

Baillargeon, R. 1990. "Young Infants' Physical Knowledge." Paper presented at the 98th Annual Convention of the American Psychological Association, Boston.

Boukydis, C. F. Z. 1979. "Adult Response to Infant Cries." Unpublished doctoral dissertation, Pennsylvania State University.

Bower, T. G. R. 1974. *Development in Infancy*. San Francisco: Freeman Press.

Bower, T. G. R. 1977. *The Perceptual World of the Child*. Cambridge, MA: Harvard University Press.

Brunner, J. 1968. *Processes of Cognitive Growth*. Worcester, MA: Clark University Press.

Damasio, A. R. 1994. *Decartes' Error*. New York: Putnam Press.

Darwin, C. 1872. *The Expression of the Emotions in Man and Animals*. New York: D. Appleton & Company. Reprinted 1965, Chicago: University of Chicago Press.

DeCasper, A. J. and Carstens, A. A. 1981. "Contingencies of Stimulation: Effects on Learning and Emotion in Neonates." *Infant Behavior and Development* 4: 19–35.

DeCasper, A. J. and Carstens, A. A. 1990. "Prenatal Influence on Newborn's Perception and Learning." Paper presented at the 98th Annual Convention of the American Psychological Association, Boston.

Demos, E. V. 1986. "Crying in Early Infancy: An Illustration of the Motivational Function of Affect." In *Affective Development in Early Infancy*, ed. T. B. Brazelton and M. Yogman 39–73. Norwood, NJ: Ablex.

Demos, E. V. 1988. "Affect and the Development of the Self: A New Frontier." In *Frontiers in Self Psychology: Progress in Self Psychology*, vol. 3, ed. A. Goldberg, 27–53. Hillsdale, NJ: Analytic Press.

Demos, E. V. 1989a. "Resiliency in Infancy." In *The Child in Our Time: Studies in the Development of Resiliency*, ed. T. F. Dugan and R. Coles, 3–22. New York: Brunner/Mazel.

Demos, E. V. 1989b. "A Prospective Constructionist View of Development." *The Annual of Psychoanalysis* 17: 287–308.

Demos, E. V. 1992. "The Early Organization of the Psyche." In *Interface of Psychoanalysis and Psychology*, ed. J. W. Barron, M. N. Eagle, and D. L. Wolitsky, 200–33. Washington, DC: American Psychological Association.

Demos, E. V. 1993. "Developmental Foundations for the Capacity for Self-Analysis." In *Self-Analysis: Critical Inquiries, Personal Visions*, ed. J. W. Barron, 5–27. Hillsdale, NJ: Analytic Press.

Donaldson, M. 1979. *Children's Minds*. New York: Norton.

Edelman, G. M. 1987. *Neural Darwinism*. New York: Basic Books.

Edelman, G. M. 1992. *Bright Air, Brilliant Fire: On the Matter of the Mind*. New York: Basic Books.

Edelman, G. M. 1998. "Building a Picture of the Brain." *Deadalus* 127, 2: 37–70.

Erikson, E. 1950. *Childhood and Society*. New York: Norton.

Field, T. M., Woodson, R., Greenberg, R., and Cohen, D. 1982. "Discrimination and Imitation of Facial Expressions by Neonates." *Science* 218: 179–81.

Fisher, K. W. and Pipp, S. L. 1984. "Processes of Cognitive Development: Optimal Level and Skill Acquisition." In *Mechanisms of Cognitive Development*, ed. R. J. Sternberg, 45–80. New York: Freeman Press.

Freud, S. 1895. "Project for a Scientific Psychology." In *The Standard Edition of the Complete Psychological Works of Sigmund Freud*, vol. 1, ed. and trans. J. Strachey, 283–387. London: Hogarth Press, 1966.

Frodi, A. M. and Lamb, M. E. 1980. "Child Abusers' Responses to Infant Smiles and Cries." *Child Development* 51: 238–41.

Galatzer-Levy, R. M. 2004. "Chaotic Possibilities." *International Journal of Psychoanalysis* 85: 419–42.

Ghent, E. 2002. "Wish, Need, Drive: Motive in the Light of Dynamic Systems Theory and Edelman's Selectionist Theory." *Psychoanalytic Dialogues* 12: 763–808.

Greenberg, J. 1991. *Oedipus and Beyond: A Clinical Theory*. Cambridge, MA: Harvard University Press.

Klein, M. 1952. "Some Theoretical Conclusions Regarding the Emotional Life of the Infant." *The Writings of Melanie Klein*, vol. 3, 61–93. London: Hogarth Press, 1975.

LeDoux, J. 1996. *The Emotional Brain*. New York: Simon and Schuster.

Lichtenberg, J. 1983. *Psychoanalysis and Infant Research*. Hillsdale, NJ: Analytic Press.

Mahler, M., Pine, F., and Bergman, A. 1975. *The Psychological Birth of the Human Infant*. New York: Basic Books.

Piaget, J. 1967. *Six Psychological Studies*. New York: Vintage Books.

Sander, L. 1969. "Regulation and Organization in the Early Infant-Caretaker System." In *Brain and Early Behavior*, vol. 1, ed. R. J. Robinson, 311–32. New York: Academic Press.

Sander, L. 1975. "Infant and Caretaking Environment: Investigation and Conceptualization of Adaptive Behavior in a System of Increasing Complexity." In *Explorations in Child Psychiatry*, ed. E. J. Anthony, 129–66. New York: Plenum Press.

Sander, L. 1982. "The Inner Experience of the Infant: A Framework for Inference Relevant to Development of the Sense of Self." Paper presented at the 13th Margaret S. Mahler Symposium, Philadelphia.

Sander, L. 1985. "Toward a Logic of Organization in Psychobiologic Development." In *Biologic Response Cycles: Clinical Implications*, ed. H. Klar and L. Siever, 19–37. Washington, DC: American Psychiatric Press.

Sander, L. 1992. "Letter to the Editor." *International Journal of Psychoanalysis* 73: 582–84.

Shapiro, D. 2000. *Dynamics of Character: Self Regulation in Psychopathology*. New York: Basic Books.

Stern, D. 1985. *The Interpersonal World of the Infant*. New York: Basic Books.

Thelen, E. 1984. "Learning to Walk: Ecological Demands and Phylogenetic Constraints." In *Advances in Infancy Research*, vol. 3, ed. L. P. Lipsett, 213–50. Norwood, NJ: Ablex.

Thelen, E. 1986. "Treadmill-Elicited Stepping in Seven-Month-Old Infants." *Child Development* 54: 1498–506.

Thelen, E., Corbetta, D., Kamm, K., Spencer, J. P., Schneider, K., and Zernicke, R. F. 1993. "The Transition to Reaching: Mapping Intention and Intrinsic Dynamics." *Child Development* 64: 1058–98.

Thelen, E. and Smith, L. B. 1994. *A Dynamic Systems Approach to the Development of Cognition and Action*. Cambridge, MA: MIT Press.

Thelen, E., Ulrich, B., and Niles, D. 1987. "Bilateral Co-ordination in Human Infants: Stepping on a Splitbelt Treadmill." *Journal of Experimental Psychology: Human Perception and Performance* 13: 405–10.

Tomkins, S. S. 1962. *Affect, Imagery, Consciousness*, vol. 1. The Positive Affects. New York: Springer Publishing Company.

Tomkins, S. S. 1963. *Affect, Imagery, Consciousness*, vol. 2. The Negative Affects. New York: Springer Publishing Company.

Tomkins, S. S. 1978. "Script Theory: Differential Magnification of Affects." In *Nebraska Symposium on Motivation*, ed. H. E. Howe, Jr. and R. A. Dunstbier, 201–36. Lincoln: University of Nebraska Press.

Werner, H. 1957. *Comparative Psychology of Mental Development*. New York: International Universities Press.

Wiesenfeld, A. R., Malatesta, C. Z., and DeLoach, L. L.. 1981. "Differential parental response to familiar and unfamiliar infant distress signals. *Infant Behavior and Development* 4: 281–95.

Winnicott, D. 1965. *The Maturational Processes and the Facilitating Environment*. New York: International Universities Press.

Winnicott, D. 1971. *Playing and Reality*. London: Tavistock.

Wolff, P. 1973. "Organization of Behavior in the First Three Months of Life." *Association for Research on Nervous and Mental Disorders* 51: 132–53.

~

The Language of Complexity Theory

Craig Piers, Ph.D.

This glossary provides a basic understanding of some of the terms and concepts of complexity theory. Good resources include books by Edward Lorenz (1993) and Sally Goerner (1994). Good online resources include *Principia Cybernetica* (www.pcp.lanl.gov/TOC) and Stephen Wolfram's site *Mathworld* (www.mathworld.wolfram.com). The bold-faced words within the definitions indicate that the word is also defined in the glossary.

assemblies: The coherent, **self-organized** coordination of a system's parts or components in response to the specific context, task demands, and past experience.

attractor: A state or point (or set of states or points) in mathematical **phase space** toward which a system evolves over time or iteration. "Attractor" is an unfortunate word because it implies that the attractor itself is drawing or "attracting" the system. More accurately, the attractor is a geometric indicator or sign of the pattern of states the system falls into.

attractor basin: States or points that near-define an **attractor** in **phase space**. Once the system falls within the basin, the evolving states of the system will move closer and closer to the attractor until the system falls on the attractor.

bifurcation: A term used to describe the qualitative shifts in the organization of a **nonlinear system** in response to slight changes in a variable or parameter of the system. A **bifurcation point** is a state or value beyond which the system will undergo qualitative shifts in organization. Another concept used to describe this critical region is the **tipping point**.

catastrophe theory: Developed by Thom (1975), catastrophe theory is the mathematical study of conditions under which the interaction of continuous causes can have discontinuous effects. Put differently, catastrophe theory demonstrates that under the right conditions, slight quantitative change in a system's parts can lead to qualitative change in a system's overall organization and behavior. In this way, catastrophe theory provides a quantitative demonstration of the **tipping point.** Zeeman (1977) extended Thom's ideas and applied them to several areas, including clinical research. Sashin and colleagues (1985, 1990) and Galatzer-Levy (1978) have applied catastrophe theory to aspects of psychoanalytic clinical theory.

cellular automaton: Deterministic, computational systems comprised of a number of identical, locally interacting components that evolve in parallel (simultaneously) or serially (sequentially) according to fixed transition rules.

chaotic systems: An extremely unstable class of nonlinear systems whose behavior is both deterministic and unpredictable. A chaotic system's long-term unpredictability derives from the system's tendency to amplify infinitely small disturbances (see **sensitive dependence on initial conditions**). When the evolving states of a chaotic system are mapped in **phase space,** they reveal the presence of a **strange attractor.**

closure: The development in a system of self-maintenance through **recursive,** self-referential acts.

coevolution: Two or more coupled and interdependent subsystems whose mutual evolution, fitness, and adaptation are inextricably bound.

complex adaptive systems: Systems that are comprised of a number of interconnected subsystems or parts that modify their organization in response to context and task demands.

complex system: A system with a large number of interconnected components or parts in which, when acting in concert, the components are able to produce coordinated patterns of behavior not available to any one component of the system in isolation. Complex systems are also systems whose overall pattern of behavior is not easily described, simulated, or reduced into simpler patterns or a mathematical solution. The paradox of complexity theory is that complex patterns of behavior can arise in **recursive systems** whose underlying processes and dynamics are rather simple.

complexity theory: An umbrella term that subsumes various formal ways of studying and modeling **complex systems**, including but not limited to nonlinear dynamic systems theory, catastrophe theory, chaos theory, artificial life, and cellular automata.

control parameter: An independent variable or constant used in an equation to specify an effect on a dependent variable. Often, the control parameter is increased or decreased experimentally to observe its impact on the dependent variable.

dissipative systems: Systems that dissipate (disperse), as opposed to conserve, energy or information over time. As such, when the evolving states of a dissipative system are mapped over time in **phase space**, the region in phase space the states occupy decreases over time (Goerner 1994). That smaller region is what is referred to as an **attractor.**

dynamical system: A system that changes over time.

edge of chaos: A term most commonly associated with work of Chris Langton (1992) and Stuart Kauffman (1995). It describes a system whose behavior is neither too orderly, stable, and predictable, nor too fluid, chaotic, and unpredictable. Systems poised on the edge of chaos are capable of both periods of relative stability as well as dramatic shifts in organization in response to slight changes in critical parameters.

emergence: The development in a system of collective and coordinated structures, functions, and patterns that are qualitatively different, irreducible, and unpredictable from knowledge of the system's preceding conditions.

energy: A power or force that drives a system's evolution.

entropy: The diminution of organization, coordination, pattern, or order.

equation: Statement of mathematical equivalence wherein the statements (usually functions, algorithms, or values) on both sides of the "=" sign are equal to one another. For instance, the nonlinear logistic equation, $x_{t+1} = r\, x_t\,(1 - x_t)$, states that the value of x at the next time step (or $t + 1$) *is equal to* "r" (**control parameter**) multiplied by the value of x at the current time step (t), multiplied again by value of 1 minus the current value of x.

feedback: The outcome of a process becomes new input to the process and, in some circumstances, can change the process itself. Negative feedback reduces deviation from the state's current state or organization, thereby stabilizing the system's functioning. Positive feedback amplifies or increases deviation from the system's current state, thereby destabilizing the system's current equilibrium. The latter increases the potential for the system to undergo qualitative transformation and change.

fitness landscape: A geometric set of changing relationships (imagined as a landscape of mountains and valleys of varying heights and depths) in which coevolving agents try to reach maximum levels of fitness or adaptation. When using fitness landscapes, researchers simulate the **coevolution** of agents and describe the conditions under which some agents can become trapped in low-lying valleys of fitness or on low local peaks of fitness, unable to reach distant and higher (more adaptive) peaks. Modeling with fitness landscapes can also capture the way one agent's movement and fitness on the landscape changes the landscape, thereby affecting the fitness of other coevolving agents.

fixed-point attractor: A system that evolves toward a single, repeating state or point over time.

fractal: The geometric shape whose dimensions are not equal to a whole number. Fractals have a nested, **self-similar** organization or structure wherein the whole pattern is comprised of infinitely smaller versions of itself.

hysteresis: Hysteresis points to the importance of a system's history and can be considered a primitive form of memory. To further explicate the concept, a nonlinear system **bifurcates** once the value of a critical parameter exceeds a certain threshold. To return the system back to its prebifurcated state, it could be assumed that we would simply need to decrease the value of the critical parameter back across the threshold. What we find, however, is that the threshold changes depending on whether we are decreasing or increasing the critical parameter across the bifurcation point. This changing threshold is an example of hysteresis. As the description indicates, the system bifurcates at a different value of the parameter depending on its immediate history or which side of the bifurcation point the system starts.

initial conditions: The state of the system (including the value of the relevant variables and control parameters) at the outset of a set of observations. Initial conditions should not be thought of exclusively in terms of origin. More often, it is used simply to designate the state of system when a researcher began making observations.

iteration: Repeatedly applying the same set of operations to a system's output and recycling the result back into the system to determine its behavior over time.

limit cycle: A system that cycles through a repeating sequence of states or points.

Lyapunov exponent: A quantitative measure of **sensitive dependence on initial conditions** that specifies the rate at which the capacity to predict the future states of a system is lost (Kellert 1993).

morphogenesis: Specifically, it is the generation of order, coordination, or pattern out of the absence of order. More generally, morphogenesis is the process of creating new patterns, structure, or organization.

neural networks: Interconnected neurons across which coordinated and organized patterns or waves of activity emerge.

neurodynamics: Changing patterns of neuronal activity.

nonlinear dynamic systems: Systems that change in discontinuous, nonproportional, and unpredictable ways.

phase space: Mathematical, multidimensional space in which the changing states of a system are mapped. The number of dimensions of phase space is equal to the number of measured variables that comprise the system. Plotting the states of a system over time in phase space reveals the system's **attractors,** or the pattern of activity that system falls into.

period: The time or number of iterations required before the system returns to a previous state or repeats itself.

recursive systems: A system wherein an identical and well-defined set of procedures, operations, or algorithms are repeatedly applied to the system's current state to arrive at the state of the system at the next iteration.

reentry: Reciprocal, bidirectional connections between coordinated **assemblies** that allow for mutual influence and systemwide coordination. The neuroscientist Gerald Edelman (1992) contends that reentrant connections lead to the coordination of neuronal assemblies across diverse and widely distributed cortical areas allowing for the binding of multimodal input (e.g., sensory, perceptual, motor, etc.) and the emergence of a single, integrated experience.

repellors: Unstable points or states in phase space. In terms of a landscape, imagine a ball delicately balanced on the peak of pointed hilltop. Providing the ball is left completely undisturbed, it could maintain this position. The slightest bump or disturbance, however, would push the ball from the peak and it would roll down a side of the hill until it came to rest at the lowest point. Which side of the hill the ball rolled down could depend on extremely small differences in the nature of the disturbance or perturbation. Finally, in this example we could think of the resting point as an **attractor.**

self-organization: Systems that organize into coordinated and coherent systemwide patterns without external direction, instruction, or top-down, centralized controls.

self-organized criticality: A concept commonly associated with the work of Per Bak (1996) and his use of sandpile models. It refers to a critical state that dynamic systems tend to organize themselves into, wherein small perturbations can lead to changes of any size in the system. Self-organized criticality is similar to the **edge of chaos** concept.

self-sameness: When a state or subpattern of states is identical or repeats the system's overall pattern of behavior.

self-similarity: When a state or subpattern of states resembles or corresponds to the system's overall pattern of behavior.

sensitive dependence on initial conditions: A term most commonly associated with the pioneering work of Edward Lorenz (1993). Often referred to as the "butterfly effect," it is a characteristic of **chaotic systems** wherein their evolution is sensitive and responsive to infinitely small perturbations. This means that long-term prediction is impossible because an infinitely small error in measuring the **initial conditions** will result in the inability to predict the long-term evolution of the system.

stochastic: Is a variable that is partially random or uncertain. It is neither completely determined nor completely random.

strange attractor (aka chaotic attractor): A name given to the **attractor** that characterizes **chaotic systems**. What is unique about strange attractors is that there are an infinite number of states or points on the strange attractor (capturing the aperiodic nature of chaotic systems), but all the states fall within a well-defined and quantifiable geometric shape in **phase space**. This is possible because strange attractors are **fractals**, with a fractal's characteristic nested, **self-similar** organization or structure.

tipping point: A variable's critical value or threshold; when this is exceeded, the entire system changes abruptly and nonlinearly.

turbulence: Noise or variant fluctuations that disturb a system's current organization and may push the system through qualitative state changes.

References

Bak, P. 1996. *How Nature Works: The Science of Self-Organized Criticality*. New York: Springer-Verlag.

Edelman, G. M. 1992. *Bright Air, Brilliant Fire: On the Matter of the Mind*. New York: Basic Books.

Galatzer-Levy, R. M. 1978. "Qualitative Change from Quantitative Change: Mathematical Catastrophe Theory in Relation to Psychoanalysis." *Journal of the American Psychoanalytic Association* 26: 921–36.

Goerner, S. J. 1994. *Chaos and the Evolving Ecological Universe*. Langhorne, PA: Gordon and Breach Science Publishers.

Kauffman, S. 1995. *At Home in the Universe*. New York: Oxford University Press.

Kellert, S. H. 1993. *In the Wake of Chaos*. Chicago: University of Chicago Press.

Langton, C. G. 1992. "Life at the Edge of Chaos." In *Artificial Life II: Santa Fe Institute Studies in the Sciences of Complexity*, vol. 10, ed. C. G. Langton, J. D. Farmer, S. Rasmussen, and C. Taylor. Reading, MA: Addison-Wesley.

Lorenz, E. 1993. *The Essence of Chaos*. Seattle: University of Washington Press.

Sashin, J. 1985. "Affect Tolerance: A Model of Affect Response Using Catastrophe Theory." *Journal of Social and Biological Structure* 8: 175–202.

Sashin, J. and Callahan, J. 1990. "A Model of Affect Using Dynamical Systems." *Annual of Psychoanalysis* 18: 213–31.

Thom, R. 1975. *Structural Stability and Morphogenesis: An Outline of a General Theory of Models.* Reading, MA: Benjamin.

Zeeman, E. C. 1977. *Catastrophe Theory: Selected Papers, 1972–1977.* Oxford, UK: Addison-Wesley.

Author Index

Abeles, M., 52, 53, 56, 75
Abraham, R. H., 54, 75
Abraham, W. C., 44, 76
Adami, C., 121, 130
Albert, M. P., 76
Aquinas, T., 20, 35
Arbib, M. A., 38, 41, 75
Artola, A., 44, 76
Axtell, R. L., 83, 85, 100–101, 108
Ayala, F., 120, 130

Baillargeon, R., 137, 161
Bak, P., 3, 4, 5, 12, 40, 58, 76, 83, 108, 169, 170
Barabasi, A-L., 124, 130
Barr, W. B., 80
Bar-Yam, Y.,
Bear, M. F., 44, 76
Beer, B., 72, 80
Berge, P., 126, 130
Bergman, A., 135, 162
Berlecamp, E., 5, 12, 121, 130
Birbaumer, N., 78
Blake, M. J. F., 63, 76
Bleuler, 16

Bliss, T. V., 43, 76
Blitz, D., 120, 130
Blumenbach, J. F., 113–15, 116, 117
Bollas, C., 119, 130
Boukydis, C F. Z., 156, 161
Bouyer, J. J., 50, 76
Bower, T. G. R., 139, 146, 161
Bressler, S. L., 58, 76
Brinciotti, M., 63, 76
Brunner, J., 145, 161
Bunge, M., 112, 130
Buzsáki, G., 51, 76

Caldwell, J.D., 36
Callahan, J., 171
Carew, T. J., 76
Carstens, A. A., 145, 147, 156, 161
Carter, C. S., 28, 35
Charcot, J.-M., 16
Chatrian, G. E., 63, 76
Chen, D. F., 68, 78
Cheyne, D., 68, 78
Clare, S., 81
Cohen, D., 162
Cohen, N. H., 49, 76

Connor, J. A., 44, 78
Conway, J., 4, 5, 12, 85, 96-97, 121, 130
Corbetta, D., 163
Crane, A. M., 79
Crutchfield, J., 6, 12, 112, 125, 130, 132

Damasio, A. R., 143, 161
Darwin, C., 115, 116, 148, 161
Deacon, T., viii, ix
DeCasper, A. J., 145, 146, 147, 156, 161
Decety, J., 79
Decorps, M., 79
DeLoach, L. L., 163
Delon-Martin, C., 79
Demos, E. V., 83, 136, 144, 149, 152, 157, 161, 162
Descrates, R., 21
Dewan, E. M., 121, 130
Dimyan, M. A., 77
Dobzhansky, T., 120, 130
Donaldson, M., 137, 162
Douglas, R. J., 52, 76
Dreyfus, H. L., 23, 35
Driesch, H., 116, 120

Eagle, M. N., 88, 108
Ebbinghaus, H., 63, 76
Edelman, G. M., 138, 140, 142, 162, 169, 170
Epstein, J. M., 83, 85, 100–101, 108
Erb, M., 78
Érdi, P., 21, 36, 38, 75
Erikson, E., 153, 160, 162
Esposito, R. U., 79

Fairbairn, W. R. D., 117, 130
Farley, J., 113, 114, 131
Felleman, D. J., 48, 49, 76, 79
Field, T. M., 145, 162
Fischer, T. M., 76
Fisher, K. W., 137, 162

Fisher, S. A., 43, 76
Flor, H., 78
Folkard, S., 63, 76
Frankl, V., 29, 35
Freeman, W. J., 17, 19, 21, 23, 24, 26, 27, 32, 35, 36, 45, 50, 51, 52, 55, 57, 58, 77, 80, 83, 109, 111, 126, 132
Freud, S., 7, 16, 35, 86, 87, 109, 116, 117–19, 127, 128, 131, 142, 147, 162
Frodi, A. M., 156, 162
Fuster, J. M., 48, 67, 77

Gabbard, G., 107, 110
Galatzer-Levy, R. M., 85, 88, 109, 136, 162, 166, 170
Gall, F. J., 49, 77
Gardner, M., 96, 109
Gati, J. S., 81
Gell-Mann, M., 3, 12
Gemignani, A., 79
Gerschlager, W., 68, 78
Geschwind, N, 16, 35, 78
Ghatan, P. H., 79
Ghent, E., 83, 109, 141, 152, 162
Gibson, J. J., 19, 35
Gillin, J. C., 63, 79
Glass, L., 16, 35, 55, 62, 63, 77
Globus, A., 77
Globus, G. G., 39, 44, 77
Goerner, S. J., 165, 167, 170
Goldberger, L., 62, 77
Goldman, P. S., 47, 77
Goldman-Rakic, P. S., 47, 77
Goldstein, J., 83, 84, 86, 103, 109, 112, 118, 119, 120, 122, 123, 125, 126, 127, 129, 131
Goodwin, B., 83, 109, 115, 132
Grajski, K. A., 79
Gray, C. M., 50, 80
Green, J. R., 76
Greenberg, J., 141, 162

Greenberg, R., 162
Grigsby, J., 41, 43, 44, 49, 59, 63, 69, 75, 77, 107, 109
Grodd, W., 78
Guastello, S., viii, ix
Guy R., 5, 12, 121, 130

Hallett, M., 77
Hampson, E., 63, 64, 78, 77
Hanakawa, T., 68, 77
Harding, G. F. A., 63, 78
Hardy, C., viii, ix
Hari, R., 68, 80
Harrington, A., 116, 132
Harris, A., 84, 109
Hartlaub, G., 41, 44, 77
Harvey, W., 113, 114
Hebb, D. O., 6, 12, 43, 78
Herskowitz, J., 63, 78
Hetke, J., 76
Hippocrates, 15
Holland, J. H., 39, 78, 126, 128, 132
Hollinger, P., 68, 78
Holt, R. R., 62, 77
Horváth, Z., 76
Hraber, P., 125, 132
Huerta, M. F., 49, 78
Hulsmann, E., 78
Humphries, P.,
Huxley, J., viii, ix
Hyland, B., 68, 78

Ilachinski, A., 89, 109
Immisch, I., 77
Ingvar, M., 79
Insel, T. R., 36
Iwai, E., 49, 78

Jantsch, E., 43, 78
Jeannerod, M., 79
Jeavons, P. M., 63, 78
Jenkins, W. M., 79
Jirikowski, G. F., 36

Jousmaki, V., 68, 80
Jung, C. G., 119

Kaas, J. H., 48, 49, 78, 79
Kamm, K., 163
Kandel, E. R., 44, 80
Kant, I, 116
Kaplan, E., 16, 35
Kauffman, S., 4, 12, 83, 94, 109, 124, 125, 132, 167, 170
Kaye, B., 127, 132
Kaye, K., 41, 77
Kellert, S. H., 168, 170
Kelso, J. A. S., 50, 58, 76, 78, 83, 109
Kendrick, K. M., 28, 35
Keverne, E. W. B., 35
Khan, M., 11, 12
Kimura, D., 64, 78
Kirkpatrick B., 35
Klein, M., 135, 137, 162
Klose, U., 78
Knowlton, B. J., 49, 78
Kowalsky, J., 77
Kozma, R., 21, 36,
Kramer, A. M., 77
Kris, A., 9, 13
Kris, E., 11, 13
Krubitzer, L., 79
Kurzrok, N., 80

Lamb, M. E., 156, 162
Lang, W., 68
Langton, C. G., 4, 13, 94, 109, 121, 124, 132, 167, 170
Laudan, L., 114, 132
Lederhendler, I. I., 35
LeDoux, J., 149, 162
Lenoir, T., 113, 115, 116, 132
Lettich, E., 76
Levy, E. Z., 80
Levy, F., 35
Lewenstein, M., 59, 79
Lichtenberg, J., 135, 162

Linden, D. J., 44, 78
Lindinger, G., 68, 78
Llinás, R., 50, 78
Lømo, T., 43, 76
Lorenz, E., 165, 169, 170
Lotze, M., 68, 78,

Mackey, M. C., 16, 35, 55, 62, 63, 77
Macready, W., 127, 133
Madore, B., 111, 132
Mahler, M., 135, 137, 162
Maier, V., 68, 78
Malatesta, C. Z., 163
Mandelbrot, B. B., 54, 79
Mangels, J. A., 78
Manger, P., 79
Manor, Y., 52, 79
Martin, K. A. C., 52, 76
Massarelli, R., 79
Matricardi, M., 76
Matthews, P. M., 81
Maurer, K., 16, 36
Maurer, U., 16, 36
McClelland, J. L., 13
McCormick, D. A., 80
Medawar, P., 120, 132
Menon, R. S., 81
Merleau-Ponty, M., 20, 36
Merzenich, M. M., 49, 79
Miles, R., 81
Miller, L. H., 76
Mitchell, M., 125, 132
Mitchell, S. A., 88, 109
Modell, A., 32, 36
Monk, T. H., 63, 79
Montaron, M. F., 78
Morand, S., 79
Mountcastle, V. B., 79

Nadim, F., 52, 79
Naito, E., 68, 79
Nauta, W. J. H., 47, 77
Nelson, R. J., 79

Newton, I., 114
Niles, D., 138, 163
Nowak, A., 59, 79

Ohl, F.W., 23, 36
Overmier, J. B., 70, 79

Palmeri, A., 68, 80
Palombo, S., 95, 109
Pandya, D. N., 49, 81
Panksepp, J., 28, 30, 36
Paré, D., 50, 78
Pavlov, I., 27
Pedersen, C.A., 27, 36
Peirce, C. S., viii, ix
Pelliccia, A., 76
Pert, A., 79
Pert, C. B., 28, 30, 36
Peterson, I., 89, 96, 109
Petersson, K. M., 79
Petrovic, P., 59, 79
Piaget, J., 24, 36, 135, 136, 137, 139,
    162
Piers, C., 84, 109, 106, 107, 110, 121,
    124, 128, 132
Pincus, D., 32, 36
Pine, F., 135, 162
Pipp, S. L., 137, 162
Ploghaus, A., 59, 81
Pomeau, V., 130
Popper, K., 120, 132
Porrino, L. J., 72, 79
Prigogine, I., 40, 79

Rapaport, D., 84, 110
Raup, D., 4, 13
Raybaudi, M., 79
Recanzone, G. H., 79
Reitman, E., 111, 121, 132
Resnick, M., 83, 85, 101, 110
Richards, R., 113, 114, 115, 118, 119,
    132
Ricoeur, P., 127, 128, 132

Ridgway, S., 79
Rocha, L. M., viii, ix
Rose, S. P. R., 43, 79
Rosenblatt, A. D., 107, 110, 121, 133
Rosman, N. P., 78
Roth, M., 68, 79
Rougeul, A., 76
Rousseau, G., 113, 133
Rowan, A. J., 80
Ruff, G. E., 62, 80
Rumelhart, D. E., 13

Sacks, O., 22, 36
Sadato, N., 68, 79
Salenius, S., 68, 80
Salmelin, R., 68, 80
Salthe, S., 125, 133
Sander, L., 149, 151, 156, 161, 162, 163
Sargant, W. W., 27, 28, 36
Sashin, J., 166, 171
Schacter, D., 107, 110
Schafer, R., 119, 133
Scheibel, A. B., 39, 77, 80
Scheibel, M. E., 39, 80
Scheich, H., 23, 36
Schneider, K., 163
Schneider, W., 50, 81
Schneiders, J. L., 41, 75, 77
Schnitzler, A., 68, 80
Schwartz, M. L., 47, 77
Seeger, T. F., 79
Segebarth, C., 79
Sejnowski, T. J., 80
Seligman, M. E., 70, 79
Shaffer, M. M., 72, 80
Shapiro, D., 103, 110, 157, 163
Shaw, C. D., 54, 75
Sherwin, B. B., 63, 80
Siegel, M., 63, 80
Siegelbaum, S. A., 44, 80
Singer, W., 44, 50, 76, 80
Skarda, C. A., 51, 57, 80

Skinner, B. F., 19, 36
Smith, L. B., 83, 110, 138, 163
Smith, S., 81
Sokoloff, L., 79
Spencer, J. P., 163
Sperry, R.W., 19, 36120, 133
Spurzheim, G., 49, 77
Squire, L. R., 78, 107, 110
Steiner, S. S., 72, 80
Stengers, I., 40, 79
Steriade, M., 51, 80
Stern, D., 135, 163
Stern, L., 7
Stevens, D., 41, 43, 49, 59, 63, 69, 75, 77, 107, 109
Stone, E. S., 79
Sulloway, F., 117, 118, 133
Sum, M., 79
Sur, M., 79
Szentágothai, J., 38, 75, 80
Szymanski, M., 79

Tang, C., 3, 12,
Teilhard De Chardin, P., viii, ix
Thaler, V. H., 80
Thelen, E., 83, 110, 137–40, 163
Thickstun, J. T., 121, 133
Thom, R., 166, 171
Tigges, J., 49, 80
Tigges, M., 49, 80
Toma, K., 77
Tomkins, S. S., 145, 146, 147, 148, 149, 150, 163
Tracey, I., 58, 81,
Trasatti, G., 76
Traub, R. D., 51, 81

Ulam, S., 89
Ulrich, B., 138, 163
Urioste, R., 76

Vahnee, J. M., 76
Van Essen, D. C., 48, 49, 76

Van Gelderen, P., 77
Verger, P., 27, 28, 36
Vidal, C., 130
von der Malsburg, C., 50, 81
von Haller, A., 114
von Neumann, J., 89

Wachtel, P. L., 88, 110
Wall, J., 79
Weiss, N., 126, 133
Werner, H., 135, 163
Westen, D., 88, 107, 110
Whyte, L. L., 112, 122, 133
Wiesendanger, M., 68, 78
Wiesenfeld, A. R., 156, 163
Wiesenfeld, K., 3, 12
Wilden, A., 119, 133

Winnicott, D., 152, 157, 163
Wise, K., 76
Wolff, C. F., 113
Wolff, P., 83, 88, 89, 110, 149, 163
Wolfram, S., 85, 89, 91–96, 97, 110,
    165
Wolpert, D., 127, 133
Wong, R. K. S., 81
Woodson, R., 162
Wuensche, A., 121, 133

Yeterian, E. H., 49, 81
Yukie, M., 49, 78

Zeeman, E. C., 166, 171
Zernicke, R. F., 163
Zukier, H., 119, 133

Subject Index

adaptation, 5, 8, 30, 39, 115
adaptive, 55, 154
affect, 11, 28, 140, 141, 144, 146, 147, 148, 149, 150, 158; modulation, 153
affordances, 19
agency, 37, 38, 40, 42, 64, 65, 67, 74, 101, 104, 156, 158, 159; *see also* intentionality
agent, 141, 145, 147
agent-based modeling, 99–101
AIM, 157–59
amplifier, 155
amygdala, 148, 149
analogue amplifier, 148
anxiety, 59, 102
art object, 128
artificial life, 121
assemblies, 165
assimilation, 20, 23, 25, 26, 27, 29, 30, 32; shared, 25
associations, 9, 12; free, 9, 30; patient's, 8; process, 10
attention, 22, 58; selective, 25
attitude, 102, 103, 105–107; unconscious organizing, 106

attractor, 23, 53, 55, 56, 125, 165; basins of, 56, 57, 58, 65, 165; chaotic, 23, 54, 55; fixed point, 54, 168; limit cycle, 54, 55, 57, 168; periodic, 54; strange, 84, 170
attunement, 11
autocatalytic sets, 126

bifurcation, 54, 57, 125, 165
binding, 50
bipedal locomotion, 138
bonding, 27, 28, 34
boundary, 125; self and other, viii

catastrophe theory, 166
cause, 29, 31, 54, 85, 88, 111, 125
cell assemblies, 39
cellular automata, 4–6, 85, 89–98, 166
chaos, 26, 28, 32
chaotic system, 54, 58, 84, 93, 166
character, 86, 87, 103, 121, 128
choice, 69–71
closure, ix, 120, 166
coevolution, viii, 1, 3, 166

coherence, 147
complex adaptive system, 5, 6, 8, 166
complexity theory, 1, 3, 6, 12, 166
compromise formation, 102, 118
compulsive hand washing, 104
computation, 6; emergence, 121;
   irreducible, 95; laws, ix
conflict, 102
consciousness, xi, 6, 23, 24, 30, 58, 62,
   124, 146, 147, 154
containers, 125, 126
context, 136, 152
critical state, 3, 6
culture, 25

defenses, 147,149, 155
deterministic, 9, 10, 126
development, 135–61
differentiation, 8
dissipative systems, 167
dissolution, 26, 27, 28, 31
dreaming, 28
drive, 117, 119
dynamical system, 167

edge of chaos, 7, 8, 9, 10, 11, 94, 124,
   167
ego, 42, 149
embryo development, 113, 118
emergence, 6, 26, 39, 40, 83–108,
   111–30, 138, 167; creative, 129
emergent property, viii, 6, 38, 39, 42,
   49, 58, 59, 61, 69, 75
emotion, 32; see also affect
empathy, 156
energy, 16, 56, 65, 119, 167; nerve, 16
entelechy, 116
entropy, 167
equation, 167; differential, 84
equilibrium-seeking process, 118
evolution, 3, 115; Big Bang, 3;
   discontinuities, 118; emergent, 120
expectancy, 22

false-self organization, 157
family members, 157
feedback, vii, 47, 49, 52, 149, 167; loop,
   103, 121, 124, 155
feedforward, 47, 51, 52
fitness, 5, 6; landscape, 167
foresight, 67–69
formative drive, 113, 114, 116
fractal, 8, 93, 127, 168
frontloading, 88, 89
frozen order, 10
fundamental rule, 9

Game of Life, 4, 5, 96–98; gliders, 5,
   97
good analytic hour, 11

hierarchical, 39, 42, 46, 48, 49, 58, 98,
   121, 143; nested, 124
history, 23, 24
hysteresis, 168

ideo-affect complex, 150, 154
imagining, 68
imitate, 145
individual variation, 138, 139, 157
infant capacities, 144
infant observation, 89
information, 17, 19, 20, 23, 28, 142;
   processing , 6; destroying, 23
instinct, 117
intention, 157
intentionality, 21, 22, 24, 27, 30, 31,
   32, 34, 158
Internet, viii
interpretants, viii
interpretation, 7
interpretive activity, vii, viii
iteration, 168

joint action, 25

kernels of redundancy, 124

language, viii, 27, 46, 47
laws, 29
learned helplessness, 70
linear systems, 85; stage theories, 135
Lyapunov exponent, 168

Markov process, 30
mastery, 128
meaning, 58
memory, 12, 24, 43, 86, 106, 107, 143, 144, 145, 146; declarative, 107, 143, 146; procedural, 107, 143, 146
mirroring, 119
modular processing, 50
modular structures, 47
morphogenesis, 111–30, 168
mother-infant relationship, 11, 152, 155; motherese, 154
motivation, 150, 159
mutual regulation, 153

natural selection, 115
negation, 126, 127, 128, 129
neural network, 6, 7, 17, 18, 19, 20, 30, 37, 38, 39, 41, 43, 44–45, 51, 52, 56, 57, 58, 72, 141, 143, 168
neurodynamics, 169
nonlinear dynamical system, 106,169
noosphere, viii
novelty, xi, 25, 113, 126, 127, 128

object relations, 107
order, 122
organization, 122
oscillatory activity, 50, 51, 52, 53
oxytocin, 27, 28

pain, 59
parameter, 125; control, 167; order, 59
pattern, 122
periodic process, 53, 169
personality, 37, 41, 42, 49, 75
phase space, 169

phase transition, 2, 7, 8, 22, 28, 40
predictable, 9, 10, 54, 85
preformation, 113, 114, 137
probability, 56
psychic coherence, 141
psychoanalysis, 1, 6, 7, 8, 12, 30, 32, 33, 86–89
psychoanalytic discourse, 9, 10
psychoanalytic process, 2, 3, 6, 10
psychotherapy, 144
psychotic, 101
punctuated equilibrium, 4

random variation, 115
reaching behaviors, 139, 159
recapitulation, 118
recognition, 157
recursive, vii, 127, 169
reentrant, 47, 169
reflex, 16, 137; orienting, 23
regression, 11, 26, 27, 28, 29, 32, 34; in the service of the ego, 11
repellor, 55, 56, 65, 169
repetition, 12, 65
repetition compulsion, 128
representation, 21, 49, 50, 58, 142; self, 57
repression, 127, 128
resistance, 11, 32

sandpile model, 3, 9
Santa Fe Institute, 3
self, 20, 24, 42, 58, 119
self-initiated action, 71–74
self-maintenance, vii, 5
self-organization, 26, 34, 39, 40, 42, 50, 111, 123, 169
self-organizing criticality, 4, 169
self-organizing system, 2, 3
self-referential, vii, 120,
self-sameness, 169
self-similarity, 12, 127, 170
self-stimulation, 72

self-transcending constructions, 127
semantic networks, viii
sensitive dependence on initial
    conditions, 54, 93, 94, 97, 168, 170
sensory deprivation, 62
signs, viii
socialization, 26, 27, 34
soft-assembly, 89
state, 38, 59, 61; organization, 149
steady state, 54
stochastic, 170
structure, 122
symptom, 86, 87, 101, 103, 122
synapse, 16, 23, 39, 142; plasticity, 39,
    43, 56, 65
syntactic autonomy, viii

theory, 31, 34
theory of psychopathology, 106
therapeutic alliance, 129
therapeutic process, 2, 7

therapeutic relationship, 8, 33
thermodynamics, 16
timing, 157
tipping point, 170
transference, 32, 34
transition rules, 4, 5, 90, 93, 102
trauma, 11, 12, 30, 55, 73, 86, 87, 149,
    155, 156
triadic model, viii
trust, 155
turbulence, 170
Turing machine, 5, 121

unconscious, x, 9, 24, 102, 147, 156;
    relational scripts, 107
unpredictable, 10, 54, 85

visual system, 48
vitalism, 116

wave packet, 22

~

Contributors

Joseph Brent, Ph.D., is a historian of ideas. He is currently president of the Semiotic Society of America and of the Charles S. Peirce Society. Dr. Brent is the author of the only full-length biography of Peirce, of which he published a revised edition in 1993.

E. Virginia Demos, Ed.D., is a senior staff psychologist and a past Erikson Scholar at the Austen Riggs Center. A clinical and developmental psychologist, infant researcher, and teacher, she is assistant clinical professor of psychology in the Department of Psychiatry at Harvard Medical School. Dr. Demos has been a teacher of early development and a clinical supervisor for over twenty years in training hospitals and at the Harvard Graduate School of Education where she was the director of the Program in Counseling and Consulting Psychology. She was also the director of a private psychotherapy clinic in Boston. Dr. Demos edited *Exploring Affects: The Selected Writings of Sylvan S. Tomkins* and has published over twenty articles and book chapters on affective development in early childhood and the central role of affect in shaping psychic organization. She has received several research fellowships and is a founding member of the International Society for Research in Emotion (ISRE). Dr. Demos graduated from Radcliffe College and received an Ed.D. from Harvard Graduate School of Education. She received postdoctoral research training at Children's Hospital in Boston, postdoctoral clinical training at the Solomon Carter Fuller Community Health Center, and the inpatient children's unit at New England Memorial Hospital, and completed course work at the Chicago Institute for Psychoanalysis.

Walter J. Freeman, M.D., studied physics and mathematics at MIT, medicine at Yale, internal medicine at Johns Hopkins, and neuropsychiatry as Fellow of the Foundations Fund for Research in Psychiatry at UCLA. He has taught brain science in the University of California at Berkeley since 1959, now as professor of the graduate school. He has received a Guggenheim Fellowship, a MERIT Award from NIH in 1990, a Pioneer Award from the Neural Networks Council in 1992, was president of the International Neural Network Society in 1994, and is a Life Fellow of the IEEE. He has published over four hundred articles and five books on various aspects of brain function, including *Mass Action in the Nervous System* in 1975, *Societies of Brains* in 1995, *Neurodynamics: An Exploration of Mesoscopic Brain Dynamics* in 2000, and *How Brains Make Up Their Minds* in 2001.

Jeffrey Goldstein, Ph.D., is professor and director of research at the School of Business, Adelphi University, as well as an associate clinical professor, Derner Institute for Advanced Psychological Studies also at Adelphi University. He has taught at Rutgers University, Columbia University, New York University, and in 2000 was a visiting professor at the NATO Advanced Studies Institute held in Moscow, Russia. He is the author of *The Unshackled Organization* (1994) and over eighty scholarly articles. Dr. Goldstein has lectured and given workshops throughout the world at leading businesses and universities. He is a member of the Institute for the Study of Coherence and Emergence, one of the editors-in-chief of the new journal *Emergence: Complexity and Organization*, and is a trustee of the Society for Chaos Theory in Psychology and the Life Sciences which publishes the internationally recognized journal *Nonlinear Dynamics, Psychology, and the Life Sciences.*

Jim Grigsby, Ph.D., is a research scientist at the University of Colorado Health Sciences Center, where he is professor in the Department of Medicine, Division of Health Care Policy and Research, and Division of Geriatric Medicine. He attended the University of Kansas and the University of Regina (formerly the University of Saskatchewan), and obtained his doctorate at the University of Colorado. The primary focus of his research has been on the neuropsychological capacity for self-regulation of purposeful behavior, the cognitive impairment associated with the Fragile X-associated Tremor-Ataxia Syndrome, and the effects of chemotherapy on the brain and cognition among women with breast cancer. With his coauthor, David Stevens, Ph.D., he wrote *The Neurodynamics of Personality*, published by Guilford Press in 2000.

John P. Muller, Ph.D., is director of training at the Austen Riggs Center. Dr. Muller is the author of *Beyond the Psychoanalytic Dyad: Developmental Semiotics in Freud, Peirce, and Lacan* (Routledge, 1996). He coauthored (with W. J. Richardson) *Lacan and Language: A Reader's Guide to Ecrits* (International Universities Press, 1982) and coedited (with W. J. Richardson), *The Purloined Poe: Lacan, Derrida, and Psychoanalytic Reading* (Johns Hopkins University Press, 1988). He is also coeditor (with J. Brent) of *Peirce, Semiotics, and Psychoanalysis* (Johns Hopkins University Press, 2000). Dr. Muller received his Ph.D. in clinical psychology from Harvard University and graduated from the Boston Psychoanalytic Society and Institute and where he twice received the Felix and Helena Deutsch Scientific Award for scholarly papers. He was the Erikson Scholar at Austen Riggs in 1992–1993 and has published over forty articles and chapters in the field of semiotics and psychoanalysis. He is the former chair of the Forum on Psychiatry and the Humanities in Washington, D.C., has coordinated the Lacanian Clinical Forum for over twenty years, and has presented his work nationally and internationally.

Elizabeth Osuch, M.D., is an assistant professor in the Department of Psychiatry at the Uniformed Services University of the Health Sciences in Bethesda, Maryland. Her medical and psychiatry training were at Michigan State University and Sheppard Pratt Hospital in Baltimore, Maryland, respectively. She completed a fellowship in clinical research within the Biological Psychiatry Branch of the National Institute of Mental Health. Currently, she conducts clinical research on the acute and chronic effects of exposure to traumatic events, and also has a private practice in general adult and adolescent psychiatry. Her research involves functional brain imaging, clinical trials, and postmortem brain tissue studies. Other areas of research interest include the neurobiology of affect modulation and how people initiate and complete novel self-motivated behaviors.

Stanley R. Palombo, M.D., practices psychoanalysis in Washington, D.C. He is the author of *Dreaming and Memory: A New Information Processing Model* and more than twenty papers on dreaming. His latest book, *The Emerging Ego: Complexity and Coevolution in the Psychoanalytic Process*, offers a radically new understanding of the therapeutic process of psychoanalysis. Dr. Palombo has taught at the Harvard, Howard, Georgetown, and George Washington University Medical Schools, the American University, the Washington Psychoanalytic Institute, and the Washington School of Psychiarty.

Craig Piers, Ph.D., is a psychotherapist and clinical supervisor in the health center at Williams College and former associate director of admissions and senior staff psychologist at the Austen Riggs Center. He frequently presents his work nationally and has published numerous articles covering topics such as personality disorders and assessment, psychotherapeutic impasse, masochism, suicide, and complexity theory. Dr. Piers is a contributing editor of *Psychoanalytic Dialogues* and also serves as a reviewer for several other professional journals. Dr. Piers earned his doctorate in clinical psychology from New School University, completed his clinical training at Dartmouth Medical School, and a four-year postdoctoral fellowship in clinical psychology at the Austen Riggs Center.